Anatomy of an Implosion

One Pastor–Professor's Diagnosis & Lament at the Mission Drift to Woke Marxism in Lutheran Higher Education

Gregory P. Schulz

Anatomy of an Implosion: One Pastor–Professor's Diagnosis & Lament at the Mission Drift to Woke Marxism in Lutheran Higher Education

Copyright (c) 2023 Gregory P. Schulz. All Rights Reserved. No portion of this book may be reproduced in any form, except for quotations in reviews, articles, and speeches, without permission from the publisher.

Cover art by Nik Ableev, putty & paint. Photograph posted at Контакты | Ставропольский край | Художник Аблеев Никита (kawstwo.wixsite.com).
Author's picture by Manning Photography, Inc., Milwaukee, courtesy of the Wisconsin Institute for Law and Liberty.

First Printing © 2023
Library of Congress Card
Lutheran News, Inc. 684 Luther Lane
New Haven, MO 63068
Published 2023
Printed in the United States of America
Lightning Source Inc., La Vergne, TN
ISBN #978-8-9895813-0-6

In Memoriam

Kurt E. Marquart, author of Anatomy of an Explosion.

Rightly honored by Concordia University Wisconsin in 2001.

Largely unheeded by its administrators and regents then as now.

Dedication

To the thousands upon thousands of pastors and parishioners, alumni and parents, who continue to petition, to write, to email, and to pray for the Concordia University Wisconsin Administration and Board of Regents to repent.

To the faithful faculty and staff at CUW who reject Woke Marxism.

To my former students at CUW and Wisconsin Lutheran College, a faithful generation for whom we continue to pray and labor in these gray and latter days, so that you can "strap on the complete armor that only God gives and, after repulsing the enemy and fulfilling our common duty, still stand your ground" (Ephesians 6:13, author's translation).

Be ever–vigilant, or someone will take you hostage by means of a hollow and deceptive philosophy—the kind of philosophy based on human ideology and worldly principles—and not based on Christ, because it is in Christ that the full nature of God resides, bodily. (Colossians 2:8–9, author's translation).

Book Recommendations

In this book, Professor Schulz performs a critical dissection of an educational institution infected by a disease. Whether called "social justice" or "diversity, equity, and inclusion," or labeled by its opponents as "woke Marxism," the result is the same: the disease corrupts the institutional host by denying the basic dignity of all human beings.

To be sure, such a malevolent theory stands in contrast to basic Christian teachings on equality. But an institution, such as Concordia, that embraces such a theory risks profound legal consequence. As the United States Supreme Court affirmed in the summer of 2023, American law demands equal treatment of all citizens, especially in the educational setting, where race should never be a factor.

Educational institutions—even private institutions like Concordia—that impose DEI or "affirmative action" policies upon a student body or faculty violate federal law, risk losing federal funding, and face the prospect of punitive damages in federal court. Higher educational institutions would do well to carefully consider not only moral and Christian teachings, but also the legal consequences of engaging in the "sordid business" of "divvying us up by race," as the Supreme Court has warned.

Attorney Dan Lennington, Deputy Counsel at the Wisconsin Institute for Law & Liberty, and a communicant member in the LCMS

Greg Schulz is perhaps not the first to sound the alarm about the current insidious drift toward Woke Marxism and Critical Race Theory within the fold of Higher Education in general or in the Concordia University System specifically—but he certainly ranks among the most qualified to do so.

What is at stake is not simply the prevalent educational ideology, policy, and terminology, but the minds and hearts of students, administrators, and teachers and their adherence to the Word of

God, to Holy Scripture, and ultimately the justification of faith through Christ alone, all in the name of church. This is the battle of our time.

In this book, Schulz is sounding the certain, clarion call of the trumpet. The church of Christ needs to prepare for battle in these latter days. We had best pay heed and have a care.

Rev Dr Karl Böhmer
Congregation of Christ Kirchdorf
Wartburg, South Africa
Free Evangelical Lutheran Synod in South Africa (FELSISA)

President Theodore Roosevelt once said, "a thorough knowledge of the Bible is worth more than a college education." This represents how our connection to God has greater worth than any university degree. Dr. Schulz has endured the ultimate pain of watching his beloved university distance itself from God, undermining its original mission. His courage to talk about the Marxism that has overtaken Lutheran colleges gives us the strength to map out a response which ensures the survival of Christian families and carries our faith forward for the next generation.

Wisconsin State Representative Janel Brandtjen

"Mission creep" is a military phrase used derogatively when the initial strategy of defeating the enemy in a combat zone has been compromised and modified for reasons unknown. The task of securing complete victory in war is transcended by extraneous purposes that lead over time to defeat in the arena of conflict.

Dr. Schulz's analysis of the rise of woke Marxism at CUW emanating from leadership within the administration is a clarion call for all fellow Lutherans who love Scripture and correctly confess and proclaim the missio Dei through the Lutheran Confessions to target, identify and remove the mission creep of woke Marxism vis-à-vis our Concordia University system.

Woke Marxism, CRT, DIE is being taught and promoted on our campuses. Dr. Schulz calls it for what it truly is: "the fentanyl of education in our churches and schools." His analysis is trenchant:

    1) Wokeism is a war against the gift of language by asserting

that meaning is meaningless and the right to interpret any text is endless.

2) Diversity is racism based upon unsubstantiated assumptions floated by the flawed and biased Harvard CRT model.

3) Inclusion's agenda is ultimately racial reparations.

4) Equity is the enforcement of all derived Diversity and Inclusion agendas by any means necessary except by rational disputation.

Any Concordia University adopting such agendas by mission creep guarantees the death of the missio Dei of that Lutheran University including loss of identity in Christ. Adoption of woke Marxism including "innocuous" experimentation will end in a mission drift assimilation into secular society and the disappearance of the Lutheran University.

No less than the heart of the Gospel is at stake at CUW. How so? Because the central teaching of Scripture—how sinful man can get right with a holy God—namely, the doctrine of universal justification is the tip of the spear that brings every thought, every teaching, and every agenda captive to the Word, Christ Jesus, the Lord and Savior of the world. The woke Marxist agenda can never be squared with Scripture.

Read *Anatomy of an Implosion* and be enlightened.

May the true church of God rise up in heroic faith, dispel the conspirators and bring every thought captive to the Word of God.

Rev. Dr. Mark J. Schreiber
CAPT, CHC, USN (Ret.)

A specter is haunting Christian colleges—the specter of Woke Marxism. Dr. Schulz offers here a stark diagnosis of this problem and issues a much-needed call for repentance.

Woke Marxism is not merely a philosophy or set of principles. On its surface, it deceitfully tempts with promises of justice and equity. In its various forms (including Critical Race Theory, DEI, Postmodernism, Queer Theory, etc.), it is in fact an insidious "anti-philosophy of revolt against privileged authority and sacrosanct texts", utterly incompatible with the most basic and important truths of the Bible. It seeks to replace God's Truth with man's subjective "truths". It seeks to divide us from God and from each other as brothers and sisters in Christ.

Its creeping influence can clearly be found in our Lutheran colleges, which have dangerously thought to borrow from the philosophies of the world for the sake of growth, sustainability, or as a result of the many strings attached to government funding. They have refused to reject and condemn it as wrong and contrary to God's Word.

Instead, Dr. Schulz himself has been condemned and exiled from Concordia University Wisconsin for condemning this devilish set of falsehoods. *Anatomy of an Implosion* clearly points us to the disease's cure: a total public rejection of the false "truths" of Marxism and Church Growth Theology and a reformation within Lutheran higher education that returns to Scripture and the Lutheran Confessions as the only standards by which all teaching can be judged.

This book must be widely read and heeded by parents, students, professors, and the leadership of our Lutheran colleges and universities—before it is too late.

Dr. Aaron J. Palmer
Professor of History / Chair, School of Humanities
Wisconsin Lutheran College

Missouri Synod Lutherans have been concerned by the swift spread of woke ideology in both secular and religious institutions of higher learning. In *Anatomy of an Implosion*, Prof. Schulz not only provides helpful analysis and testimony, but also twenty-one appendices filled with primary documents and articles.

For those who wish to understand the woke infiltration of Concordia University Wisconsin and Ann Arbor in particular and the Concordia System in general, Prof. Schulz has provided an invaluable resource.

Pastor David Ramirez

As an educator of Constitutional Law in a public college, I knew immediately when I read about Woke Marxism that it violates our United States Constitution. When I noticed that Concordia University Wisconsin (CUW) students were being directed to the same woke conferences as students at my public college, when the presidential search for a new university president for CUW wanted a person to implement woke policies on campus, when the institution of a bias reporting system was implemented, and when Ibram Kendi's writings were recommended, I became alarmed.

Professor Gregory Schulz, Professor of Philosophy at CUW, spoke out and identified how Woke Marxism violates our beliefs as Lutherans which stem from the Bible and The Book of Concord. In *Anatomy of an Implosion*, he faithfully traces the history of these problems at CUW, the mission drift and shift that occurred, in what way Woke Marxism violates Christian beliefs, and what may be the result.

This is a must read for anyone concerned about the state of higher Lutheran, Christian, or public education.

The Honorable Nancy Bekx, Wisconsin District VII Reserve Judge, retired

---

It is a gift when a person can diagnose a poison. It is even more a gift when that writer can prescribe the antidote.

Greg Schulz diagnoses what he refers to as Woke Marxism. "Woke Marxism" is not an uncommon cry in the current context, but Schulz is doing much more than throwing around some current cliché. With the eye of a philosopher (Schulz has a PhD in philosophy) he is able to define his terms and describe the effect of the poison, demonstrating how Woke Marxism is not only a "deceptive philosophy" but an attack on "the Incarnate Logos Himself." Here the reader benefits not only from the author's gimlet eye, but also from his pastoral heart.

To pierce the problem of Woke Marxism with clarity (again, not for the sake of just hurling cliches at political adversaries) is an important undertaking. The dissidents of Eastern Europe would speak of Marxism ("woke" was not a live term back then), of socialism, of "the Ideology," of dialectical materialism (or Diamat), in describing this movement. Thus, one could study Marxism by reading those who could analyze theoretically (Kenneth Minogue, Eric Voegelin, Karl Popper; in America, Thomas Sowell; and many others), or one could read the writers (the "dissidents") who lived under the oppression (Czeslaw Milosz, Vaclav Benda,

Vaclav Havel, Solzhenitsyn, and many others).

The theoretical discernment is crucial, but the actual "lived" accounts put flesh and bone in front of the reader's eye. Greg Schulz delivers both: a piercing diagnosis of the problem, and a "lived" account of seeing the poison face–to–face, not only in witnessing the "university's philosophy of education," but also in having his voice suppressed by those unable to contend openly with any opposing voice. As Schulz notes, then, "this is not an academic exercise." Rather, it is real life under the pressures of Woke Marxism (dialectical materialism by whatever name).

This is where we see the profound gift Greg Schulz delivers to the reader. Having diagnosed the poison, having described its "philosophy of education," having given a factual account of the suppression of his own voice, Schulz brings out the one thing needful: the antidote.

If, as Schulz contends, Woke Marxism is a "revolt against God, the Bible, and language," and, thus, against the Incarnate Word, the answer is the justification of the sinner and our Baptismal identity. This rescues us from the relativistic language of Woke, delivering us back to the bedrock of confessional language, specifically, the "central article of Justification."

This concise book is a great benefit not only for its historical account, but also for the clarity and comfort of the teacher or pastor wanting to discern the problem and to rightly speak our Lord's Word in these troubled days.
Pastor Warren Graff

The casual observer of the current travails of academic and broader cultural life is often tempted to wonder "Why all the fuss about including a few bits of the woke agenda into college curricula and life? Colleges exist to teach students and society to evaluate, discern, judge and sift out bad ideas. What can it hurt?"

Professor Schulz has documented and given us the answer in *Anatomy of An Implosion*: the woke agenda can, and already has, hurt plenty, and in the case of the Concordia Universities of the Lutheran Church—Missouri Synod, promises to be fatal to the institutional life and soul of any organization that seeks to moderate between wokeness and the original meaning and purpose of these institutions. Schulz makes an excellent case: To ask "What harm can a little wokeness do?" is like asking "What harm can a little cyanide do?" or "What harm can a little polonium do?"

In the case of Christian colleges, the smallest embrace of wokeness will destroy or at least seriously damage the institution's "immune system" of reason and discernment derived from natural law and the created order as it has been historically understood.

The particularity of Schulz's work also lends it strength. The acknowledged predecessor of his effort here is Kurt Marquardt's *Anatomy of An Explosion*, and Schulz does much to update Marquart's analysis of similar events at Concordia Seminary Saint Louis in the early 1970's by applying Marquardt's rationale to his own institution, Concordia University Wisconsin. More generalized and broader "anatomies" exist (such as Burtchaell's Dying of the Light and even Whittaker Chamber's Witness), but the prospective reader will find that Prof. Schulz has an excellent ability to make difficult concepts understandable to the general reader, and to those who come from a variety of different educational backgrounds.

And for those readers who may find themselves indifferent to wokeness, or even in favor of various aspects of its agenda, Implosion might serve as a way to challenge their assumptions. If, as just one example, colleges can now mandate reading lists to "challenge the unconscious assumptions of supremacy" which include works such as those by Ibram Kendi and the 1619 project, why would they not "challenge the unconscious assumptions of wokeness" on the part of their students by requiring they read Orwell, or Solzhenitsyn, or even the authors mentioned above?

Implosion, like its predecessors, points to a cure that could potentially benefit not just a specific college and Church, but also a larger academic and cultural environment.

The greatest beneficiaries of the work, however, may ultimately be the students of Concordia Wisconsin, who chose the institution because of its repeatedly stated fidelity to the theology, doctrine, practice and academic life of the historic Lutheran church. Implosion may ultimately make the gap between the education they were promised and the education they actually receive much smaller in the future.

Gordon Bynum
Chaplain, The Saint Timothy Society for Lutheran Seminary Scholarship

---

In his 1978 work, *Anatomy of an Explosion*, the now–sainted Rev. Prof. Kurt E. Marquart not only chronicled the dramatic events of the firing of the liberal faculty at Concordia Seminary and the subsequent Seminex Walkout, he also provided historical, sociological, and theological contexts and analyses of the causes of the "explosion."

In his 2023 work, *Anatomy of an Implosion*, the Rev. Prof. Gregory P. Schulz chronicles not only the historical events of his own ongoing crisis regarding "wokeism" at Concordia University Wisconsin, he also provides similar analyses of the philosophical, linguistic, and theological underpinnings of this "implosion" of nearly a half–century later.

Schulz relies on Marquart as a muse, quoting him frequently, as well as a kind of Virgil taking Schulz on a tour of the inferno of Critical Theory and the political infestation of DEI (Diversity Equity and Inclusion), which Schulz describes as DIE, as it amounts to the putting of rational discourse to death.

In Implosion we see the common philosophical roots between the two events: relativism, the deconstruction of sacrosanct texts, and ultimately, the attack on the Logos Himself.

Whereas Prof. Marquart wrote his *Anatomy* a few years after the fact as a kind of post–mortem analysis, Prof. Schulz writes his *Anatomy* in the midst of the still–unfolding tumult, in hopes that the LCMS can once again beat back what is a very similar assault grounded in Marxist premises. We would do well to pay heed to the writings of both professors.

Pastor Larry Beane

"Take heart," says the Lord. Why should that be? The answer to that question relies upon how we take His Word into our hearts. It is hearts that Dr. Schulz concerns himself with in this courageous volume, namely to turn hearts and minds from the attractive, but deceptive, lies of our age, and to the unchanging truth of Christ and His saving Gospel as confessed by the united voice and heart of our forefathers in the Faith, the Book of Concord.

As every faithful pastor, Dr. Schulz knows that what we speak (or fail to speak) with our mouths reveals just as much of what is present in our hearts as what we commit with our hands. Dr. Schulz contends that we have abandoned ship: we have omitted from our lips the words and content of our Confessions, as well as the way that they proceed to unfold and explain the scriptures. For too long, we have been able to be ambivalent about our confession. For too long, we have not known the contempt of the world which Christ says hounds after His disciples (Matt. 5:12). The result is that we do not take the confession of our forefathers in the faith with the seriousness that they did. To our detriment we treat our confession merely as a "faith tradition" with the same standing as every other "faith tradition" whether of Christendom or beyond it.

The aversion, which now grips not only the culture of the world but our Church as a whole, our institutions, and our own hearts, to conform the confession of our lips in content and in practice to the Word of God and to the Lutheran Confessions is a warning sign that what is now proceeding from our hearts comes from flesh and blood and not, as with Peter, "From the Father in Heaven."

If we are to have the sort of courage required by the Law of Christ to resist the world and the satanic spells that rule it, then we must first receive God's whole counsel and not only the portions which make us comfortable. This includes such rebukes as those that God sends by no other means than through His called and authorized pastors and professors. This volume is a rebuke and warning to those who think that the ascription of the name Lutheran is enough to provide us with substance. Friendship with the world however, does not announce itself loudly. It is obvious only in such occasions where courage to offend the world is required. Where the material threat to one's well-being is real. Such is the substance of confession, and the reason why all pastors must submit to our confession—we must be willing to die for the sake of words. Yet it is not such men alone who have the duty and responsibility to know and confess. It was the distinctive conviction of the Missouri Synod that every faithful Christian—that is to say, every Lutheran—ought to know the content and procedure of the Book of Concord. Theology is not confined to the Theology department.

If indeed we as a Church are to be "Lutheran" to be "confessional" to be "biblical" then we must ask whether we—individuals, congregations, colleges, synod—are willing to be limited, defined by, normed by the Word of God. If we are, then we abide in Christ and He in us, and His blessing, including cross and trial will be upon us. The promise of Christ sacrificial and atoning death, in bloody agony, and His glorious resurrection—this alone gives us the confidence and courage we need to stand against the world. "Take they our life, goods, fame, child and wife" cannot be empty words to the confessing Church, but are real possibilities. May God and His Christ grant that through the admonition of this little volume, we may again have such courage, and in consequence, such Concord.

Pastor Christopher and Mary Durham

Anatomy of an Implosion is a timely and provocative book. Dr. Schulz provides a detailed critique of the ways in which aspects of 'wokeism' (and various derivatives) infiltrate one specific Lutheran school of higher education. He finds both sins of commission and omission, resulting in mission drift from the original purposes and goals of confessional Lutheran education. His critique is a warning to Lutheran higher education specific to his own university, but also in general. The erosion of Lutheran distinctives (e.g. Justification!) is not a phenomenon limited to only some Lutheran colleges or universities. The corrosive effects of modern culture need to be addressed with discernment and commitment to the biblical and confessional foundation of the Lutheran church and not a "it can't happen here" complacency.

Dr. Schulz voices a "call to arms" much needed today. He is to be thanked for what has been his lonely and often trying work of love for the truth, for contending "earnestly for the faith which was once for all delivered to the saints" (Jude 3).

Rev Thomas Rank
Professor of Religious Studies
Bethany Lutheran College

Annotated Table of Contents

Preamble .... **Page 1**

1. **Studied Ignorance of the Text that Makes Lutheran Schools Lutheran**..**Page 9**

    *The aim is simply to highlight what has always been considered basic and decisive among confessing Lutherans, in order to have in hand a **frame of reference** within which to make sense of our present debates* (Kurt Marquart, *Anatomy of an Explosion*).

    1.1 The 1580 *Formula of Concord* is the authoritative and sacrosanct text for Lutheran churches and schools. It is our frame of reference.

    1.2 The *Formula* (with its Epitome) is authoritative regarding (a) the *content* of Lutheran teaching as well as (b) the *methodology* of Lutheran teaching.

    (a) In terms of content it mandates, for example, teaching the total depravity of our human nature, alongside the perfect human nature and divine nature in the singular Person of Jesus of Nazareth, who is the only source of good in this life and the next.

    (b) In terms of methodology it requires pastors and professors (a) to believe, teach and confess everything Jesus has commanded us in the Bible, and (b) to reject and condemn false teaching.

    1.3 In contrast to the content and methodology of Lutheran teaching, Woke Marxism rejects *all* authority, including especially Christ's authority, and therefore all sacrosanct texts such as the Bible and the Lutheran Confessions, of which the *Formula* is the official summary.

    1.4 At my Concordia university many Regents, the Interim President, and the current President have been quashing at least one confessional pastor–professor for rejecting and condemning Woke Marxism as false doctrine. This is lamentable, both educationally and in terms of our presumed common confession.

2. **Breaking the Concordia Fellowship: A Hollow and Deceptive Philosophy of Language..........................Page 29**

   *It is important to see that the uncompromising supremacy of 'scientific' reasoning in the ... **critical method** is not an excess or an abuse which can somehow be tempered. On the contrary, it is of the essence of the method. [Social and Political] Science **has no room for privileged authorities or sacrosanct texts** (Kurt Marquart, Anatomy of an Explosion).*

   2.1 Woke Marxism is a violent and *mythological* ideology which is flourishing in higher education based on a false presupposition regarding the divine gift of language.

   2.2 This presupposition is the accomplishment of wholesale relativism, better known as *postmodernism*.

   2.3 The hollow and deceptive presupposition is this: "Language is utterly without (divine or even human) authority; therefore, *no text is authoritative or sacrosanct*."

   This presupposition of Woke Marxism:
   (a) is the very definition of hollow and deceptive philosophy in Colossians 2:8–9;
   (b) undercuts the ultimate first principle of the incarnate Logos Himself (John 1:1–3 and 14);
   (c) contradicts the content and methodology of Lutheran teaching, namely, (a) believing/teaching/confessing the Word of Christ, and (b) rejecting and condemning false doctrine; and
   (d) depletes the atmosphere of the university.

   2.4 We must diagnose Woke Marxism at my Concordia university as Marquart diagnosed the false doctrine of Seminex: The [social, political, pseudo–] science of Woke Marxism has no room for privileged authority (especially the divine authority of Jesus, Matthew 28) and has no room for canonical or authoritative texts (especially not for the sacred, efficacious, verbally inspired texts of the Hebrew and Greek Scriptures, Psalms 1 and 119 and 2 Timothy 3).

For examples of Woke Marxism at CUW replacing Christ's authority and related sacrosanct texts, consider:

(a) the promotion of DIE (Diversity, Inclusion, Equity) throughout most of 2021–2022 at CUW and the philosophy of language employed to defend it;

(b) Ibram Kendi's false doctrine in the university's Black Student Union;

(c) the entire Marxist reporting and planning apparatus at CUW; and

(d) the studied ignorance of the authority of the Confessions. For example, Luther's explanation of the 8th Commandment in the Large Catechism, by the university's Administration and Regents. This lack of confessional integrity is lamentable.

3. **Cringing toward Social Justice and Marxist Identity and Drifting away from Universal Justification............Page 57**

Theology had fallen into a confusion of tongues. **Old words were used in new and vague senses.** *Even liberals on occasion felt threatened by the all–enveloping double–talk* (Kurt Marquart, *Anatomy of an Explosion*).

3.1 Universal justification (which is *not* universalism) is (a) the central article of the Lutheran believing/teaching/confessing biblical doctrine and (b) the point of the spear for rejecting false doctrine. It is a CHRISTological first principle (John 1:1–24 and 14:6, and Jeremiah 23:6).

3.2 Social Justice/Racial Justice/LGBTQ2SA+/Marxist Identity, and all the Hydra heads of Woke Marxism, are socially constructed in opposition to the Bible, as shown in The Dallas Statement on Social Justice and the Gospel (Appendix T).

3.3 "But how does God deliver the reality of universal justification into the lives of human beings who are, as we confess in the first section of the *Formula*, fountainheads of corruption?" This is the question that determines the means by which we exist as LCMS churches and schools, such as Concordia universities.

3.4 Universal Justification, as taught in the normative Scriptures and the biblically normed Lutheran Confessions, is delivered *nisi per Verbum*, that is, exclusively via the Word of God. The infallible and efficacious Word delivers universal justification and establishes *Baptismal identity* by means of the Word, which Woke Marxism suppresses via its postmodern Expressionist Semiotics philosophy of language (Romans 3 and 6).

(a) Lutheran pastors and professors believe, teach and confess that the Old and New Testament Scriptures and the sacraments authorized in the New Testament Scriptures, such as Baptism and Holy Communion, are *the* only *means by which God* saves human beings in this life and for the life to come.

(b) By working through these exclusive means God establishes our *Baptismal identity*.

(c) Lutheran pastors and professors therefore reject the false doctrine of the DIE–ing ideology of Woke Marxism, both

   (i) because it rejects the divine authority of Christ and His verbatim Word, and

   (ii) because DIE seeks to overwrite the crucial importance of the doctrine of universal justification with Marxist identity theory in opposition to our Baptismal identity.

(d) One Concordia very recently claimed, "Our Lutheran identity is central to all we do, including our Diversity, Equity, and Inclusion (DEI) work. We recognize that DEI is an important issue and believe that our efforts in this area align with Lutheran theology." That is to say, "We are not Lutheran or biblical; our identity is not based on the Word and on our Baptismal identity alone, but on Marxist identity theory." This is lamentable because it is harmful to the soul of a Lutheran university and to the souls therein.

3.5 The infallible and efficacious Word delivers universal justification and establishes *Baptismal identity* (Romans 3 and 6), for which Marxist Identity is a poor, unbiblical substitute.

4. **Cringing toward Woke Marxism and away from the Lutheran/ biblical Understanding of Church and Ministry..........Page 87**

   What is divinely instituted, according to Scripture and the Confessions is ... the glorious and permanent (2 Corinthians 3:11) ministry of life and justification. The Gospel and sacraments themselves—not organizational chains of command— are the content, nature, task, and power of the office... the evangelical ministry is not manipulative. It relies totally on **God's working through His holy means** *"when and where he pleases"* (Augsburg Confession, 5, 20)—*not when and where human surveys, strategies, and "goal–settings" may predict or prescribe* (Kurt Marquart, *The Church and Her Fellowship, Ministry, and Governance*, 122–123).

   4.1 The Lutheran teaching of Church and Ministry follows from that practical question about universal justification: "But how does God deliver the reality of universal justification into the lives of human beings who are, as we confess in the first section of the *Formula*, fountainheads of corruption?" This is the question of the only means by which we exist as Concordia universities (see 3.3). That is, it is the question of the office or work of the Gospel ministry and spiritual leadership written in the requirements, for example, of the university President.

   4.2 The cringe toward Woke Marxism at my Concordia university has included a studied ignorance of sacrosanct texts regarding Christ's Church and its Gospel ministry. For example, there appears to be a studied ignorance of Saint Paul's apostolic texts on the office of the ministry in Ephesians 4 and in his pastoral epistles such as 1 Timothy 2 and 5 as well as of the *Formula*. This cringe– and–drift maneuvering is a lamentable mission drift from what the *Formula* calls "our public common writings" (*Formula*, Of the Comprehensive Summary, Foundation, Rule, and Standard, paragraph 1).

This studied ignorance is evident in

(a) CUW's process by which the Board of Regents elected the new President;

(b) CUW's transgressions of the Scriptures and our Lutheran Confessions in so–called "reconciliation processes"; and

(c) CUW's doctrinal innovations regarding the Lutheran teaching and practice of Church–and–Ministry in the current anatomy/culture/educational philosophy of the university.

4.3 Note well: The cringe toward Woke Marxism at my Concordia has also affirmed for this generation *the continuing relevance of Kurt Marquart's diagnosis of the Seminex explosion and Martin Luther's Lutheran stance at the Diet of Worms.*

Afterword .... **Page 125**

Author's Church and Academic Biography .... **Page 138**

Appendices .... **Page 140**

A. My response to censorship by the Provost and the Dean of the School of Arts and Sciences, January 2021.......p143

B. My essay, "Woke Dysphoria at Concordia" in Christian News, February 14, 2022..p148

C. Preaching on Psalm 32, one of the Seven Penitential Psalms, March 6, 2022...p154

D. Reporting in *The Federalist*, "Christian University Bans Professor From Campus For Critiquing Its Dive Into 'Equity' And 'Inclusion,'" March 7, 2022....................p160

E. Letter of Censure from AFA, Academic Freedom Alliance, February 28, 2022..p165

F. Letter of Censure from FIRE, Freedom and Individual Rights in Education, March 4, 2022...........................p168

G. Essay from FIRE, "Concordia University Wisconsin Must Reinstate Professor Suspended without Due Process for Article Critical of the University's 'Woke Dysphoria,'" FIRE, March 8, 2022... p173

H. Letter to the Board of Regents from LCMS President, May 9, 2022... p176

I. Reporting in *The Federalist*, "Christian University Still Hasn't Reinstated Professor It Kicked Out After He Criticized Identity Politics," May 16, 2022................p180

J. My essay, "Dem Dry Bones: Can Academic Freedom Live Again at My Religious University?" *Christian News*, June 5, 2022... p183

K. My Response to the Interim President's Complaint seeking my termination, August 29, 2022..................p188

L. Brief to the Review Committee hearing determining the outcome of the "reconciliation" process seeking my termination, November 29, 2022.............................. p207

M. The Eighth Commandment, concluding paragraphs from Martin Luther's *Large Catechism*...........................p216

N. Kurt Marquart, "The Question of Procedure in Theological Controversies," in *Australian Theological Review*, April–September 1966................................. p217

O. Christian Preus, "Bad Company Corrupts Good Character: The Only Way to Keep a Lutheran College Lutheran," *Christian Culture: A Journal for Lutherans*, Spring/Summer 2022... p226

P. Dietrich Bonhoeffer, "The Successful Man," from his unfinished *Ethics*, translated by Eberhard Bethge, 1949... p234

Q. Reporting in *The Federalist*, "Professor Banned For Calling Out Racism at Christian University Negotiates His Return," February 23, 2023................................ p236

R. Reply to the President–Provost "Agreement" Memo, March 18, 2023... p240

S. Essay, *"Cur Verbum Verba,"* to the First Annual Convention of Luther Classical College, June 6–7, 2023... p246

T. The Dallas Statement on Social Justice and the Gospel.. p256
U. Luther's 1521 Speech at the Diet of Worms................ p262

Preamble

For the better part of two years, from 2021–2022, my Lutheran university publicly announced its search for a new President who exhibits a "demonstrated belief in and commitment to equity and inclusion" and who promotes racialized "diversity in all its myriad forms." Various university Regents, Administrators, and professors had a part in this. Some supported this declaration actively while others supported it by not speaking up when they should have.

This presidential search was an effort to turn Concordia University Wisconsin (CUW) away from Lutheran doctrine and practice and move it toward Woke Marxism.

After doing everything I could to address this directly with Administrators, Regents, and others, I published an essay in February 2022, "Woke Dysphoria at Concordia." I wrote, "My Concordia university is experiencing dysphoria because it is coming under the influence of Woke–ism (that is, a potent cocktail of Progressivism, Neo–Pragmatism, and Marxism)."

Dysphoria means the "restlessness" or "disquiet" caused when people are diverted from rest in Christ alone. In this case, by the alienation from God that atheistic Marxism creates. Next, I explained the meanings of the words written in that very public announcement.

> These are aggressive–progressive Woke mantras. *Diversity* refers to a racialized diversity with unsubstantiated assumptions of white privilege and systemic (national and institutional) racism that form the mythological basis of Harvard's Critical Race Theory and the 1619 Project. *Inclusion* is an aggressive, almost violent version of what used to be known as affirmative action, now construed as racial reparations—again, on the basis of the mythological thinking from Critical Race Theory. *Equity* is the enforcement of Diversity and Inclusion by any means

necessary—excepting by means of thoughtful, reasonable, and honest writing and discussion.

The lynchpin issue is this: *The Woke agenda (*DIE, for *Diversity, Inclusion, Equity) is utterly opposed to texts and to textual authority.* In theory (such as it is) and in practice, the Woke agenda being championed by our BoR [Board of Regents] committees is literally an illiterate philosophy of education that has no place for authoritative texts" (see Appendix B for my complete essay).

My university's announcement of its plans for a Woke President was eventually removed from its website without comment and without repentance. Subsequently, our university and church leadership—some of my faculty colleagues and a few of my fellow Lutheran pastors—feel that Woke Marxism is no longer a problem because that ghastly anti–Christian announcement has been deleted and now the university has a new President. They are wrong. They are wrong because they have misdiagnosed the situation.

The problem is not that announcement, as bad as it was, telling the church and the world that individuals with institutional power and influence intended to remake Concordia University Wisconsin into Concordia University Woke. No, **the problem is the *conditions* at CUW that led to the public explosion.** In other words, the real problem is *the university's philosophy of education* and how its philosophy was and is being lived out.

There was an explosion over that public, two–year long announcement. This is a well–documented historical fact. Now we urgently need a careful study of the culture, the internal structure, the *anatomy*, so to speak, of the university—a religious, conservative Christian university!—which created such an explosion. This little book is my response as a confessional pastor in The Lutheran Church—Missouri Synod (LCMS) and as one Professor of Philosophy at Concordia University Wisconsin.

Clearly, if the culture of the university is not properly diagnosed and then biblically and confessionally re–formed, the same thing is bound to happen again and again. In addition, without a proper diagnosis and appropriate treatment of the university's philosophy of education, it is reasonable to say (as I am saying in this book) that the explosion is still in progress, out of sight. Of course, this would mean that the Woke Marxist announcement at the heart of the presidential search was really a symptom of an institutional implosion that has been underway for some time at Concordia.

In fact, the implosion was underway during the last years of the President who retired, leading to the search for a new university President. After all, it was his Board of Regents and his Administrators, some of whom engineered, some of whom promoted the *putsch* for a Woke university President. It was on his watch that faculty training in the Woke Marxist values of white supremacy and anti–racist racism took place.

The implosion was undeniably underway during the tenure of the Interim President, who had been responsible for faculty development under the retired President for decades. The implosion is still underway in these early days of the new President, as is evident in his refusal immediately to lead the university to repent of its Woke Marxism and to dismantle the Woke Marxist apparatus at CUW. It is evident as well in his continuation of the university's assault on academic freedom, which is also an assault on Lutheran disputation and debate. Regarding the university's Woke Marxist apparatus being left in place by the new President and his assault on academic freedom, see Appendices Q–S.

As military people would say, it is clear as crystal that CUW has been and still is undergoing mission drift. Those of us who teach and study missiology would further analyze this theologically as mission drift away from our *Missio Dei*, the divine mission that Jesus the Messiah has given us (Matthew 28:18–20).

Here in *Anatomy of an Implosion: One Pastor–Professor's Diagnosis & Lament at the Mission Drift to Woke Marxism in Lutheran Higher Education*, I provide a philosophical and theological diagnosis of CUW's drift away from biblical Lutheran doctrine and practice and toward the doctrine and practice of Woke Marxist values at my Lutheran university.

I believe this diagnosis has wider application to our

Concordia University System as well. I am also concerned about the implosive conditions at Bethany Lutheran College in Mankato, Minnesota, nearby Martin Luther College, and Wisconsin Lutheran College in Milwaukee, Wisconsin, where I taught for nearly twenty years.

But my urgent concern here and now is with my university, Concordia University Wisconsin, in Mequon. CUW is the university to which I have a divine call to preach, teach, and confess according to the inerrant Scriptures and the doctrines of the Scriptures as taught in the Lutheran Confessions, and to reject the false teaching which these sacrosanct texts reject. I've taken a sacred oath to do this, as has each of the pastors on faculty at my university.

The Woke Marxism taking root in our Lutheran and Christian universities is not just an incursion of Newspeak and Wokespeak. In fact, it is a full-scale war against the foundation of Christian and Lutheran churches and schools everywhere. It is a war against the Word incarnate—a campaign against the small-l *logos* of Western civilization as clearly as it is war against the incarnate *Logos* revealed in the Gospel according to Saint John.

Woke Marxism is a demonic attack on us and our children, aided and abetted by university Administrators, Regents, and certain professors "in the unconfident departments of American universities" (Ronald Dworkin) who seem willing to take every thought captive—not to Christ (2 Corinthians 10:5)—but to terrorists in tunnels, to the archetypes of Tolkien's Balrogs, and H.G. Wells' subterranean Morlocks, who are blowing up the foundations and dragging our children into the abyss.

Beneath our feet and beneath our notice, Woke Marxism (the Hydra headed monster of LGBTQ-ism, Social and Racial Justice, Marxist identity, and DIE-ing ideologies of education) is waging war against the essence of our human being. That is, the war is against flesh and blood and what Aristotle identifies as the formal characteristic of our human being—an understanding with which readers of Luther and Lutheran doctrine, for example, are remarkably familiar—namely, *language*.

The queer and rebellious vocabulary that Woke Marxist Administrators and professors are pounding into the minds of our children, resulting in the maiming of their souls and bodies, depends upon a hollow and deceptive philosophy of language (Colossians 2:8–9). This grounding philosophy of Woke Marxism is the philosophy articulated by Derrida, delivered via the IED of DIE: 'I want to keep the right to read these texts [the Bible and all authoritative texts] in a way that has to be constantly invented and *no one gets to tell me that I'm wrong!*'

The truth that Woke Marxists and their academic allies are suppressing is this: although it can be surrendered, language can never be destroyed (Matthew 24:35). Strap on your armor. Take and read, as Augustine writes in *Confessions*.

I am also writing with a heart for schools beyond the Lutheran churches in my church body, other Christian schools at home and abroad.

I have in mind, for example, the Christians in South Africa who are right now fighting the good fight against Marxism in their country and especially in their schools and universities. For example, my friend and brother in the ministry, Karl Böhmer, divinely called pastor of the steadfast and confessional Kirchdorf Lutheran congregation; as well as my friend Simon Brace, Director of Ratio Christi in South Africa, who is mightily fortifying Christian students with the inerrant Word of God against their Marxist professors; and my friend and academic colleague Daniel Maritz and his fellow faculty at Akademia, who are forming a Christian liberal arts university to overcome the mythologies of Marxism besieging their beloved country, with the incarnate capital–T Truth of Christ and His Word. These believers are standing firm against the onslaught with the whole armor of God as their everyday work–clothes. We here in the United States should do the same.

In his *Republic,* Plato recommended the *polis* or "city–state" of his day as a large–scale model that would help everyone to consider deeply the interrelated dimensions of the human soul. After searching for a scale model that will help us examine very carefully the working of Christ (Hebrews 3:1) in the CHRISTian university, I am recommending that we *think of the Christian university as a submarine.* Like a military submarine, each religious university or college, such as my Concordia university, has several interrelated dimensions. For example, the religious university is under tremendous external pressures, making a catastrophic implosion an ever–present possibility. I do refer to these external pressures based on a recent essay by a brother LCMS pastor (see Appendix O), but my main concern is with (a) the structural integrity of the university/submarine, (b) the atmosphere needed to sustain the crew, and (c) its mission readiness.

Please understand, this is not an academic exercise. This is the real deal. This anatomy or cultural analysis of my Concordia university is urgently needed if we want to avoid a *postmortem* of Concordia University Wisconsin, the kind of analysis that we in the LCMS appear to be undertaking over our Concordia university in Texas. That southern Concordia has straightforwardly declared its secession from Lutheran doctrine and the LCMS. Another postmortem analysis has been offered of three additional Concordia–class universities that have imploded in recent years. See Appendix N for evidence that it was their drift toward Woke Marxism that led to the loss at sea of our Concordias in Selma, Alabama; New York, New York; and Portland, Oregon.

My analysis is patterned after Kurt Marquart's *Anatomy of an Explosion: A Theological Analysis of the Missouri Synod Conflict*. His book is also something of a postmortem analysis. My fervent prayer is that my shorter and less academic little book will reach our people, pastors, and leaders in the LCMS, and our university professors (as well as Administrators at our conservative Lutheran colleges and universities) in the rest of the country in time to avoid the level of carnage produced by the Seminex professors and Administrators.

But I am haunted by the words of my church body's President in his May 9, 2022, letter to my university's Board of Regents, calling for them to repent of their Woke Marxism: "I fear you will continue to reject my advice, to the continued detriment of Concordia and our life together" (Appendix H).

What Marquart wrote about Seminex at our Concordia Seminary, St. Louis, a generation ago applies equally to the drift toward Woke Marxism at CUW: "[This] neo–Lutheran with–it–ness is not the theology of the cross ... but a cultural cringe to secular values." *Cringe* means "to bow down to." That CUW presidential search announcement—which still has not been repudiated and rejected at the time I am writing—was a bowing down to the secular values of Woke Marxism, a "taking a knee" to Lutheran and biblical teaching. It was not bowing down to the Lord Jesus in fear, love, and trust, but bowing down to an ideology utterly opposed to Him and His Church.

Make no mistake, Woke Marxism is a secular religion that is utterly and maniacally opposed to all authority (especially to the divine authority of Jesus, Matthew 28) and has no room for canonical or authoritative texts (especially not for the sacred, efficacious, verbatim texts of the Hebrew and Greek Scriptures, 2 Timothy 3:16) as I explain in my second chapter. My first chapter sets out the Lutheran method and philosophy of education from which my university has been drifting for far too long. My third and fourth chapters outline two articles of Lutheran and biblical doctrine that CUW has been contradicting in word and deed because of its continuing cringe toward the secular values of Woke Marxism.

In my chapter–by–chapter argument, please keep your eyes on my attention to our Lutheran and Christian commitment to the means of grace and language as the means–by–which we teach in our churches and schools. This is a fundamental or foundational reality for us as human beings, as I explain in fine-grained detail. Language is fundamental because it is the means–by–which our Lord God, the incarnate Logos of John 1, has chosen to speak with us human beings.

Written in the (much louder and far more educated) footsteps of Professor Marquart, I am writing *Anatomy of an Implosion: One Pastor–Professor's Diagnosis & Lament at the Mission Drift to Woke Marxism in Lutheran Higher Education* to provide "rank and file Christians," pastors, people, and professors, "with information [and analysis] needed to face the present crises in Christendom" regarding education in our churches and schools. It is an analysis of Woke Marxism versus Christ and His Word in four interrelated essays, with a not so brief Appendices of primary texts.

To paraphrase Marquart, *without* contempt *of the world and the worldly ideology of Woke Marxism, we cannot love, much less proclaim, the eternal things of God*. A worldly philosophy of education in our churches and schools leads instead to a despising of that very suffering and cross which open our eyes to the priceless grandeur of the "visible and lowlier" things of God (*Anatomy of an Explosion*, 140–141)!

In the fellowship of His sufferings,

Greg Schulz
Professor of Philosophy
Lt Col, USAF/CAP (retired)
Lutheran Philosopher at https://lutheranphilosopher.com

A Note of Thanksgiving

Thanks to my entire Lutheran Philosopher Aircrew and Team for your support, prayers, and insistence that I write boldly! Especially, thanks to Virginia (Ginny) Valleau and my brother in the Gospel ministry, Paul Arndt. Ginny graciously edited this book. Pastor Arndt graciously involved me in his online study of our *Formula of Concord*, With Intrepid Hearts, which continues to be a Godsend for my thinking and writing.

I am grateful as well to Pastor Philip Hale, editor of *Christian News*, and his passionate and professional staff. In this, I also speak for many, many other confessional Lutherans.

As always, I am thankful to our Lord for my favorite poet and helper, my beloved wife Paula, without whom I would only rant, but because of whose steadfast love and example I write.

My thanks to the Lord for the Administration and Board of Regents at Concordia University Wisconsin who imposed on me a two-year forced sabbatical. As Joseph would say, "As for you, you meant evil against me; but God meant it for good in order to bring about this present result" (Genesis 50:20). That present result is this book and the good that it will, Lord willing, do for religious universities who are under the thrall of Woke Marxism—especially the good that it will do for my fellow pastors and professors with the courage in Christ to call out for Administrators and Regents in our Lutheran colleges and universities to repent of their mission or *missio Dei* drift into the soul-crushing and anti-Christ dogma of Woke Marxism.

Finally, thanks to Attorney Mark Leitner of Laffey, Leitner & Goode; and to Attorney Dan Lennington and the generous donors to WILL, the Wisconsin Institute for Law and Liberty, whose resolve to protect academic freedom has made my work possible these past two years.

Chapter One

Studied Ignorance of the Text that Makes Lutheran Schools Lutheran

*The aim is simply to highlight what has always been considered basic and decisive among confessing Lutherans, in order to have in hand a **frame of reference** within which to make sense of our present debates* (Kurt Marquart, *Anatomy of an Explosion*).[1]

Concordia is not a brand; it is a confessional covenant—a covenant with an institution's church body and with its students and professors. My university's very name, Concordia, highlights the importance of the *source* of whatever we confess, good or bad. As our Lord explains, the source of good or bad confessing is one's heart: "A good man out of the good treasure of his heart brings forth good; and an evil man out of the evil treasure of his heart brings forth evil. For out of the abundance of the heart his mouth speaks" (Luke 6:45). When His explanation is translated into Latin, "heart" becomes *cor,* as in "core curriculum" or "core values."

So, *heart* is at the core of the name Con–*cor*–dia. The next question is whether a Concordia university, my Concordia for example, has a Lutheran heart. This brings us to the question of what a Lutheran university with the name Concordia is confessing. *Confessional* means "to speak in line with texts." In this case, the texts must be the entirety of the verbatim biblical text as well as our Lutheran Confessions. The Lutheran

---

[1] Kurt Marquart, *Anatomy of an Explosion: A Theological Analysis of the Missouri Synod Conflict* (Concordia Theological Seminary Press 1977; Reprinted 1978 by Baker Book House Company), 9. Unless otherwise footnoted this is the book from which quotations or ideas attributed to Professor Marquart are taken. All of these attributions except for this opening quote and the epigraph for my Afterword are from Chapter 5, The Counter–Biblical (Critical) Attack, 107–146.

Confessions are authoritative because they are completely reliable doctrinal reflections and summaries of what Jesus teaches in the entire, verbatim biblical text. A Lutheran university or college either confesses all of these texts without qualification or it is not Lutheran at its core. Think here of our Lord's commission to be "teaching them to obey *everything I have commanded you*" (Matthew 28:20).

Is Concordia University Wisconsin (CUW) confessional? While many of my fellow professors are clearly and blessedly confessional in what they believe, teach, and confess, the Administration—especially the academic leadership—is plainly not. Because of its upside-down organizational structure, in which a morbidly obese administration rules the roost,[2] the present culture of Concordia is anything but confessional, as I will explain.

Confessional. *Confessional* is a term with a deep history in the German Reformation of the 1500s which was in turn rooted in the New Testament Scriptures. It means "to speak in line with Christ and His inerrant Word, the Bible." For example, consider Augustine's book, *Confessions*, written about 400 A.D. Every chapter of his *Confessions*—every biographical reflection and every philosophical investigation—is framed and deeply informed by God's words, which Augustine knows by heart. Consider too the apostle John and his first epistle. In 1 John 1:9 the apostle explains that if we say we have no sin then the truth is not among us. He goes on to say that only if we *confess* our sins—his Greek word for confessing, *homologomen,* means "speaking the same Word"—will God cleanse us from all unrighteousness or injustice.

Too often these days, the word *confessional* is used by people who self-identify themselves, their churches, their schools as "confessional," as if simply uttering that deeply historical word again and again proves that they and therefore their institution are genuinely Lutheran: "I'm confessional! I'm confessional! I'm confessional!"

---

[2] For more on this stultifying development in modern universities, including especially religious universities, see Benjamin Ginsberg, *The Fall of the Faculty: The Rise of the All–Administrative University and Why It Matters* (New York: Oxford University Press, 2011), especially Chapter 1, The Growth of the Administration, and Chapter 7, What Is to Be Done?

But as Kurt Marquart wrote about the kerfuffle of Seminex, "Theology had fallen into a confusion of tongues. Old words were used in new and vague senses." The same thing is true of the tumult of Woke Marxism at my Concordia university.

The real question is, "Confessional *with what?*"

It's like saying, "I am a person of integrity!" as if mouthing the word proves something all by itself. From decades of teaching military core values and command leadership to people in uniform I know that this virtue of integrity is almost always misunderstood and abused.

Integrity is not a matter of being an officer who successfully imposes his will and vision on his subordinates. Integrity is about the ultimate authority a military officer lives, leads, and is ready to die by.

Authority is the lynchpin issue for integrity as it is for being confessional.

This understanding of integrity and ultimate authority applies as well to officials and leaders in institutions such as Concordia university, which self-identifies as "a Lutheran institution of higher learning." The right question to pose when someone asserts that, or acts as if he is "a leader of integrity" is this: "Fine, but *what exactly are you integrous with*? What is your ultimate and therefore your daily authority in practice?" Think for instance of what the Scriptures tell us of the integrity of the centurion stationed in Capernaum. "Lord ... just say the word... For I also am a man under authority" (Matthew 8:5–13). Think as well of the opening verse of Job, where we learn that Job was a man of integrity, meaning that he was integrous *with the LORD God, his Kinsman–redeemer.*

Confessional integrity is textual. Speaking of integrity and authoritative texts, in my church body, The Lutheran Church—Missouri Synod (LCMS), "all authority over Synod activities and agencies such as our Concordias is a sacred trust granted by the Synod's congregations to specific officers and boards in the interest of actively maintaining and furthering the congregations' common confession and constitutional objectives in all aspects of the work of the Synod and its agencies." Our Bylaws make it clear as crystal. All are to carry out their responsibilities "in a manner reflecting the highest degree of integrity and honesty consistent with the Scriptures, the Lutheran Confessions, the Constitution, Bylaws, and resolutions of the Synod" (for more, please see Appendices K and L).

Concordia University Wisconsin has been acting apart from the authority of the texts of Scriptures and the Lutheran Confessions for so long that its top-down culture is no longer confessional and Lutheran.

For example, as the LCMS President wrote to CUW in May 2022, "As a result of these very significant concerns, some of which have been made public across the Synod and in news reports beyond the church, many pious laypeople and congregations of the Synod have lost trust in the university's faithfulness to genuine Lutheranism and her mission to raise up both church workers and faithful citizens in other vocations, all while reaching the lost with the Gospel of Christ." See Appendix H.

Concordia University Wisconsin broke from the Scriptures and the Lutheran Confessions in 2021–2022 by publicly and officially declaring its search for a new President who exhibits a "demonstrated belief in and commitment to equity and inclusion" and who promotes racialized "diversity in all its myriad forms." This was a violation of our confessional covenant—a major explosion set off by the university's Administrators and Regents and a few faculty. That explosion is a symptom of the un-confessional and un-Lutheran culture of my university.

In the case of my Concordia, the question at this point is to find out what, if anything, the university is integrous with. What is its foundation, rule, and standard? In ethics we speak about this foundational standard as the *norm*. What is normative at CUW? What is normal? Are its leaders, for instance, administering as confessional Lutherans, or do they merely invoke the word *confessional* as needed for public relations or to persuade potential students and donors?

As with being a person of genuine integrity, so it is with being a genuinely confessional Lutheran. There is always that vital element which Martin Luther calls the *extra nos*, that outside–of–us authority or authoritative texts. The question is, "What are you believing, teaching, and confessing—is it our common Lutheran confession?" As Kurt Marquart put it in his *Anatomy of an Explosion* of Seminex a generation ago, this is the purpose of this chapter: "The aim is simply to highlight what has always been considered basic and defining among confessing Lutherans, in order to have in hand a frame of reference within which to make sense of our present debates."

CUW has not been thinking or acting confessionally. How can we tell? The giveaway is that the university has been studiously ignoring *The Formula of Concord*. This is not a theoretical matter, "For out of the abundance of the heart, the *cor*" comes the content and the method of teaching at my Con–*cor*–dia university.

University as a submarine. To understand the problems that stem from Concordia's ignorance of the *Formula*, it will help to think of my university as a military submarine. A submarine operates under substantial, potentially fatal water pressure, while a religious university operates under substantial worldly pressure. The inner hull of a submarine must withstand water pressure, or it will implode. Similarly, a religious university must withstand worldly pressure, or it will implode. A submarine crew depends on the atmosphere in their submarine. A university faculty depends on the atmosphere within their vessel.

There are two ways to address the Woke Marxism incident from the recent Presidential search. One way would be to pretend, with the election of a new University President, that all is well. This would be to imitate the "reset" button presented to the Russians by the US Secretary of State in March 2009, which ironically featured a Russian word that did not mean "reset" but "overload." This way does not, of course, address the problem at all, but constitutes a coverup of a potentially fatal situation for the university/submarine—something very much like the administrative culture at NASA which suppressed the warnings from engineers about a loss of integrity in the solid rocket booster O-rings for the Challenger space shuttle.

From CGT to CRT. A second way to analyze the situation is in terms of the university leadership's commitment to Church Growth practices in recent decades. According to Church Growth Theory (CGT), norms and standards from the social and behavioral sciences take precedence over biblical and confessional norms and standards. In CGT the way to do education is not according to Psalm 119 or Deuteronomy 6, but according to social science metrics. Scripture may be invoked, but not normatively; only as a religious veneer for visions, policies, and programs that are dictated by the social sciences such as Political Science, Anthropology, Culture Studies, and so on.

Over the past couple of decades this has been the strategy of the Administration and Board of Regents. It is CGT that made CUW vulnerable to Woke Marxism and Critical Race Theory (CRT). CRT is the militant version of CGT.

During the long tenure of the recently retired university President, the university moved from teaching and planning according to the means of grace, that is, via teaching God's Word to future seminary students and Lutheran teachers, to teaching and planning according to the non-biblical and anti-Christ means of CGT. The university drifted away from the rule and standard of the means of grace—the *norm* of faithfulness—to the means-by-which the social sciences operate.

Mission drift = *Missio Dei* drift. This was and is mission drift, the kind of drift from mission statements and so on to which non-profit organizations are prone. But in the case of my religious university, it is far worse, far more dangerous. In the second chapter I will explain how profound the danger is. At present, let me unpack some of the consequences of CUW's mission drift, first into CGT and then into the depths of CRT. This drift is, I am saying, a direct consequence of what the university has *not* been doing. It has *not* been thinking and acting confessionally because it has chosen *not* to live by the authority of Scripture and our Confessions.

In the case of Concordia University Wisconsin, its mission drift is *missio Dei* drift. That is, it is a departure from our *mission from God*, a drift away from Scripture and the Confessions toward a deeper and deeper commitment to social science metrics to assess success numerically, in terms of demographics, finances, and so on. In line with my submarine/university analogy, this is a completely predictable drift which is bringing us closer and closer to crush depth and a fatal implosion. It is a mission drift that is also a clear dereliction of duty. "But what then is the duty [we have been given]? Well, the duty is precisely the expression for God's will" (Søren Kierkegaard).[3]

"How can the young keep his way without fault? Only by observing Your words. With all my heart I seek You; do not let me stray from Your commandments" (Psalm 119:9–10).

The outcome of its devotion to CGT is that Concordia's planning, programming, and curricula are no longer primarily about sowing God's Word but are focused instead on "measurable success." For a Lutheran and biblical criticism of this squishy notion of scientifically measurable "success" see Dietrich Bonhoeffer's "The Successful Man," Appendix P.

Another way to express this systemic problem of imposing CGT or Church Growth Theory on my Lutheran university, as one of our exceptionally well qualified parish pastors has done in point–for–point detail, is to recognize the consequences of a church growth strategy for universities such as mine. The consequences include (a) a nearly debilitating financial dependency on the federal government, (b) making confessional Lutheran students into a minority in the CUW student body, and (c) reducing the percentage of confessional Lutheran professors on faculty, and so on.

Woke Marxist accreditation. The consequences of CGT also include financial dependence on accreditation from a Woke Marxist agency. This is the tipping point where the CGT at the heart of the university becomes CRT. This dependency is now malforming the *missio Dei* of CUW.

> Accreditation has played a role in this also. When Dr. Gregory Schulz publicly stated that accreditation concerns played a role in the woke agenda at Concordia Wisconsin, the administration openly retorted that this was a lie. It was not a lie. It was and is obvious and it's embarrassing not to admit it.
>
> The Higher Learning Commission (HLC), which accredits all of the Lutheran colleges in the Midwest, has a five-year plan called EVOLVE 2025, where it states that "an equity framework should permeate… all levels of institutions (e.g., students, staff, faculty

---

[3] Søren Kierkegaard, C. Stephen Evans and Sylvia Walsh, editors, *Fear and Trembling* (New York: Cambridge University Press, 2006), 52.

and governing boards)" and then further states that "HLC will ensure that concepts of equity, diversity, access and inclusion are demonstrated in its mission and other foundational statements."

HLC's visitation teams lecture the administration and faculty on how overly white and non-diverse our Lutheran colleges are. The expectation is for more women in authority, more non-white faculty, staff, students, and regents, and more public acceptance or toleration of LGBTQ or BLM-type groups.

If any of our Lutheran colleges or universities loses accreditation they will go bankrupt almost immediately. Enrollment will dip so drastically that it would be impossible to sustain their enormous budgets. Every regent knows this and every administrator knows this. The fact that HLC is openly woke and pushes wokeness on the institutions it accredits is a problem and an obvious factor in the leftward shift (for the complete essay, see Appendix O).

Let me summarize my focus this way. My concern is primarily with the hull integrity and the atmosphere of the submarine. These two factors are interdependent. Think of the hull integrity of CUW as integrity with the Bible and our Lutheran Confessions, particularly *The Formula of Concord*. There is clear evidence of metal fatigue and hull failure as I explain in the next few pages.

The atmosphere of the university submarine is also being depleted. Although it may not seem obvious yet in this first chapter, the Administrators, with the support of the Regents, are well along in the process of replacing the linguistic foundation of our Lutheran confessional philosophy of education with the very philosophy of language that supports Woke Marxism in higher education and in Western society and beyond. This hollow and deceptive philosophy of education is what the apostle Paul cautions against in Colossians 2, as we shall consider in detail in the next chapter.

1.1 The 1580 *Formula of Concord* is the authoritative and sacrosanct text...

Confessional frame of reference. Now it is time to apply Professor Marquart's 1977 analysis of the problem with Seminex to the problem at my Concordia university today. "The aim is simply to highlight what has always been considered basic and decisive among confessing Lutherans, in order to have in hand a *frame of reference* within which to make sense of our present debates."

The frame of reference for confessing Lutheran churches and schools is *The Formula of Concord*. The common name of our Concordia universities is taken from a paragraph in the opening pages of the *Formula*.

> Since for thorough, permanent unity in the Church it is, above all things, necessary that we have a comprehensive, unanimously approved summary and form wherein is brought together from God's Word the common doctrine, reduced to a brief compass, which the churches that are of the true Christian religion confess ... [the creeds, catechisms and other Lutheran confessions are mentioned]...
>
> In the pure churches and schools these public writings have been always regarded as the sum and model of the doctrine which Dr. Luther, of blessed memory, has admirably deduced from God's Word and firmly established ... and has expressly drawn this distinction, namely, that the Word of God should alone be and remain the only rule and standard of doctrine, to which the writings of no man should be regarded as equal, but to which everything should be subjected (*The Formula of Concord*, Of the Comprehensive Summary, Foundation, Rule, and Standard, paragraphs 1 and 9).

The meaning of *Concordia* is baked into the text of the *Formula*. The first line of paragraph 1 highlights the means to "thorough and permanent unity" in Christ's Church. The Latin word translated as "unity" is *concordiam*. This brings us again to the matter of being a confessional person—or being a confessional institution. As you look at the word Concordia, you see the middle syllable, *cor*, which is "heart." Not heart in a vague romantic sense, but heart as the *core* (there's our Latin word again) of one's being or the core values of an institution.

Lamentably, the *Formula* is not at the core of Concordia University Wisconsin. It is not anywhere to be found—except in the faithful work of the confessional professors I mentioned. The LCMS President identified three departments where confessional professors can be found: the Theology, Philosophy, and Science departments. See Appendix H.

1.2 The *Formula* (...Epitome) is authoritative regarding... content...methodology of Lutheran teaching.

The *Formula of Concord* frames what it means to be a Concordia in two dimensions. First, it provides the *core content* of Lutheran teaching. Second, it provides the *basic methodology* for Lutheran teaching.

Lutheran core content. For the core content of Lutheran teaching, be sure to read for yourself the first part of the *Formula*, Of Original Sin. Here are two excerpts. The first is about human nature after Adam and Eve's insurgency in the Garden of Eden.

> And first, it is true that Christians should regard and recognize as sin not only the actual transgression of God's commandments; but also that the horrible, dreadful hereditary malady by which the entire nature is corrupted should above all things be regarded and recognized as sin indeed, yea, as the chief sin, which is a root and fountain-head of all actual sins.
>
> And by Dr. Luther it is called a nature–sin or person–sin, thereby to indicate that, even though a person would think, speak, or do nothing evil (which, however, is impossible in this life, since the fall of our first parents), his nature and person are nevertheless sinful, that is, thoroughly and utterly infected and corrupted before God by original sin, as by a spiritual leprosy; and on account of this corruption and because of the fall of the first man the nature or person is accused or condemned by God's Law, so that we are by nature the children of wrath, death, and damnation, unless we are delivered therefrom by the merit of Christ (Paragraphs 5–6).

This is human nature after the Fall, fatally affected by the malady of sin. Think of the consequences of this reality for how we professors teach and how our students learn. Consider that the only way to address this reality is in terms of *human nature*, a concept suppressed in most of our PhD programs, in the professional journals and textbooks of many of our disciplines and—not incidentally—in Critical Race Theory (CRT) and Woke Marxist ideology, not to mention global media and government schools, especially secular institutions of higher learning.

Someone may object that Western and biblical concepts such as *nature* can be done away with and replaced by other cultural conceptions. My reply is to agree that this is precisely what is being done in university classrooms today. But the consequences are dreadful. The notion that our traditional concepts such as the *Formula's* term *nature* are replaceable is precisely what has enabled professors and others to promote transgenderism and a multitude of evils against our sons and daughters. If there is no such thing as human nature, there is no prohibition against human experimentation. Just as bad, by deleting *nature* from classroom and campus discussions our children and grandchildren are denied the exact vocabulary to see for themselves what is being perpetrated against them.

The concept of *human nature* is required for Lutheran teaching because it is the classical, biblical, and confessional way of thinking about ourselves as human beings. This way of thinking is at the heart and core of Western culture. It is also, as you can see, at the core of our Lutheran confessions, summed up and presented in the *Formula* as the Sole Rule and Standard for Lutheran teaching "in our churches and schools." Not to teach the concept of nature and not to teach the reality of the total corruption of all human beings but instead to teach self-esteem, developmental theories or ethics that assume an essential goodness in the human being, and so on—this is to teach in contradiction to biblical, Lutheran, and LCMS doctrine. It is also to contribute to the destruction of Western culture.

Western culture is shared moral judgments handed down from one generation to the next according to Greek forms of thinking and further informed by the Old and New Testaments (adapted from Roger Scruton).[4] So, any other formulations of our human kind of being (Darwin's, Marx's, Freud's, for example) are intellectually flawed (a) because they are very recent theories and essentially untested, but also (b) because they either deny or refuse to consider the divine wisdom and clarity of the Hebrew and Greek Scriptures. "What is man that you are mindful of him, the son of man [human being] that You care for him?"

This dialog from Psalm 8, the dialogue initiated by God with His human creatures, is unknown and unknowable if our anthropology—that is, our understanding of ourselves and our students—is taken from Darwin, Marx, and Freud and their disciples.

There is also the matter of God's human nature and the way in which He has taken our human nature (though without sin, Hebrews 4:15) up into His divine nature, these two natures being forever after united in the singular Person of Jesus the Messiah!

> Secondly, in the article of Redemption the Scriptures testify forcibly that God's Son assumed our human nature without sin, so that He was in all things, sin excepted, made like unto us, His brethren, Heb. 2:14. Hence all the old orthodox teachers have maintained that Christ, according to His assumed humanity, is of one essence with us, His brethren; for He has assumed His human nature, which in all respects (sin alone excepted) is like our human nature in its essence and all essential attributes; and they have condemned the contrary doctrine as manifest heresy.
>
> Now, if there were no distinction between the nature or essence of corrupt man and original sin, it must follow that Christ either did not assume our nature, because He did not assume sin, or that, because He assumed our nature, He also assumed sin; both of which ideas are contrary to the Scriptures. But inasmuch as the Son of God assumed our nature, and not original sin, it is clear from this fact that human nature, even since the Fall, and original sin, are not one [and the same] thing, but must be distinguished (*The Formula of Concord*, Of the Comprehensive Summary,

---

[4] Roger Scruton, *Culture Counts: Faith and Feeling in a World Besieged* (New York: Encounter books, 2007), see especially Chapter 1, What is Culture? And Chapter 5, Teaching Culture.

Foundation, Rule, and Standard, paragraphs 43–44).

This is God's ultimate response to the question He teaches us to ask Him in Psalm 8, "What is man that you are mindful of him, the son of man [human being] that You care for him?" The Epistle to the Hebrews tells us that the son of man is the Son of Man Himself.

> For He has not put the world to come, of which we speak, in subjection to angels.
>
> But one testified in a certain place, saying:
> "What is man that You are mindful of him,
> Or the son of man that You take care of him?
> You have made him a little lower than the angels;
> You have crowned him with glory and honor,
> And set him over the works of Your hands.
> You have put all things in subjection under his feet."
>
> For in that He put all in subjection under him, He left nothing *that is* not put under him. But now we do not yet see all things put under him. But we see Jesus, who was made a little lower than the angels, for the suffering of death crowned with glory and honor, that He, by the grace of God, might taste death for everyone (Hebrews 2:5–9).

What is the content of confessional Lutheran thinking and teaching? It is this world-shattering, life-changing reality that our human nature has been taken up and forever fused with God's divine nature in the person of Jesus the Christ. This is what Lutheran pastors preach, what Lutheran teachers teach, and what Lutheran professors profess. This is what we believe, teach, and confess. This is what gives content and form to Lutheran teaching.

The place to see whether there is Lutheran content in the teaching at my Concordia is to consider faculty development. As my department chair has been arguing for decades, our university should be operating on the subsidiarity principle, where teaching and curriculum decisions and policies are made and implemented by the professors. Regrettably, the university operates in a heavy-handed top-down manner. For the way this top-down academic faculty "development" works in respect to Lutheran content in our classrooms see Appendix A.

The Administrator in charge of faculty development is the

Provost, the latest way of referring to what used to be called the Academic Dean. There has not been a single time, as far as I can discover, when the university's provosts have ever cited the *Formula*, much less made the *Formula's* Sole Rule and Standard for Lutheran churches and schools the rule and standard for the faculty, or for their own work of supervising the faculty.

What they have done instead is provide Woke Marxist training and Woke Marxist "options" for the faculty—training and opportunities that align with their Woke Marxist accrediting agency: "The university also maintains a 'bias reporting system.' Those are widely known to enable attacks against students or colleagues. Campus trainings on the system led by CUW Administrators under the previous President ... allege 'unconscious bias' as a cause for filing such a report." See Appendices D and Q.

Lutheran methodology. The second dimension of the *Formula* is the basic methodology for teaching that it mandates for Lutheran teaching.

> *Affirmativa*
>> The Pure Doctrine, Faith, and Confession...
>> 1. We believe, teach, and confess...
>> 2. We believe, teach, and confess...
>> 3. We believe, teach, and confess...
>
> *Negativa*
>> Rejection of the false opposite Dogmas
>> Therefore we reject and condemn...
>
> (*The Formula of Concord*. Epitome, I. Of Original Sin, paragraphs 1–9).

Mettle fatigue. Why, why has Concordia University Wisconsin not rejected and condemned Woke Marxism? In viewing the university as a submarine, we could think here of problems with the hull such as metal fatigue. At this point, with the *Formula's* required methodology stated in black and white ("We believe, teach, and confess" everything Jesus has commanded us, plus "We reject and condemn" the false and opposite doctrines) we should consider the "mettle fatigue" of CUW leadership.

This is *mettle* in the sense of "testing their mettle," that is, assessing the character and abilities of CUW's Administrators, Regents, and those program directors and professors who condone and celebrate CGT, CRT, and Woke Marxism. For the record, here is what confessional Lutherans in this situation would say: "It has been our purpose to state and declare plainly [categorically], purely, and clearly our faith and confession concerning each one of these [controversies]" (*Formula of Concord*, Of Articles in Controversy, paragraph 19).

For anyone who objects that the Bible, and not our *Formula*, should be the frame of reference for education at our Lutheran university, I respond this way. While serving as pastor at my last congregation on Milwaukee's North Side, there was a storefront church with the slogan on its sign, "No Creed but Christ, No Book but the Bible."

Would you send your children or grandchildren to a church or church school with that motto? This is a slogan to conjure with. The motto provides wiggle room for a preacher or teacher to say whatever he wants to say and not say whatever he does not want to say about the Christ. He can do whatever cherry-picking of God's written Word that he needs to keep his job. Anything goes, according to this pious pandering, this mushy notion of "creed" and hasty mention of "Bible." Every heretic who ever misrepresented the two natures in the one Person of Christ would be comfortable with this motto.

The Seminex professors of Marquart's time could have used this motto to justify their undercutting of the privileged authority of the Bible with their quasi-scientific method of biblical interpretation.

Woke Marxist professors such as Ibram X. Kendi could use this slogan to deny the divine authority of Christ as well as the form and content of "these Scriptures that testify of Me" (John 5:39–40). "Racially divisive actions, committees, and public statements from CUW that *The Federalist* highlighted last year [2022] are still present on university websites. The university's Black Student Union recommends the fact-challenged and racially biased 1619 Project to students, as well as making purchases based on a vendor's skin color. It also recommended author Ibram X. Kendi's work." See Appendix Q.

Even with such a brief sampling of its dogma, every Christian should acknowledge that Woke Marxism is in fact a rejection of Christ and His Word—a false, anti-Christ dogma which we must, according to the *Formula*, reject and condemn as damnable. The official Latin for "we reject and condemn" is "we reject and *damnamus*."

1.3 In contrast to…Lutheran teaching, Woke Marxism rejects *all* authority…

Woke Marxism = rejection of all textual authority. In opposition to confessional, *Formula of Concord* Lutheran education, Woke Marxism is a secular religion[5] that is utterly and maniacally opposed to authority (especially to the divine authority of Jesus, Matthew 28) and has no room for canonical or authoritative texts (especially not for the sacred, efficacious, verbally inspired texts of the Hebrew and Greek Scriptures, 2 Timothy 3). Like the serpentine Hydra in Greek mythology, Woke Marxism has many heads and is constantly sprouting more: Cultural Marxism, CRT, LGBTQ2, Wokeism, Critical Theory, and so on.

Fundamentally, Woke Marxism is an anti-philosophy of revolt against "privileged authority and sacrosanct texts," to use Marquart's words for the science at the root of Seminex heresy. Remember that Woke Marxism is the militant version of Church Growth Theory (CGT).

Marx himself insisted that the Christian religion is the opium of the people. "Religion is the sigh of the oppressed creature, the heart of a heartless world, and the soul of soulless conditions. It is the *opium* of the people" (Critique of Hegel's Philosophy of Right). He did not write this conviction in his critique of his philosophical father, Hegel, to provide a soundbite. Marx's rejection of the revealed Word of God, branding it as a mass narcotic, is the heart and core of his socialist atheism. For Woke Marxists, religion is an opiate; but for us Christians, Marxism is the fentanyl of education in our churches and schools.

Woke Marxism is not a bushel basket of deplorable ideas;

---

[5] John McWhorter, *Woke Racism: How a New Religion Has Betrayed Black America* (New York: Random House, 2021), especially the Preface, xii–xv.

actually, it is a religion of revolution against all authority. For example, consider its revolution against the sacrosanct texts of the United States. *Sacrosanct* means "sacred" or set apart, but the term emphasizes the inherent *authority* of sacred texts. As I wrote in "Woke Dysphoria at Concordia" in February 2022:

> These are aggressive–progressive Woke mantras. *Diversity* refers to a racialized diversity with unsubstantiated assumptions of white privilege and systemic (national and institutional) racism that form the mythological basis of Harvard's Critical Race Theory and the 1619 Project. *Inclusion* is an aggressive, almost violent version of what used to be known as affirmative action, now construed as racial reparations—again, on the basis of the mythological thinking from Critical Race Theory. *Equity* is the enforcement of Diversity and Inclusion by any means necessary—excepting by means of thoughtful, reasonable, and honest writing and discussion.
>
> The lynchpin issue is this: *The Woke agenda (*DIE, for *Diversity, Inclusion, Equity) is utterly opposed to texts and to textual authority.* In theory (such as it is) and in practice, the Woke agenda being championed by our BoR committees is literally an illiterate philosophy of education that has no place for authoritative texts. For example, Woke–ness has no place for authoritative texts such as the Constitution or the Declaration of Independence (Appendix B).

False dogma. Marx's false teaching—a confession in violent opposition to our common Lutheran confessional texts and to *all* authority and authoritative texts—has been taught and is tolerated at CUW. In step with Marxist atheism, Ibram X. Kendi's false doctrine, as expressed in his writings and on social media, is that Jesus the Messiah is not a Savior from sin but only a role model for Marxist revolution and the implementation of Critical Race Theory. As mentioned, Kendi has been taught and promoted by the Black Student Union program at CUW. This false teaching has not been rejected or condemned. See Appendices D and Q.

This is another indication that the two-year putsch at my Lutheran university for a new President who exhibits a "demonstrated belief in and commitment to equity and inclusion" and who promotes racialized "diversity in all its myriad forms"—the vocabulary of Woke Marxism, including its use of Critical Race Theory and so on—was not an isolated explosion, but rather is an indication of an ongoing implosion. As long as Woke Marxism goes unrepudiated at my university, and if the Administrators and programs that support or tolerate Woke Marxism remain in place, you will know that my university is not confessional. Ultimately, the submarine/university will implode and be lost at sea. She already appears to be out of her depth.

We should also consider that the entire Concordia-class fleet is at risk of implosion. At the time I am writing, to my knowledge none of our Concordias (all of my church body's universities are called Concordia) has repudiated and condemned Woke Marxism. It seems reasonable to ask whether the other members of the Concordia University System fleet are in sync with *The Formula of Concord* academically and programmatically, since my Concordia is often held up as "the flagship of the Concordias."

The major cause of this implosion, remember, is the lack of structural integrity, the systemic squelching of the confessional identity with which my self-identified "Lutheran institution of higher learning" was christened at its launch.

1.4 ...[University Administrators]...have been quashing... [a] professor–pastor for rejecting Woke Marxism...

Contradicting the *Formula*. How deep does CUW's studied ignorance of the *Formula* go? The university's disdain for the *Formula* is so profound that the Interim President and now the new University President, both supported by the Board of Regents, *condemn and reject a pastor–professor for condemning and rejecting the false doctrine of Woke Marxism* at their "Lutheran institution of higher learning." They've been at it for nearly two years now.

I will address the public scandal of their ongoing attack on academic freedom in a later chapter. At this point, though, let me quote one of the national organizations that have censured CUW in order to show how opposed CUW has become to the teaching methodology mandated in our Lutheran Confessions. And how transparent the university's hypocritical conduct is to observers outside of the LCMS. In February 2022, the Academic Freedom Alliance wrote:

> Schulz is not challenging accepted Lutheran doctrine or subverting the mission of the university as a Christian institution. He is criticizing the policy decisions of the university administration and whether the administration's actions should be regarded as consistent with Lutheran commitments properly understood. For the university to punish and suppress speech of that sort would be to dramatically limit professorial speech and call into question whether Concordia is capable of operating as a recognizable institution of higher education.
>
> Of course, Professor Schulz has a responsibility not to "advocate a position contrary to that of the Synod," but here he is participating in a public debate on what the implications of the Synod's positions might be for the university. If faculty at the university must refrain from speaking in public about the future of the university and the fidelity of the university's activities to the positions of the Synod, then the university's commitment to the faculty to value their individuality and to engage in intellectual inquiry will be an empty promise (Appendix E and Academic Freedom Alliance [AFA], February 28, 2022, blog about the Appendix E letter).

Is Concordia University Wisconsin "capable of operating as a recognizable institution of higher education" that self-identifies as *Lutheran* or *confessional*? It appears that the university leadership is not.

Because I follow the teaching methodology mandated in the *Formula* to "believe, teach, and confess" the Bible and our Lutheran Confessions as well as "rejecting and condemning" false teaching that opposes Christ and the Scriptures, I have been condemned and put on trial by my university's administrators and Board of Regents (Appendices K–L). The Regents include the LCMS South Wisconsin District President and the former LCMS Michigan District President who supervised our adjunct campus in Ann Arbor, Michigan. The new Concordia President has apparently endorsed rejecting and condemning me for doing my confessional due diligence. He has insisted on my forced retirement and demanded my signature in agreement with his demand that he and his Provost can terminate me at any time "at their sole discretion." See Appendix R.

How can this happen at a "Lutheran institution of higher education?" The studied ignorance of *The Formula of Concord* is one part of this confessional crisis at my Lutheran university. Loss of confessional integrity is the obvious portion of the university's anatomical or structural failing—obvious to national organizations and their lawyers concerned with academic freedom, if not to Administrators, Regents and District Presidents.

The other part of CUW's structural problem is so obvious that no one seems to be able to recognize it. That part of the culture problem at my university is the topic of our second chapter.

Chapter Two

Breaking the Concordia Fellowship: A Hollow and Deceptive Philosophy of Language

*It is important to see that the uncompromising supremacy of 'scientific' reasoning in the ... **critical method** is not an excess or an abuse which can somehow be tempered. On the contrary, it is of the essence of the method. [Social and Political] Science **has no room for privileged authorities or sacrosanct texts** (Kurt Marquart, Anatomy of an Explosion).*

Six months after the Woke explosion in February 2022, the university's Interim President acknowledged that seventy Lutheran students and families had withdrawn their applications to attend Concordia University. This was because the university had broken fellowship with them.

Breaking fellowship goes much deeper than you may realize. Underneath the Woke Marxist discord coming from my Concordia university there was and is another breaking of a fellowship—breaking the fellowship of language, which is the stealth technology on which Woke Marxism depends.

A far-reaching consequence of suppressing the *Formula*. The consequence of the studied ignorance of the Lutheran framework at my religious university, specifically its suppression of the *Formula of Concord* which we considered in our previous chapter, is the adoption of a radically anti-Christ philosophy of language, as I will explain in this chapter. Concordia University Wisconsin's (CUW's) Administrators, Regents, and I am afraid, a growing number of faculty, appear to be acting on the basis of the same hollow and deceptive philosophy of language that undergirds the neo-Marxism or Woke Marxism plaguing secular universities and other corporations and institutions.

There is no more properly basic, foundational issue than language. To paraphrase the apostle Paul speaking to the Athenian philosophers, it is in language that we live and move and have our human being (Acts 17:28). This is because we human beings are in our essence *logos* or language beings. This is because our God, the Life of all mankind, has revealed Himself as *the Logos* in human flesh (John 1:1–14).

In terms of my analogy between a military submarine and the university, this philosophy of language has to do with the atmosphere on which the crew, the faculty and students at the university, depends. As I will show, particularly in the conclusion of this chapter, the leadership at CUW is in effect depleting the atmosphere of the institution. They have been leaching the atmosphere of the oxygen that is necessary for a university to be a university and for a Lutheran university to be a Lutheran institution of higher learning. One symptom of this is their strategy of cancelling, censoring, shutting down academic conversation and Lutheran disputation. In this way they are asphyxiating the crew. Recall the observation from the Academic Freedom Alliance in the first chapter.

> Schulz is not challenging accepted Lutheran doctrine or subverting the mission of the university as a Christian institution. He is criticizing the policy decisions of the university administration and whether the administration's actions should be regarded as consistent with Lutheran commitments properly understood. For the university to punish and suppress speech of that sort would be to dramatically limit professorial speech and call into question whether Concordia is capable of operating as a recognizable institution of higher education (AFA February 28, 2022, blog about the Appendix E letter).

"Criticizing the policy decisions of the university administration and whether the administration's actions should be regarded as consistent with Lutheran commitments properly understood"—this is precisely what one pastor–professor has been up to. See Appendices A–S. In this chapter I am criticizing the apparent basis for their actions, namely, their hollow and deceptive philosophy of language. This deceptive philosophy of language is why Woke Marxism is able to be so successful in our institutions, especially in our educational institutions.

Two competing philosophies of language. It will help to have side–by–side definitions of the two philosophies of language that are at issue. To see why Woke Marxism needs a philosophy of language other than the philosophy of language followed by Luther and the Lutheran Confessions, it will help to realize that these are two *opposed* philosophies of language. The labels for these two competing philosophies are verbatim from Cary.[1] The brief summaries are mine, gleaned from Phillip Cary and the Lutheran texts that inform his books.

1. *External Efficacious Means of Grace.* This is the recognition that the biblical text is itself meaningful and effective. We could say of the text what we say of the sacrament of Holy Communion. There is a real presence here. God is present, speaking in, with, and under the texts of the Holy Scriptures. The infallible and efficacious words of the biblical text are the means by which God Himself does His work among us. Cary notes that this view is held by Aquinas and Luther.

2. *Expressionist Semiotics.* This is the view that the biblical text is nothing but signs to be decoded, that what really counts is what is going on in one's soul or mind. So, the ***semeia*** or signs are incidental and serve only as opportunities for us to express our individual inner convictions. This *Neoplatonist* view, Cary explains, is held by Augustine and Calvin.

The External Efficacious Means of Grace philosophy is the biblical and Lutheran philosophy. It is the philosophy of language maintained in the Lutheran Confessions such as the *Formula*. It is the view of the language of Scripture held by every confessional thinker from Luther onward. For example, here is Johann Gerhard:

> With the name "Scripture" we must understand not so much the external form [formulae] or signs (that is,

---

[1] Phillip Cary, *Outward Signs: The Powerlessness of External Things in Augustine's Thought* (New York: Oxford University Press, 2008), Preface, especially the sections, Powerless Externals and Thesis and Argumentation, viii–x: "I was led into this investigation by Luther, that great enemy of the religion of inner experience. According to Luther, God gives Himself to us through the external Word..."

the shapes of the letters)—the acts and utterances of writing by which the divine revelation is put into writing—as the material itself or what is designated, and indeed the very thing that the writing denotes and signifies, namely, the very Word of God, which instructs us in the essence and will of God.

Some state this in such a way that the Word of God is taken either essentially, as the very meaning that God expresses, or adventitiously, according to what has happened, which are preaching and writing.

For as in every writing brought about by a cause that is understanding or intellectual, so also in this prophetic and apostolic Scripture we must consider two points: first, the very letters, syllables, and phrases that are written—the external symbols that signify and express ideas of the mind—and second, the very meanings that are, as it were, something signified and expressed by those external symbols of letters, syllables, and words. Consequently, we include both—and principally the latter—when we use the word "Scripture" here.[2]

This is the external effective means of grace disposition toward language and Scripture. It is the way Scripture presents itself. It is the classical Lutheran view. It is the orthodox view. Please note that, while Gerhard uses the word *signified* in his explanation of homonyms for Scripture, he clearly does not espouse a semiotic philosophy of language. Here is why. Gerhard's mention of the *symbols and significations* of Scripture is congruent with our Lutheran and biblical understanding of Holy Baptism.

We confess that baptism symbolizes our union with Christ in His death and in His resurrection, but also that it in fact unites us with Him in His death and resurrection (Romans 6). This is not a metaphor; it is the literal, metaphysical truth. What we reject is any claim that baptism *merely* symbolizes God's grace to us. Our confession in the catechisms, for example, is that baptism is a means of grace, not a metaphor.

Similarly, as Gerhard says, the Word of God has an external form, namely, the letters, syllables, and words that God breathed

---

[2] Johann Gerhard, Richard Dinda, translator, *On the Nature of Theology and on Scripture* (Saint Louis: Concordia Publishing House, 2009), 36–37.

out through His writers, but the Word is not merely a collection of (arbitrary) signs and (pointless or endlessly interpretable) signifiers. It is a means of grace, not a free-playground for semiotic linguistic theorists. As Gerhard says with crystal clarity, "the external symbols [both] signify *and* express" because the Word of God, the biblical text, is to be taken "essentially [this is the robust vocabulary of the Creed, as in the Son is of one substance], as the very meaning that God expresses." The Word of God, the written Scriptures, are external and effective according to what happens in the preaching and writing of "those external symbols of letters, syllables, and words."

The Expressionist Semiotics philosophy of language is in direct opposition to the External Efficacious Means of Grace model and should therefore, according to the *Formula*, be rejected and condemned as false dogma. This is precisely what I intend to do in this chapter.

To see through the camouflage—that is, to see that there is a radically different philosophy of language at work wherever Marxist Wokeism is accepted—we first need to return to the *Formula's* term *nature*, which is about *human nature* and not about Nature.

The starting point for the confessional understanding of human nature and language is a passage from Aristotle, written about 350 B.C. The best place to see what this has to do with being confessional and Lutheran in our thinking and teaching is to consider Martin Luther's 1536 "Disputation Concerning Man."

Disputation Concerning Man. Before answering the question, "What then is man?" in terms of Psalm 8, Romans, and the rest of biblical revelation, Martin Luther stipulates the basic, minimal definition of our type of creature, the human kind of being, from Aristotle's *Politics*, Book 1. *Politics* is the Greek word for "town" or "city-state," communities populated by human beings, so I am translating it as "community." Pulling together several sentences of *Politics* 1 into one brief definition, Aristotle can be quoted as saying, "The human kind of being is *zoon logon echon*, 'an animal (not a rock or a plant) possessing language'." Here are some of the forty propositions or theses at the opening of Luther's disputation which show how he used Aristotle to get the ball rolling.

1. Philosophy or human wisdom defines man as an animal having reason, sensation, and body.
2. It is not necessary at this time to debate whether man is properly or improperly called an animal.
3. But this must be known, that this definition describes man only as a mortal and in relation to this life.
4. And it is certainly true that reason is the most important and the highest in rank among all things and, in comparison with other things of this life, the best and something divine.
5. It is the inventor and mentor of all the arts, medicines, laws, and of whatever wisdom, power, virtue, and glory men possess in this life.
6. By virtue of this fact it ought to be named the essential difference by which man is distinguished from the animals and other things.
7. Holy Scripture also makes it lord over the earth, birds, fish, and cattle, saying, "Have dominion..." [Genesis 1:28].

...

11. Therefore, if philosophy or reason itself is compared with theology, it will appear that we know almost nothing about man.

...

32. Paul in Romans 3 [:28], "We hold that a man is justified by faith apart from works," briefly sums up the definition of man, saying, "Man is justified by faith."

In *Politics* 1, Aristotle also observes that *logos* or "language" is the medium of fellowship among human beings. "For *nature* [this is the concept that informs the *Formula's* content regarding human beings and then our incarnate Savior], as we declare, never does anything without purpose; and man alone of the animals possesses language... for it is the unique idiom of man— in distinction from all animals—that he alone has perception of right and wrong and the other moral qualities in the community... A man who is incapable of entering this community fellowship [of language beings] ... must be either a lower animal or a god" (*Politics* 1, 1253a, 10–12).

Language and fellowship. Aristotle's word for "fellowship" (*koinonia*) is the same Greek word used by Saint Luke in Acts of the Apostles for *fellowship* with God and with one another in faith, communion, and the community of the first-century believers who followed "the Way."

This is the starting point for understanding the fundamental importance of language. *Woke Marxism depends upon breaking our human fellowship, the human fellowship that we have because of, and only within language (logos in Greek) by breaking language.* Christian readers are no doubt thinking ahead to the first chapter of the Gospel According to Saint John, where Jesus is revealed as the *Logos*. I am headed for the conclusion that Woke Marxism depends on a philosophy of language which is opposed to Christ the *Logos*. I will explain more both in this chapter and in the next chapter when we turn to the means–by–which God delivers universal justification to human beings via the external efficacious means of grace.

But on the way, we should first experience together the way that Luther grounds his philosophy of language on that vital term *nature* from our *Formula*, (a) human nature and then (b) human nature as justified and recreated by Christ's work alone. To put this another way, the divine gift of language shows up in our human nature.[3] It is the way we have been created. It is the central feature of the image of God in which we human beings—unique among all the other kinds of beings in God's creation—were and are created and preserved by God Himself (Genesis 1:24–31 and Psalm 139).

Here, to become familiar with language as to what Aristotle discovers to be the *formal* or *essential cause* of our being human beings, is a brief tutorial on Luther's 1536 "Disputation Concerning Man." His theses or propositions are in italics; my comments are in regular print. For my complete essay, *Cur Verbum Verba*, "Why does the Incarnate Word Reveal Himself to Us in Words?," please see Appendix S.

Disputation, *Thesis 1.* *Philosophy or human wisdom defines man as an animal having reason, sensation, and body.*

Luther is stipulating Aristotle's definition of man in *Politics*,

---

[3] For an argument that language cannot be accounted for by evolutionary theory, see Hauser, Marc D., Charles Yang, Robert C. Berwick, Ian Tattersall, Michael J. Ryan, Jeffrey Watumull, Noam Chomsky, and Richard C. Lewontin, "The Mystery of Language Evolution," 2014, *Frontiers in Psychology* 5 (1): 401.

Book 1. There the philosopher categorizes man as *zoon logon echon*, an animal type of being characterized by *logos*. Aristotle takes stock of all the different types of beings in the cosmos and sets about learning what a thing is, "always and for the most part," by determining its kind. A thing's kind of being is determined by asking, "What is this kind of thing *essentially*?" Today we call this *ontology*, the study of beings. The second word in the compound term for this discipline, onto–*logy*, preserves the fact that study and discovery take place in the medium of *logos*, that is, in language—that it takes place in informed conversation, in discourse, and in disputation.

Significantly, Aristotle also identifies *logos* or language as the medium of fellowship (*koinonia*) among human beings. What Aristotle could not dream of, but what is revealed in the Person and words of Jesus the incarnate *Logos*, is that *language is also the medium of fellowship with God Himself*.

The human being is, at the core of his being, a language being fitted by the Creator for the *verba* of the Redeemer by the work of the Sanctifier.

An attack on language is, therefore, a crime against humanity, an abolition of man. The suppression of language—say, by canceling, censoring, restricting debate, disputation and the thoughtful application of authoritative texts which inform these activities—is a violation of the rights with which our Creator has endowed all us members of the human, *logos* species.

If it is true that The Word reveals Himself in words (*Verbum verba*, according to our Latin title for this essay), then the suppression of language and words is insurgency against the second person of the Holy Trinity Himself.

As Kurt Marquart said of the insurgency against the Word by the queer hermeneutics at St. Louis late last century, censoring and punishing professors and others "hits at the inmost nature of biblical Christianity. The written Word is about the Incarnate Word and is of a piece with Him." It is, to invoke Tolkien, "the breaking of the fellowship."

Disputation, *Thesis 11.* *Therefore, if philosophy or reason itself is compared with theology, it will appear that we know almost nothing about man.*

Here Luther is talking about what Paul refers to as "the hollow and deceptive kind of *philosophy*." In the first century A.D., *philosophy* did not refer to one university department among many; rather, it referred to all learning and studying. It's hollow and deceptive because it depends entirely on human tradition and the basic principles of this world. For example, see atheistic Marxism.

Instead, the apostle mandates the kind of philosophy and education that depends on Christ (Colossians 2:8–10). Christianity is the true *philos–sophos,* or philosophy, because it is the befriending and loving of Christ, who is Himself the *sophos* of God in a singular Person (1 Corinthians 1:22–25). Thus, Luther's theology of the human being is also a Christological anthropology.

Luther is understandably leaning forward, toward a major upcoming thesis for disputing, debating, and understanding our human kind of being Christologically in terms of justification, Thesis 32. But there is an important point regarding his mention of *reason* and rationality at this point. When the Greek term *logos* is carried over into Latin, there is a fork in the road. As we all know, "When you come to a fork in the road, take it" (Yogi Berra). The fork in this case is that the one Greek word, *logos*, forks into two diverging Latin words, namely, *verba* and *ratio*.

The single Greek word for language, *logos*, can be translated by *ratio* or *verbum* in Latin. *Verbum* is the far better translation. To modern ears, *ratio* sounds like a reference to rationality as something apart from language and apart from God's Word.

Perhaps the medievals were able to keep both terms in mind, side by side, but the choice of *ratio* as the Latin translation for *logos* inevitably leads us moderns down the wrong road. It leads those of us after Descartes to think that *logos* is fundamentally about our private mental processes; but on the contrary, our mental capacities *originate in and depend upon language. Ratio* invariably leads to Platonism and to thumbing one's nose at language and written texts, material liabilities and incidentals such as they are to Plato and Plotinus. We should take the road less traveled.

Verba is the better translation. It's also the road taken in our Lutheran Confessions. For example, the text of the Apology of the Augsburg Confession, the article on the chief article of doctrine, justification, reads, "God cannot be treated, He cannot be apprehended, *nisi per Verbum*, except via the Word."

Disputation, *Thesis 32*. *Paul in Romans 3[:28], "We hold that a man is justified by faith apart from works," briefly sums up the definition of man, saying, "Man is justified by faith."*

Since this thesis is definitional, as Oswald Bayer says, we would do well to translate it as "The human being is human in that he is justified by faith."[4] In other words, while we have grown up learning to think of the human being as *homo sapiens*, on the basis of the thicker anthropology which we have only from the incarnate *Verbum* by way of His revelation of Himself in His own *verba*, it would be much more accurate to think of the human being as *homo justificans*, since we are the kind of being that seeks to be justified: either we acknowledge that we are justified by God's grace alone in Christ or we waste our time of grace as language beings trying to justify ourselves apart from Christ and His words—a deeply frustrating and upsetting project for any member of the language species!

By the way, as Lutherans we should see more clearly than most Christians because of our inherited commitment to the means of grace and faith in Christ's words alone (the *solas* of the Lutheran Reformation), that the Woke Marxist notions of diversity, inclusion, and equity (DIE) are ineffective replacements for the central doctrine of universal justification ("All .. are justified..." Romans 3, especially verses 23–24) brought to us solely by God and solely through His means of grace.

Woke ideology insists that people will find meaning and purpose, not in praising God for universal justification, but in constant revolution, class against class, everyone in unending violent rebellion against the sacrosanct texts and the God of creation and order. But Marxism is a lie.

---

[4] Oswald Bayer, Thomas Trapp, translator, *Martin Luther's Theology: A Contemporary Translation* (Grand Rapids, Michigan: William B. Eerdmans Publishing Company, 2007 edition), Chapter 7, The Human Being: In the Image of God, especially 154–162.

2.1 Woke Marxism is a violent and *mythological* ideology...

Because of its disdain for "privileged authority and sacrosanct texts," as Professor Marquart would say, Marxism disdains the External Efficacious Means of Grace philosophy of language. Since Marxism depends on mythology to win comrades and influence people, it depends upon the Expressionist Semiotic view. In the quote which heads this chapter, Marquart refers to the pernicious methodology of the *critical methodology* that informed the interpretive heresy of Seminex. Critical theory comes from Marx and Freud.

It is helpful to think of critical theory as cultural Marxism or cultural materialism. *Cultural materialism*, the worldview of Hegel, Marx, and Woke Marxists, insists that culture is a closed social process—no room for God or His Word—and that language, especially written texts, is just a bunch of semiotic or merely symbolic "signifiers" whose meaning comes exclusively from social forces such as power over oppressed people.[5]

Critical theory. Critical theory is in concord with Church Growth Theory (CGT), which was the Trojan Horse at my Concordia for Critical Race Theory (CRT), as I explained in our first chapter. What critical theory and CGT have in common is prioritizing social science methodology over the means of grace In this chapter, I am arguing, much as Marquart did in regard to Seminex, that "critical method is not an excess or an abuse which can somehow be tempered. On the contrary, it is of the essence of the method. [Social and Political] Science has no room for privileged authorities or sacrosanct texts." In the case of Woke Marxism, however, it has become even clearer that what Professor Marquart identified as "a critical [Marxist] method" is a philosophy of language, the Expressionist Semiotics philosophy of language, which is in opposition to the External Efficacious Means of Grace character of language, which is the biblical and confessional understanding of language.

When I say that Woke Marxism depends upon mythology to influence people, I am speaking about the history of ideas. We are used to the phrase, "Politics is downstream from culture." It

---

[5] See David Macey, *The Penguin Dictionary of Critical Theory* (New York: Penguin Books, 2000), entries for *critical theory, cultural materialism,* and *ideology.*

is also the case that culture is downstream from philosophy because ideas have consequences.[6] Ultimately, politics is downstream from culture and culture is downstream from philosophy—but the stream itself is language, from its source to its mouth!

If we are thinking in tune with Aristotle's recognition that our *polis* is the community in which we human beings, characterized as we are by *logos* or language, enjoy fellowship by virtue of language—then we can cut to the chase and say that everything flows because of *logos*. This suggests a word from Heraclitus of Ephesus, who died in the early fifth century B.C. at the time that the prophet Malachi was completing the Hebrew Old Testament. *Panta rhei*, "Everything flows," is sometimes attributed to him (although it does not actually appear in his surviving writings). If you lean on Heraclitus's favorite word, *logos*, to complete the thought, you could conclude that we know everything flows only because we are in the swim of things as *logos* beings.

But Karl Marx and his twenty-first century followers have no time or patience for the *logos* of Greek thought, anymore than they have patience and regard for the *Logos* of the Scriptures. Marx graduated from his gymnasium school as a Christian but then decided to live out the philosophy of Georg Wilhelm Friedrich Hegel, team captain of nineteenth-century German Idealism. Marxism is cribbed from Hegel.[7] One of Hegel's major contributions was to treat the individual human being as little more than a pawn in the development of the state.

Here is another hand–me–down. Hegel taught that the way states or cultures become better is when conflicting ideas in society clash violently against each other. This is the famous Hegelian thesis–antithesis–synthesis business, deduced from Hegel's prodigious writing. Marx, eager—not to learn and teach, but fundamentally to change Western culture completely, created conflicting identity groups such as workers and owners, and then incited them to clash violently against each other. This was his way to generate communist societies.

---

[6] Richard Weaver, *Ideas Have Consequences: Expanded Edition* (Chicago: University of Chicago Press, 2013).

[7] Bruce Mazlish, *The Meaning of Karl Marx* (New York, Oxford University Press, 1984), Chapter IV, Father and Son, and the Ghost of Hegel, 45–53.

Philosophical mythologies. Hegel's method is known as *dialectical materialism*. Dialectic materialism is a closed-minded version of philosophical dialogues such as Plato's Socratic dialogue *Euthyphro*. Whereas Plato and Socrates looked for an ultimate norm or authority for their ethical dialogues wherever their dialogues led them, including to gods or "the god," Hegel insisted on a closed philosophical system with no room for gods or the God, or for the Word of God, the Bible. As did his Padawan, Karl Marx.

> The permanent value of German idealism consists in its poetic apprehension of empirical phenomena, its artistic appreciation and religious insight. The idealistic school was preoccupied with the meaning of events, with their relevance to human experience, not with recording and interpreting facts. The metaphysical systems in which Hegel and his contemporaries cast their thought may well be called *philosophical mythologies*. Their claim was ... to comprehend in creative vision the meaning of the world, natural, human and divine...
>
> "Everything that from eternity has happened in heaven and on earth, the life of God and all the deeds of time simply are the struggles for mind to know itself, and finally to unite itself to itself; it is alienated and divided, but only so as to be able thus to find itself and return to itself." This is the great Hegelian mythology and philosophic vision... [8]

"Creative" in this philosophical summary means "disruptive" in a violently anti-God and anti-human sense. Having rejected the understanding of human nature based on Greek thought and the impact of the biblical view of man in Christ, Marxism relies on philosophical mythologies—made-up identity groups incited to violence against one another. Philosophical mythologies after the first advent of God in the flesh, after the incarnation of God and Wisdom Himself, are silly. But when philosophical mythologies become the tool for creating violence between made-up castes and classes of human beings, this is immoral.

This strange work of doing philosophy and changing Western culture by means of philosophical mythologies comes to a head

---

[8] J. Glenn Gray, *Hegel and Greek Thought* (Harper & Row, 1968), vii and 68.

in Nietzsche's analysis of where this gets us culturally. In his Story of the Madman, Nietzsche provides his anatomy or diagnosis of Western culture after the Enlightenment and its seductive sequel, German Idealism. His Madman—think of how often in literature it is hard to tell the difference between a madman and a prophet—has been searching for God with a bright lantern even though there is bright early morning sunlight everywhere. The fashionable atheists standing around have been mocking him just as Elijah mocked the prophets of Baal on Mount Carmel.

> Then the madman transfixed them with his laser-like stares. "'Where did He go?' Alright, let me tell you! We have killed him—you and I. All of us are God's murderers. 'How have we done this,' you are beginning to wonder? How were we able to make the sea evaporate? Who came up with the means to obliterate the horizon of our planet? How did we manage to untether the earth from its sun? Where is it careening off to right now?
>
> "Where are we headed? To a reality with no suns at all? Look! We are in perpetual freefall—backward, sideward, forward—a non-directional freefall! Absolutely no point of orientation! Do you seriously imagine that there is any up or down anymore?
>
> "Still don't get it? We are adrift aimlessly through an infinite n o t h i n g. You do feel it, don't you—a frozen breath of empty space, the absolute coldness of maximum entropy? It is black, starless night. It is night with nothing but more lightless night to follow. We are at the point that lanterns have to be lit in the morning hours too.
>
> "Listen! Don't you hear the rumblings and shovelings of the gravediggers who are burying God? Don't you smell the stench of God's decomposition? Gods too decompose. God is dead. God remains dead. Moreover, we have killed him.
>
> "Think it through! How shall we, the murderers of all murderers, comfort ourselves? What was holiest and most powerful of all that the world could ever know has bled to death under our knives. Who will wipe this blood off us? What baptism is there for us to wash ourselves clean? What holidays of atonement, what sacred games

shall we have to invent? Are not the consequences of the deed too, too overwhelming for us? Must we not become gods ourselves simply to live up to it?" (*The Joyful Science*, Book 3, entry 125, my translation).

By the way, this is a logical point to mention that our English translation of Luther's Catechism Question as "What does this mean?" is problematic. This translation of his German leans toward German Idealism. Luther's actual wording is *Was ist das?* and ought to be translated, "What is this?" Luther was not preoccupied with creating "meaning relevant to human experience;" he was preoccupied with the sacred and unsurpassably authoritative written text of the Scriptures. Luther, as Cary says, and we confessional Lutherans ought to say as well, held to the External Efficacious Means of Grace philosophy of language out of fear, love, and trust for God.

So, what about the Expressionist Semiotic philosophy of language? To say that language is merely semiotic, that is, a matter of more–or–less incidental symbols, is to say in a sophisticated way that there is no inherent meaningfulness in language. Whereas language or *logos* is inherently meaningful, even brimming over with meaningfulness, as we know from experience, the presupposed philosophy of language in our day is opposed to the *logos* and to the *Logos* incarnate. *Presupposed* means that the Expressionist Semiotic view of language is so widely taken for granted that no one notices what's being assumed. This leads us to the source of the stealthy and unhealthy philosophy of language that is sucking the oxygen out of the atmosphere in our universities, including my Concordia Lutheran university. That source is postmodernism.

2.2 A false presupposition...wholesale relativism...postmodernism...

Postmodernism is a perennial problem or Shingles-like virus that has plagued Western thought from its beginnings in Greece. Think of the words of Protagoras: "Man is the measure of all things: of things which are, that they are, and of things which are not, that they are not" (quoted by Plato in *Theaetetus* 152a). Protagoras was a moral and cognitive relativist, the type of philosopher who would be called in our day "postmodernist."

In art history, postmodern art is the type of art that comes after distinctly modern art. In literature, postmodern novels are the sort of novels that come after distinctly modern novels. But this is not how it works in philosophy and intellectual life considered more broadly. In philosophy, postmodernism is an intellectual (or more accurately, an anti-intellectual) mindset simultaneously opposed to Heraclitus's *logos*, the essential orderly feature of the cosmos and of our human being, and to John's *Logos*, God incarnate.

"I get to say that words mean whatever I want them to and no one can tell me, 'No, you're wrong!'" The postmodernist Jacques Derrida took the Expressionist Semiotic philosophy of language to its logical conclusion by teaching that since language was nothing but semiotics, that is, nothing but signifiers or symbols, written texts were open to unlimited interpretations. I have only one of Derrida's forty-some books on my shelves (and an anthology), to be as scholarly as necessary toward this frustratingly destructive writer. To paraphrase Emily Dickinson, to figure out what Derrida is up to I will "tell it slant," that is, by catching his responses to questions in interviews, rather than in any of his forty-some books. Only in his interviews is Derrida intelligible.

There are two interviews with Derrida that will serve to illustrate my point that the Expressionist Semiotic philosophy of language leads invariably to this: *Everyone is entitled to say whatever he thinks a text means, and no one is entitled to say, "No, you are wrong."*

Since I have already referred to Augustine's *Confessions* as a prime example of being confessional, that is, speaking and writing in line with the biblical text, here is what Derrida feels free to do with Augustine's text. This is from a 2001 roundtable discussion with Derrida about his book, *Circumfession*.

> The confession or circumfession, which is not a confession, this strange thing that I call circumfession, this hybrid of Judaism, already a strange sort of Judaism and Christianity, is a monstrosity... Perhaps there is a confession, but if there is confession, no one would be entitled to sign the confession. If I sign the confession, that would be perhaps useful for the police or for God, but I wouldn't call this a confession... The

> whole text [of *Circumfession*], which cannot be summarized in one sentence, challenges the possibility of saying, "I confess," as well as saying "I give" or "I forgive" or "I decide."[9]

In an earlier, 1994 roundtable discussion—coincidentally, right after making a comment about Augustine and then his own monstrous book, *Circumfession*—Derrida speaks about his view of the Bible, which is also an expression of his commitment to a philosophy of language that sees canonical and authoritative texts as playthings for himself and for everyone else, including Marx.

> First, I have no stable position on the texts you mentioned, the prophets and the Bible. For me, this is an open field, and I can receive the most necessary provocations from these texts as well as, at the same time, from Plato and others. In *Spectres of Marx* I try to reconstitute the link between Marx and some prophets through Shakespeare.
>
> This does not mean that I am simply a religious person or that I am simply a believer. For me, there is no such thing as "religion". Within what one calls religions—Judaism, Christianity, Islam, or other religions—there are again tensions, heterogeneity, disruptive volcanos, sometimes texts, especially those of the prophets, which cannot be reduced to an institution, to a corpus, to a system.
>
> I want to keep the right to read these texts in a way that has to be constantly reinvented. It is something which can be totally new at every moment.
>
> Then I would distinguish between religion and faith. If by religion you mean a set of beliefs, dogmas, or institutions—the church, for example, then I would say that religion not only can but should be deconstructed, sometimes in the name of faith.[10]

The hollow and deceptive (and never–to–be–challenged) philosophy is this: "Language is utterly without (divine or even

---

[9] John Caputo and Michael Scanlon, editors, *Augustine and Postmodernism: Confessions and Circumfession* (Bloomington and Indianapolis: Indiana University Press, 2005), 32-33.

[10] John Caputo, editor, *Deconstruction in a Nutshell: A Conversation with Jaques Derrida* (New York: Fordham University Press, 1997), 21.

human) authority; therefore, *no text is authoritative or sacrosanct.*" This explains why people in Human Resources in our workplaces demand that we respect everyone's self-chosen pronouns and gender identities, or we will be fired; why Supreme Court Justices feel free to alter the definition of *marriage*; why educated professors claim that the term "servile arts" is racist and condemn anyone who uses the term; and why academic deans meeting with the Provost say one professor who uses the term "China Virus" is racist and should be censored. See Appendix A.

Against all reason, people assume that language is their plaything to do with whatever they please, and no one gets to correct them. This is why Woke Marxists in education and government feel empowered to censor, to cancel, to destroy the rest of us. This is why people in the corporate media feel justified in lying. These people believe that language—especially normative, authoritative texts—is open to whatever interpretation they want to give it at any given moment. In addition, they are angry and alienated people who hate anyone who dares to correct them. They are the heirs of Marx the angry revolutionary and of Derrida, who said, "I want to keep the right to read these texts in a way that has to be constantly reinvented. It is something which can be totally new at every moment." It's just what they do.

The fundamental, bedrock, existential problem is that our bosses, our government, and our university Administrators have abandoned the External Efficacious Means of Grace philosophy of language and have bought into the anti-Scriptural, anti-authority, anti-logos, anti-Christ, anti-human Expressionist Semiotic philosophy of language as promulgated by postmodernists such as Derrida. They want no part of the fellowship of language and, as a consequence, see people either as gods or as lower animals, just as Aristotle said.

Objection and reply. At this point someone may object, "Wait a minute! Even if your analysis is correct, how can you expect Administrators, Regents, and professors who are not theologians or philosophers to agree with you?" My response is in two parts. First, I am not writing to prove a point; I am writing this book for the same reason that I wrote my essay "Woke Dysphoria at Concordia." That reason is: to lead my university leadership to repent and to repudiate the anti-Christian dogma of Woke Marxism, to get rid of it and the practices that brought it about, root and branch. There can be no accommodation, no appeasement with this evil dogma. What do you suppose is the cause of the restlessness and dysphoria at Concordia—as in almost all of our universities and institutions? I have explained at great length and for years where the problem lies, so the question is whether the institution cares to do anything about it.

In the Preamble I stated that, as my church body's President wrote in 2022, I do not expect Regents and Administrators to agree. I expect them to dig in their heels as they have been doing all along, in keeping with their philosophy of language, their disregard for authoritative texts, and their hatred of anyone who dares to correct them. To date, they have been in lockstep with Derrida, and I do not anticipate any change in their philosophy of language. They "want to keep the right to read these texts in a way that has to be constantly reinvented."

That said, I am a pastor–professor with responsibilities—moral and contractual responsibilities, certainly, but more importantly, with divine–call responsibilities, to do what God has called me to do for His people. I am a confessional Lutheran Professor of Philosophy and therefore I profess *kata Christon*, according to Christ and His Word (Colossians 2:8–10) as I have been doing for decades, by His grace. I also have beloved former students, children, and grandchildren to whom I feel accountable in the Lord to set an example. This from the Table of Duties in Luther's Catechism.

Secondly, my university's Administrators, Regents, and others are responsible (a) for the suppression of the Lutheran Confessions at CUW, the authoritative texts which alone could and would have inoculated the university community against what they have been doing, that is, from publicly seeking a Woke Marxist President and refusing to repent of it.

They are also responsible for (b) rejecting and condemning one pastor–professor who sounded the (doctrinal and philosophical) call to General Quarters. The new President is continuing the attack on academic freedom launched by the

Interim President—in both cases, with the (at least tacit) consent of the Board of Regents (see Appendices D–G, I–L, and Q–R).

I am fulfilling my responsibilities; they are not. Apparently, they have bought into the philosophy of language that entitles them to say whatever they want to say about authoritative texts and to lie about other texts as they see fit, all the while pretending that no one is entitled to tell them, "No, you are wrong!" Look, for example, at their use of language such as "conduct unbecoming a Christian," "harassing students," and "insubordination." Look at their willingness to reinterpret authoritative texts to suit their purposes. See Appendices D–G and K, for examples.

2.3 ...the deceptive presupposition is...language is without authority...no text is authoritative...

To return to my analysis, we must diagnose Woke Marxism at my Concordia university as Marquart diagnosed the false doctrine of Seminex. The [social, political, pseudo-] science of Woke Marxism has no room for privileged authority (especially the divine authority of Jesus, Matthew 28:18–20 and has no room for canonical or authoritative texts (especially not for the sacred, efficacious verbally inspired texts of the Hebrew and Greek Scriptures, Psalms 1 and 119 and 2 Timothy 3). As I have argued, this is, at bottom, a matter of which philosophy of language people at my university hold to and live out.

Isaiah hath foretold it. We are used to citing Isaiah 55 as if the prophet's and His Lord's only purpose in this chapter is to point out how far beyond our way of thinking God's thoughts are. But there is more. Isaiah 55 is a seventh-century B.C. rejection of the Expressionist Semiotics philosophy of language as taught by Derrida and the postmodernists—and taken for granted by Woke Marxism. Take and read.

> Ho! Everyone who thirsts, Come to the waters;
> And you who have no money, Come, buy and eat.
> Yes, come, buy wine and milk Without money and without price.
> Why do you spend money for what is not bread, And your wages for what does not satisfy?
> *Listen carefully to Me, and eat what is good, And let your soul delight itself in abundance.*

Incline your ear, and come to Me. Hear, and your soul shall live;
And I will make an everlasting covenant with you—
The sure mercies of David.
Indeed I have given him as a witness to the people,
A leader and commander for the people.

Surely you shall call a nation you do not know,
And nations who do not know you shall run to you,
Because of the Lord your God, And the Holy One of Israel; For He has glorified you."

Seek the Lord while He may be found, Call upon Him while He is near.

Let the wicked forsake his way, And the unrighteous man his thoughts; *Let him return to the Lord*, And He will have mercy on him; And to our God, For He will abundantly pardon.

"For My thoughts are not your thoughts,
Nor are your ways My ways," says the Lord.

For as the heavens are higher than the earth, So are My ways higher than your ways, And My thoughts than your thoughts.

For as the rain comes down, and the snow from heaven,
And do not return there, But water the earth,
And make it bring forth and bud, That it may give seed to the sower And bread to the eater,

So shall My word be that goes forth from My mouth; It shall not return to Me void, But it shall accomplish what I please, And it shall prosper in the thing for which I sent it.
(Isaiah 55:1–11, NKJV, italics added).

Don't misunderstand. As Luther wrote in A Mighty Fortress, the battle hymn of the German Reformation, "The Word, it cannot not remain, they're just not thankful for it!" Just as we can empirically verify the falsity of predictions of nuclear winter or climate change catastrophe by holding on to God's promise to Noah in Genesis 8:22, we can verify the falsity of the postmodern Expressionist Semiotics philosophy of language by holding on to His promise in Matthew 24:35: "Heaven and earth will pass away, but My words will by no means pass away" (NKJV). Still, we cannot stand idly by while our future seminary students, Lutheran teachers, and all of our sons and daughters and grandchildren go to school in an atmosphere that is being depleted by Woke Marxism and a hollow and deceptive philosophy of language.

2.4 ...diagnose Woke Marxism...as Marquart diagnosed the false doctrine of Seminex...

In the light of our careful study of language according to the Scriptures and the Lutheran Confessions, let's conclude this chapter by sampling the philosophy of language being lived out by the leadership at Concordia University Wisconsin.

First, there is the language of the presidential search for a Woke Marxist university President.

> When our BoR committees announce their intentions to install a president who exhibits a "demonstrated belief in and commitment to equity and inclusion" and promotes racialized "diversity in all its myriad forms," they are announcing their plan to disrupt the authority of the biblical text and in this way to transform our university from an institution of Lutheran higher education to ... who knows what. They are announcing their intention to transform this LCMS (The Lutheran Church—Missouri Synod) institution into a DIE–ing institution. See, for instance, the language and content of the Office of Multicultural Engagement on the university's website at cuw.edu.
>
> Not incidentally, the BoR committees' posted announcements are unsurprisingly Woke in their cavalier altering of texts. True to the Woke mindset of the Presidential Search postings, someone or some committee presumed to alter the pronouns in their posted version of our LCMS bylaws. As one of my faculty colleagues pointed out, in that posting the first two sentences of the LCMS Bylaw 3.10.6.6, addressing "Concordia University System Presidents," read: "The president of the institution shall be the executive officer of the board of regents. He shall serve as the spiritual, academic, and administrative head of the institution." The first two sentences under "Role of the 9th President of Concordia University" in the Presidential Prospectus, however, read: "The president of Concordia University is the chief executive of the institution, reporting to the Board of Regents. The president serves both as academic head

of the faculty and as spiritual leader of the institution."

Notice, my colleague explained, how closely the posted Presidential Prospectus follows the exact language of Bylaw 3.10.6.6. in its first sentence "The president," "executive," "of the institution," "the board of regents"—but then *avoids using the masculine pronoun "He"* at the beginning of its second sentence. One might also ask why *Presidential Prospectus* places "spiritual" *after* "academic" instead of keeping "spiritual" first as the bylaw has it, and why *Presidential Prospectus* uses the term "leader" with "spiritual," as "leader" is not found anywhere in Bylaw 3.10.6.6 when describing a Concordia University president.

Whether the BoR committees alter their posted, online statements, or not—without a detailed and equally widely published retraction of their Woke desires and commitments, the Woke dysphoria at Concordia will continue. After all, this is not a PR issue but a matter of repentance and showing the fruit of faith (Appendix B).

"Oh, sons of men, how long will you be dull of heart? How long will you love vain words and seek after lies?" (Psalm 5:6).

Second, there is the language of the Interim President in response to my published call to repent of that language. His interview about the Woke Marxist mantra of diversity, inclusion, and equity (DIE) is an illustration of such language.

The Administrator who introduces the topic is concerned with only a personal, subjective view of language. The Interim President does not correct him but proceeds as if the words are there for him to say whatever he wants to say they mean. Like Derrida, he offers what he classifies as an academic, professorial assessment in which he says that definitions of words (which he implies are part of the church's doctrinal vocabulary) change over time and cannot be specified. He admits that Critical Race Theory is an "ideology" related to diversity, inclusion, and equity, but imagines that this has a place in the church. Although gesturing toward official doctrinal statements from his church body, he apparently has not read or applied these authoritative texts. And so on.

Administrator: Dr. Cario, there is, you know words are used in different ways and there's certainly some—there is concern out there about the words that are used at times that include diversity, equity, and inclusion. Could you talk about—a number of people have asked about that. What do those words mean to you?

I know again that you can't speak for the Board, the Board speaks for itself, but how do you use those words? What do those words mean to you as the Interim President at Concordia?

Interim President: That's a very interesting question and probably more that my, my response could take up the rest of this time but let me try to be succinct. That's tough for the history prof to do, to tell the truth but let me see what I can do here.

Let me start out by saying words, the definitions of words, have tended to change over time and the DEI acronym, diversity, inclusion, equity, seems now to be tied to the CRT movement or at least, I should be careful, CRT is not necessarily a movement, it is an ideology that several different groups in our world, especially in the secular world, are taking, are making use of all right.

Um, diversity, equity, and inclusion I think have some specific meanings in this new world with CRT most specifically—equity, there is some evidence that while in general our American society has talked about equality and often meant equality of that opportunity, the change that the emphasis on equity tends to mean equality of results and that is just my sense of a change looking back.

I don't know that we have always been, in the church—been so unwilling to use the words, perhaps different meanings... For example, when I look at back at some of the CTCR documents about race and understanding how the church responds to the issues of that we're encountering in our world, I have seen, certainly diversity is used in those documents and I believe I've seen one or two times the definition the word inclusion used, so perhaps not in the same meaning that we have today.

I believe that this change in definition is happening

before our eyes. There is a lot of debate and discussion in the church about how to respond to that and while I don't believe that the Missouri Synod has specifically identified definitions and some of these things, and have specifically responded to CRT, I think that process is happening.

Where I think we all have at least some understanding is that, that our Christian faith recognizes that there is unity of all people in terms of creation, in terms of God's redemption, he offers redemption to all people, there is a certain unity of all. But within that, different individuals, there is a diversity of, there's male and female, there are different races and ethnicities.

I believe our church recognizes that there have been inequalities and issues, that our country and our world has had to deal with in terms of race. I think it's pretty clear that the church condemns racism.

Again, that term is being redefined and obviously that's a big part of CRT. So, my answer is, as you can see, a bit nuanced. I believe that Concordia is very willing to follow the church's lead on some of these definitions and understandings, but this is what I would describe at least from my academic mind.

At this point we're still working through some of this stuff so I guess I would encourage, at least within the church some willingness to dialogue about this.

Let me stop there.[11]

Third, to state what is painfully obvious, the university's two-year war against academic freedom springs from its postmodern philosophy of language. This is not a problem of communication; it is a philosophical divide. The Administration and Board appear to be committed to asphyxiating any professor who calls them to account for their departure from the authoritative texts of Scripture and the Lutheran Confessions. They are clearly committed to violating the lesser authorities of freedom of speech in the U.S. Constitution and even their own policy manuals—although, in keeping with the postmodern view that texts can be endlessly reinterpreted, they constantly note that their written

---

[11] From a CUW "Townhall" on March 21, 2022, at https://www.youtube.com/watch?v=u0FCc72PJ-4, accessed 15 August, 2023.

policies can be changed at any time, at their discretion. It's Derrida again. They "want to keep the right to read these texts in a way that has to be constantly reinvented."

Objection and reply. Someone might object that the purpose of academic freedom is to enable Administrators to deal with professors who teach and publish things that Regents and Administrators cannot agree with. I reply first by saying that this is an absurd idea. For example, see the brief and inspiring model Statement of Academic Freedom on the last page of Appendix R. Second, the notion that there is any correcting at all to be done is irrelevant in the case of one pastor–professor. Remember what the Academic Freedom Alliance wrote.

> *Principles of free speech include the right of professors to speak in public on matters of public concern without the threat of sanctions by their university employer.* We call upon Concordia University Wisconsin to live up to its free speech commitments in the case of Professor Gregory P. Schulz ...
>
> Of course, Professor Schulz has a responsibility not to "advocate a position contrary to that of the Synod," but *here he is participating in a public debate on what the implications of the Synod's positions might be for the university. If faculty at the university must refrain from speaking in public about the future of the university and the fidelity of the university's activities to the positions of the Synod, then the university's commitment to the faculty to value their individuality and to engage in intellectual inquiry will be an empty promise.* [Italics added.]

Following my explanation of the pervasiveness of the postmodern philosophy of language at work in our universities, you can see that the ongoing assault on academic freedom at CUW from the Interim President to the current President, is evidence that its leadership is breaking the fellowship of language. They do not want academic dialogue or Lutheran disputation. There are major problems with confessional hull integrity and the atmosphere is stifling in the submarine. If the implosion doesn't get us, the atmosphere will.

Summary. In these first two chapters we have seen that my Lutheran university has studiously ignored *The Formula of*

Concord, an authoritative and biblical text which serves, as Kurt Marquart wrote, as "a frame of reference for the current debates" in our Lutheran churches and schools. We have seen as well that, in the absence of biblical and Lutheran texts teaching us the philosophy of language to which confessional Lutherans such as Luther and Gerhard were deeply committed, the anti-Scriptural philosophy of language known as the Expressionist Semiotic and postmodern view becomes the default position. This anti-Lutheran and anti-Scriptural philosophy of language is what undergirds Woke Marxism in our universities and beyond.

As I have explained, it is their hollow and postmodern philosophy of language that makes both (a) fruitful dialog and (b) Lutheran disputation (which is philosophical and doctrinal) impossible. To reiterate, this is not a problem of communication; it is a philosophical divide. It is the philosophical divide which Saint Paul writes about in Colossians 2:8–9, with Christ on one side of the divide, the traditions of men and the ABCs of the secular world on the other. Hence the personal violence of Woke Marxism at my university and the violence in society at large.

In the concluding two chapters I will explain that the combination of the longtime institutional suppression of the *Formula* in combination with the prevalence of a demonstrably anti-biblical and anti-confessional view of language has led to systemic transgressions of at least two articles of biblical and Lutheran doctrine at my university. Those two articles are Universal Justification and Church and Ministry.

Chapter Three

Cringing toward Social Justice and Marxist Identity and Drifting away from Universal Justification

Theology had fallen into a confusion of tongues. **Old words were used in new and vague senses**. *Even liberals on occasion felt threatened by the all–enveloping double-talk* (Kurt Marquart, *Anatomy of an Explosion*, 111).

A little Woke Marxist leaven goes a long, long way (Galatians 5:9). Woke Marxism did not disappear, just because the Board of Regents finally elected a President, and the university belatedly took down its plans for a Woke President from its website. Far from it. The problems with the confessional integrity of the hull and the depleted atmosphere at Concordia University Wisconsin (CUW) continue to threaten implosion.

Nowhere is this more painfully obvious than in my university's retreat from the core article of Lutheran doctrine, the article of Justification. **This retreat is a consequence of its adulterous affair with the Racial or Social Justice Movement**, another head of the Hydra serpent known as DIE ideology, CRT, Marxist identity theory, BIPOC, LGBTQIA+, and so on.

While my university is, as Professor Marquart would say, *cringing* or bowing to Social Justice, there are pastors and others in my church body, The Lutheran Church—Missouri Synod (LCMS), who are preaching and teaching the same thing. For example, this is what is happening in a group called "Lutherans for Racial Justice."

To show how weak-minded and shameful this move away from the biblical article of Justification and toward Social or Racial Justice is, I will first explain our Lutheran and biblical recognition of the article of Justification as the central feature of biblical doctrine as a whole. There is no such thing as cafeteria

Lutheranism; it's all or nothing, as Jesus the Messiah clearly says in Matthew 28:18–20, but our Lutheran commitment to Justification is our core doctrinal value. This is in keeping with the apostle Paul's thesis or core thought in his first-century A.D. Epistle to the Romans.

Justification is a Lutheran core value. The heart of the matter is this: Absolutely everything depends on the Gospel of Christ, which delivers God's righteousness or justice to human beings. Paul's Greek term, *dikaiosune*, can be translated both as "righteousness" and as "justice."

> I am not ashamed of the Gospel. The Gospel is the power of God leading everyone who believes in it to salvation, the Jew first, then the Greek. For in the Gospel is revealed the justice of God which begins and ends with faith; as Scripture says, "The just man will live by faith" (Romans 1:16–17, NAB).

I will show that there is a first principle here—a principle which, if we ignore it, shows us to be ashamed of Christ Himself and His Word, the Bible. At the same time, ignorance of this first principle hamstrings the teaching and mission work of our churches and schools. The suppression of the Gospel of Justification leads inevitably toward mission failure and toward the implosion of church institutions—as is evident at my Concordia and in three other Concordia universities already lost because of Woke Marxism.

Following my explanation of this first principle I will introduce you to Voddie Baucham Jr., Dean of the School of Divinity at Africa Christian University in Lusaka, Zambia. Professor Baucham provides an exceptionally clear analysis of the anti-biblical, anti-God presuppositions upon which CRT (Critical Race Theory), the mythology behind the Social Justice Movement, is based. His book, *Fault Lines*, includes an Evangelical or Reformed Confession which is a brief but thorough debunking of the notion of "justice" in the name of the movement. I have included this Evangelical confession, "The Dallas Statement on Social Justice and the Gospel," in Appendix T.[1]

---

[1] Voddie T. Baucham, Jr., *Fault Lines: The Social Justice Movement and Evangelical's Looming Catastrophe* (Washington, D.C.: Salem Books, 2021).

The Dallas Statement on Social Justice and the Gospel. As the Dallas Statement shows, the very term "justice" in "Social Justice" and "Racial Justice" is not about justice at all but is a case of what we recognize as the logical fallacy of *equivocation*: using the same word in a deceptive way to make people feel comfortable with what you are really doing. As Professor Marquart said of Seminex, "Theology had fallen into a confusion of tongues. *Old words were used in new and vague senses.* Even liberals on occasion felt threatened by the all–enveloping double-talk." In keeping with their acceptance of the hollow and deceptive philosophy of language (the Expressionist Semiotic view of postmodernism) on which Woke Marxism depends, this is exactly what the Social or Racial Justice people are doing.

Their notion of social justice has nothing to do with *justice* in Western culture or the sacrosanct texts of the United States Declaration of Independence and the Constitution, much less with the biblical revelation of God's justice. As I will explain, *justice* and *justification* are intimately tied to the person and work of Jesus the Christ. Racial and social "justice," in opposition to the Word of God, is all about the stuff of the Political and Social Sciences—the CGT (Church Growth Theory) that paved the way for CRT and Woke accreditation at CUW. Mentioning a few Bible passages does not clean up the dishonest equivocation, it only makes it worse.

While I am grateful for the Dallas Statement as well as Baucham's wonderfully clear analysis, showing that Social Justice or Racial Justice is based on Marxist identity theory; still, the Dallas Statement is not everything that a biblical and Christian confession ought to be. I will be arguing that our Lutheran understanding of universal justification and our recognition that Holy Baptism is a means of grace is the full-throated response to the myths and lies of the Social Justice Movement.

In a nutshell, I will be saying that *Baptismal identity* is the Lord's response to the Marxist identity promoted by disciples of Social Justice which includes Black Lives Matter, Antifa, and secular universities such as Harvard. Social Justice has also infected Evangelical churches and schools—which poses a looming catastrophe for Christian churches and denominations, as Baucham warns. These evils have also infected and compromised Lutheran churches and schools. My Concordia university, for example. Because of Universal Justification and our attention to the means of grace, we Lutherans are even more culpable. To whom the *solas* of the German Reformation have been given, from them shall much be expected.

First, we need to know what a first principle is, and then we must be clear about exactly what (or Who) the first principle of confessional Lutheran thinking is.

3.1 Universal justification is the central article for teaching and for rejecting false doctrine…

A first principle is not "a good idea" or an arbitrary starting point of some sort. Nor is a first principle something that philosophers invent. First principles are discovered, not made. So, a first principle is not a social construct.

A first principle—and there are only two or three—are the *archai* (Greek), the artesian wells, so to speak, which account for the central phenomena of existence being the enduring and significant phenomena that they are. For instance, John 1:1, with John's deployment of the Greek term *arche*, could be translated, "In first principle terms, the *Logos* already was with God." The first principle that I am most concerned with here is the first principle of theology, *nisi per Verbum* from our Lutheran Confession, *The Apology to the Augsburg Confession*, Article 4, On Justification.

The first principle of Justification. But in order to understand what it means to call Justification a first principle or *the* first principle, let me share with you a brief tutorial on (1) the first principle of noncontradiction, (2) the first principle of ethics, and (3) the first principle of the *Logos*. Aristotle lights up the first principle of noncontradiction this way: "The same thing cannot be said both to be and not to be (a) for the same person or thing, (b) at the same time, and (c) in the same respect" (Aristotle, *Metaphysics* IV 3, 1005b19–20, my paraphrase). Introducing this in class, I often invite everyone to imagine that two students at the farthest corners of the classroom are texting back and forth.

"So Prof. Schulz isn't here today!" texts the first student. "But Prof. Schulz is here!" texts the second student. At first blush it sounds like the students are contradicting each other, but maybe not. It so happens that there are two Prof. Schulz's on our two Concordia campuses. First, then, suppose that they agree that they are both referring to the same person, namely, Prof. Greg Schulz. Second, they could text the same texts back and forth a second time, verbatim. Are they contradicting each other now? Probably not, since they may have different times in mind, say, one thinking that I am here on campus today and the other seeing that I am not in the classroom this minute. But what happens if they also agree that "here" in their texts means "here in this classroom during this class period"? Third, they could repeat the exact same texts a third time, but there is one more issue to agree on. What do they each mean by saying that I "am here" today? One could mean that I am not mentally present, that I seem unprepared and befuddled, while the other means that I am physically present.

Now what happens if, having clarified (a) which person they have been texting about, (b) which time and place they have in mind, and (c) in what respect they are referring to my "being here today," they both stick with their original texts? Well, if they agree that I both am and am not here in this classroom this period physically—if they in effect agree that what is true for one writer is not necessarily true for the other writer and everyone else in class feels the same way—then the jig is up. Accepting such contradictory texts as the norm would be the end of all texts—the end, in fact, of all communicating, all thinking, all writing, all person–to–person relationships. As the T-shirt says, "Gravity: It's not just a Good Idea; it's the Law." The principle of noncontradiction is a natural law for communication. It's the law. It's Torah. It's a first principle.

There is a first principle for ethics too. Ethics is a normative discipline, a standard-based inquiry that befits us as human beings within God's creation. The perennial, generation–after–generation question that leads us to do ethics is the question, "How ought we act and not act toward one another as the kind of creature or being that we are, namely, human beings?" The first principle for ethics is the principle of Good and Evil: "Do the good, avoid the evil." In other words, "Do no harm."

When C. S. Lewis argues in the three essays that comprise his 1943 book *The Abolition of Man*, that "the Innovator" always ends up depending on moral principles whenever he tries to make his case that there is no such thing as morality, he is depending on this first principle. When Nietzsche (whom I take to be "the Innovator" in *Abolition*) attacked the very concept of morality in the waning years of the nineteenth century, he titled one of his attacks "Beyond Good and Evil," thereby expressing his intent to demolish the first principle of ethics. The principle of Good and Evil is a natural law of ethics. No Good and Evil, no ethics. It is a first principle (see also Romans 12:2–13 and 7:14–25).

Heraclitus's *logos* is a first principle. I would even refer to it as "the first principle of first principles." The first principle character of the *logos* is what we read in these quotes from his surviving *Fragments*.

> This *Logos* holds always but humans always prove unable to understand it, both before hearing it and when they have first heard it. For though all things come to be in accordance with this *Logos*, humans are like the inexperienced when they experience such words and deeds as I set out, distinguishing each in accordance with its nature and saying how it is. But other people fail to notice what they do when awake, just as they forget what they do while asleep. (DK 22B1)

> For this reason it is necessary to follow what is common. But although the *Logos* is common, most people live as if they had their own private understanding. (DK 22B2)

Here is another way to look at Heraclitus's discovery of this first principle or *arche*. Plato referred to Heraclitus as the philosopher of radical flux. In one of his dialogs Plato puts it this way: "Heraclitus, I believe, says that all things go and nothing stays, and comparing existents to the flow of a river, he says you could not step twice into the same river" (Cratylus 402a).

So far, so good. But if everything, absolutely everything, is constantly changing, we could never know that everything was constantly changing. This is because we would be fluxing, so there would be no individuals to know anything. The cosmos would be utter chaos and not a coherent cosmos, so there would be no universe to know. Language would be nothing, no thing, not language at all, so there would be no way to know. If all is in flux, there would be nothing to know, no knowers, and no language.

However, given that things continue to exist as the things that they are, there must be a source and explanation for their continuing identity over time. If we know the universe as an orderly and dependably consistent unitary reality, then there must be a source and explanation for our coherent knowing. This is what Heraclitus means by the *Logos*. *Logos* is both the source and fundamental order of the cosmos.

It is, as I said, the ultimate first principle—as is clear when we translate *logos* not as *ratio*, or "mental rationality" (the wrong fork in the road from Greek to Latin) but as *Verbum*. Verbum is the Latin term—the correct term that is more faithful to the Greek—used in the Apology: "God cannot be treated, He cannot be apprehended *nisi per Verbum* or, in English, Except via the Word." It's just as you see on the fashionable black T-shirt marketed by my former students at Concordia seen from coast to coast across the United States, the T-shirt with the cross and the white lettering, "nisi per Verbum."

In Heraclitus's hometown of Ephesus, one-half millennium after his discovery of the first principle of the *Logos*, St. John revealed this first principle to be a two-natured person, the second person of the Holy Trinity. "In terms of the archaic or first principle, the *Logos* already existed with God ... The *Logos* became flesh and tabernacled among us, and we apostles have seen His glory, the glory of the only-begotten, full of grace and truth" (John 1:1 and 14).

The centerpiece of Heraclitus's philosophy is the *logos*—the Logos Who, it turns out, is God in the flesh—but postmodernist philosophers such as Jacques Derrida who are incredulous of the orderliness of all creation, glom onto the notion of flux instead of *logos*. Derrida, for example, famously wanted to "decenter the *Logos*," meaning both Saint John's *Logos* and Heraclitus first principle of the *Logos*. These postmodernists are, even *before* all is said and done, committed disbelievers—Lyotard defines postmodernism as "incredulity toward all metanarrative"[2]—so reality as it is remains beside the point for the Woke Marxists who follow in their train.

Notwithstanding postmodern disbelief, in a philosophical sense as in the biblical sense you cannot serve two masters. You cannot have flux and chaos as your guiding principle because such a position is not a position; it is nothing more than a stubborn denial of the orderliness of creation as it is. Despite all of this, postmodern philosophers love the flux dimension of Heraclitus, especially to give them philosophical cover for imposing their endless reinterpretations on language and texts. They suppress Heraclitus's philosophical claims in support of the common, universal, ordering first principle of the *logos* and language. The postmodern suppression of texts and especially authoritative or normative texts is, as we discussed in the first chapter, of a piece with Concordia university's suppression of the authoritative Lutheran and biblical *Formula of Concord*.

This brings us back to Derrida and his deceptive, anti-Logos philosophy of language: "I reserve the right to utilize texts however I want to, constantly reinventing their interpretation, and no one gets to tell me that I'm wrong!"

This is what Harvard teaches with its CRT. This is the pandemic laying waste most universities in the United States. This is the disease that CUW refuses to reject and condemn. It has flared up in its search for a Woke Marxist President. It is there in the Black Liberation Theology of Ibram X. Kendi taught to the university's students in its Black Student Union.

It is mainstreamed in the university's bias reporting system, mainlined in CUW's concessions to Woke Marxist accreditation standards, in the academic sympathies with BIPOC, Black Lives Matter, Social and Racial Justice, and on and on. A little leaven leavens the whole lump (Galatians 5:9). Woke Marxism is the fentanyl of the educated masses. Get rid of the leaven. Get rid of the fentanyl.

While commenting on religion in an interview we sampled in

---

[2] Jean–François Lyotard, *The Postmodern Condition: A Report on Knowledge*, trans. Geoff Bennington and Brian Massumi (Minneapolis: University of Minnesota Press, 1993), xxiv.

our previous chapter, Derrida goes on about Jesus the Messiah, whom he deconstructs down to a tiny abstraction that he can interpret however he chooses.

> When I insisted in *Specters of Marx* on messianicity, which I distinguished from messianism, I wanted to show that the messianic structure is a universal structure. As soon as you address the other, as soon as you are open to the future, of waiting for someone to come: that is the opening of experience. Someone is to come, is *now* to come. Justice and peace will have to do with this coming of the other, with the promise. Each time I am opening my mouth, I am promising something… So the just one speech act among others, every speech act is fundamentally a promise… this is what I call the messianic structure. This messianic structure is not limited to what one calls messianisms, that is, Jewish, Christian, or Islamic messianism, to these determinate figures and forms of the Messiah.[3]

Remember, as we saw earlier, Derrida has "no stable position on the texts you mentioned, the prophets and the Bible." He insists, "I want to keep the right to read these texts in a way that has to be constantly reinvented." In this passage, he acknowledges that "justice and peace" come only from a concrete, personal Messiah—*which he rejects in favor of his queer notion of "messianic structure" and "messianisms."* This right to reinvent Bible texts constantly—this is the problem with Christians who insist that social justice is about biblical justice.

3.2 …all Hydra heads of false teaching are…in opposition to the Bible…

For example, consider how the Dallas Statement on Social Justice and the Gospel (Appendix T) contrasts the biblical term *justice* with the way the word is used equivocally in "Social *Justice*" or "Racial *Justice*." This is further proof that those committed to Woke Marxism reject the External Efficacious Means of Grace philosophy of language—*even while they claim to be following the Bible!*

III Justice
WE AFFIRM that since he is holy, righteous, and just,

---
[3] *Deconstruction in a Nutshell*, 22–23.

God requires those who bear his image to live justly in the world. This includes showing appropriate respect to every person and giving to each one what he or she is due. We affirm that societies must establish laws to correct injustices that have been imposed through cultural prejudice.

WE DENY that true justice can be culturally defined or that standards of justice that are merely socially constructed can be imposed with the same authority as those that are derived from Scripture. We further deny that Christians can live justly in the world under any principles other than the biblical standard of righteousness. Relativism, socially-constructed standards of truth or morality, and notions of virtue and vice that are constantly in flux cannot result in authentic justice.

Scripture: Genesis 18:19; Isaiah 61:8; Micah 6:8; Matthew 5:17–19; Romans 3:31

Consider as well how the Dallas Statement contrasts the biblical understanding of *race* with the equivocation in "*Racial Justice*."

XII Race / Ethnicity

WE AFFIRM God made all people from one man. Though people often can be distinguished by different ethnicities and nationalities, they are ontological equals before God in both creation and redemption. "Race" is not a biblical category, but rather a social construct that often has been used to classify groups of people in terms of inferiority and superiority. All that is good, honest, just, and beautiful in various ethnic backgrounds and experiences can be celebrated as the fruit of God's grace. All sinful actions and their results (including evils perpetrated between and upon ethnic groups by others) are to be confessed as sinful, repented of, and repudiated.

WE DENY that Christians should segregate themselves into racial groups or regard racial identity above, or even equal to, their identity in Christ. We deny that any divisions between people groups (from an unstated attitude of superiority to an overt spirit of resentment) have any legitimate place in the fellowship of the redeemed. We reject any teaching

> that encourages racial groups to view themselves as privileged oppressors or entitled victims of oppression. While we are to weep with those who weep, we deny that a person's feelings of offense or oppression necessarily prove that someone else is guilty of sinful behaviors, oppression, or prejudice.
>
> Scripture: Genesis 1:26–28; Acts 17:24–26; 1 Corinthians 13:4–7; 2 Corinthians 12:16–18

In biblical terms, disciples of Social and Racial Justice are "waging war according to the flesh," that is, according to made-up human ideologies of race. *Ideologies* are ideas that are generated on the basis of made-up human and worldly principles, rather than philosophy based on Christ Himself (see Colossians 2:8–9). The current Provost at my university, for example, has recommended Black, Indigenous, People of Color (BIPOC) conferences for faculty members. During the 2020–2021 Academic Year she commended a professor from CUW's stepchild campus in Ann Arbor for participating in a Racial Justice seminar. Concordia Ann Arbor's logo was included on the posting for this project.

Contrary to this academic Administrator's ideas, this is not how the apostles did things.

> We do indeed live in the body, but we do not wage war with human resources. The weapons of our warfare are not merely human. They possess God's power for the destruction of strongholds. We demolish sophistries and every proud pretension that raises itself against the knowledge of God: we likewise bring every thought into captivity to make it obedient to Christ... You view things superficially... (2 Corinthians 10:3–7, NAB).

That said—and this brief contrast between the Bible and Social or Racial Justice, so-called, is well said indeed in the Dallas Statement; there are two more dimensions to justice and justification that we confessional Lutherans can contribute to Baucham's brave and biblical writing and speaking. These two major contributions are (a) Universal Justification (which is *not* universalism) and (b) equating *justice* with God's righteousness in the person and work of Jesus the Messiah.

3.3 ...how does God deliver the reality of universal justification...

Kurt Marquart wrote, "What ought to be crystal clear is that any retreat from biblical facts and history is a retreat from the Incarnation itself. Any driving of wedges ... between fact and faith, between history and theology, hits at the inmost nature of biblical Christianity. The written Word is about the Incarnate Word and is of a piece with Him" (*Anatomy of an Explosion*, 125). Here is one way to see the intimate relationship between Jesus and His Word and Universal Justification, which is God's view of justice.

The First Principle of *Logos* in Confessional Lutheran Thought

1. "God cannot be treated with, God cannot be apprehended *nisi per Verbum*, except through the Word" (*Apology of the Augsburg Confession*, Article 4, On Justification).
2. *Nisi per Verbum* is derived from Jesus' identification of Himself, and of His utterly unique work of reconciling humanity with His Father, *nisi per Me* (John 14:6 in Latin).
3. Jesus the *Verbum* is the *Logos* incarnate (John 1:1–14).
4. *Logos* means "language," the essential difference between the human kind of being and all other types of animals (Aristotle, *Politics* 1, the minimal definition of humankind stipulated by Luther in his 1536 Disputation Concerning Man).[4]
5. Therefore, everyday language is a divine gift intimately from Christ, the incarnate *Logos*.
6. The difference between everyday human language

---

[4] For a study of *logos* that is accessible to all English speakers, see Geoffrey Bromiley, editor, *Theological Dictionary of the New Testament Abridged in One Volume* (Grand Rapids: William B. Eerdmans Publishing Company, 1985), 505–514. "The word [*logos*] is not just what Jesus said, but the mystery of God disclosed in Christ (Colossians 1:25ff)... This shows that Revelation 19:13 is expressing something integral to the whole Christian message when it says that [Christ's] name is the Word of God."

and Holy Scripture is that Scripture is inerrant, efficacious, and God-breathed, word–for–word; whereas everyday language is not. Scripture is the very words of the Word incarnate, whereas everyday language is not.

7. There is thus a contiguity of the very words of the *Logos* incarnate in Scripture and everyday language. This contiguity, created and preserved by the *Logos* incarnate, makes language means–of–grace–like, so to speak. This basis of language in Christ the *Logos* is what accounts for the External Efficacious Means of Grace philosophy of language (Colossians 2:8–9).

8. On the same basis, that is, the means of grace view of language based on Christ Himself, any philosophy of language in opposition to the External Efficacious Means of Grace philosophy is a philosophy of language in opposition to Christ the *Logos* (Colossians 2:8–9).

The Word, not the world. The trouble for Social Justice and Racial Justice warriors who also claim that they are standing up for Jesus is that Social Justice and Racial Justice are frontal attacks on Jesus Himself. Furthermore, the peace that these Woke Marxist movements deliver is not the peace which Jesus gives; it is the peace that the world gives, because these are worldly movements (John 14:27).

Considering Marquart's analysis of the Seminex explosion in our Concordia Seminary, Saint Louis, two generations ago, how shall we respond to the incursion of God-less Woke Marxism in our Lutheran universities today, accompanied by the censoring of debate and disputation against this retreat from the Incarnation? Well, let us live not by lies. Let us instead oppose the lies with the Truth Himself.

The Word, the Word, the words. We should heed Marquart's proposition that the written word is about the Incarnate Word and is of a piece with Him. Adopting and adapting the title of a recent book by Jeremy Holmes, *Cur Deus Verba*, let me unpack and apply Marquart's proposition by asking with a slightly different accent, *Cur Verbum Verba*, "Why has the Word revealed Himself in words?"

In this way we can expose and then refute the presupposition on which Woke Marxism depends—that is, we can refute Woke Marxism with Christ the Incarnate Word and thereby establish that the means of grace are the only means by which we can do Lutheran and Christian education. A come-along feature of this refutation would be to reestablish disputation or argumentation as the hallmark of Lutheran teaching and learning. This refutation, then, will be of help not only to Lutherans, but to every Christian praying and laboring to save Christian schools from the anti-Christian assault of the latest version of Marxism in Social Justice, Racial Justice, and so on.

As we consider how to put this first principle of *Logos* and language into practice, here are a few crucial terms, by way of a reminder. Remember, *Woke Marxism* (also known as Cultural Marxism, Identity Marxism, Diversity/Inclusion/Equity, Critical Social Justice, etc.) has two components, as I have explained. One is obvious, the other is suppressed. On the one hand, it involves the Marxist social engineering of society by means of disruption and violence resulting from the invention and incitement of diverse identity groups (see Karl Marx, *The German Ideology* and *The Communist Manifesto*). This is the obvious component.

On the other hand, there is a component that is *presupposed*, meaning that it is so widely taken for granted that it hardly ever comes up for debate or discussion (even in churches and schools where debate and discussion are possible). If anyone asks about this presupposed foundation, his question will most often be poo pooed. (*Poo pooing* is an actual philosophical term that amounts to an outright dismissal of someone's argument by the *ad hominem* tactic of insinuating that he is being ridiculous—or racist.)

The unacknowledged presupposition of Woke Marxism is postmodernism's cynical disbelief regarding the inherent meaningfulness of the divine gift of language. This presupposition that language is open to infinite interpretation—and furthermore, that "No one has the right to tell me that my interpretation is wrong!"—has to do with the means–by–which Woke Marxism is promulgated. As we saw in the previous chapter on my university Administration's hollow and deceptive philosophy of language—and as we will see again in the case of the university's Regents and Administrators abuse of tried–and–true words and texts regarding the office of the ministry—Woke Marxism is anti-text because it is anarchic, or anti-authority. Just look at Woke Marxism's cavalier overthrow of personal pronouns, sacred propositions, and all words, as they see fit. Woke Marxism depends upon the Expressionist Semiotic philosophy of language, as we have seen. So do groups such as Lutherans for Racial Justice.

In truth, our universities, secular and religious, have been neglecting philosophy of language and shunning sacrosanct texts, particularly the Scriptures, for a long while. This is not unique to Concordia universities such as CUW and Concordia University Texas. Pre-censoring classical texts in theory and in practice is a major reason contemporary universities are vulnerable to Marxism. In C.S. Lewis's essay collection, *The Abolition of Man*, of which his book, *That Hideous Strength*, is a novelization, he puts the problem this way: "The task of the modern educator is not to cut down jungles, but to irrigate deserts."

Woke Marxism thrives in a desert environment. Therefore, it detests irrigation and sources of living water (Psalm 1:3).

Speaking of sources and texts, *Western culture* is a term that must be understood normatively, that is, in terms of moral authority. This is important because our Woke adversaries always follow the understanding of culture taught by the social sciences (such as Anthropology, Political Science, and Psychology). But the Social Science understanding of culture is merely descriptive. It is without authority and without moral content. It just paints a picture, just produces graphs and metrics. You cannot make moral judgments based on scientific data or hypotheses, no matter how detailed or widely believed your hypothesis may be. This is the nature of science. As Marquart wrote in his anatomy of our earlier crisis in Lutheran education, "Science has neither use nor room for privileged authorities or sacrosanct texts. It recognizes only observations, experiments..."

As T.S. Eliot wrote in Choruses from the Rock, just before lamenting, "Where the Life [Christ] that we have lost in living?"
> Endless invention, endless experiment,
> Brings knowledge of motion, but not of stillness;

>Knowledge of speech, but not of silence;
>Knowledge of words, and ignorance of the Word.
>All our knowledge brings us nearer to our ignorance,
>All our ignorance brings us nearer to death,
>But nearness to death no nearer to God.

Cultural implosion in society. Trafficking on widespread ignorance of the Word, of the texts and ultimate authority of the Word of Christ, Woke Marxism is a Social Science experiment conducted with utter disregard for the individual and utterly void of moral authority. It is a global transgression of the Nuremberg Code regulating human experimentation after the ghastly social and physical experiments of the Nazis.

Readers of C.S. Lewis's *That Hideous Strength* will recognize that N.I.C.E., the National Institute for Continuing Experimentation on animals and human beings, is a foreshadowing of ideologies and social phenomena such as Woke Marxism, with its queer undermining of all morality and its physical and mental experimentation on the bodies and souls of our children at all levels of formal and media education.

Cultural implosion in the university. In late twentieth-century and early twenty-first century universities, there are IRB's, Institutional Review Boards, to scrutinize and supervise the treatment of animals and human beings in scientific and social science experiments. However, the social experiment of Woke Marxism, Social Justice, Racial Justice, transgendering (as in LGBTQ2S+), and so on apparently slides by without scrutiny or supervision. Schools of Education in universities such as mine should be scrutinizing and supervising this social education/indoctrination business, but instead they are cranking out Doctors of Education (EdD's) who promote Woke Marxism.

This is a cultural and societal implosion because of institutional implosion. Western culture is best defined as *culture* in the normative or authoritative sense of the passing on of moral judgments and values from one generation to the next. This is a philosophical definition in contrast to the mere descriptions that come from the social sciences. What distinguishes it as *Western* culture is that it passes on moral judgments (a) in Greek forms of thinking and (b) with the material content of the Hebrew and Greek texts of the Scriptures (Roger Scruton).

The Greek forms of thinking that formed Western culture are Socratic and Platonic dialog, argumentation, logic—the stuff of argumentation, debate, and disputation for the sake of capital-T Truth which take place, of course, *in the medium of language.*

Language has us, not vice versa. The twentieth century German philosopher, Martin Heidegger, provides a philosophical antidote to the "I can interpret it however I want and you don't get to tell me that I'm wrong" view of Woke Marxists. You may be interested to know that Heidegger regularly read his Greek New Testament and his Weimar Edition of Luther's Works. Unlike Lutherans who cooperate with Social Justice/Racial Justice ideology, Heidegger (for all his moral and political failings) recognized that we do not own language, to interpret it however we choose. Rather, it is the case that language is ultimate (there is nowhere to stand outside of language) and language forms us—not the other way around. He understands language as *logos*, not the way the Social Justice people do, as an opportunity to interpret words such as "justice" however they choose, while insisting that no one gets to tell them, "No, you're wrong."

> To reflect on language ... demands that we enter into the speaking of language in order to take up our stay with language, i.e., within its speaking, not within our own. Only in that way do we arrive at the region wherein it may happen—or also fail to happen—that language will call us from there and grant us its nature. We leave speaking to language. We do not wish to ground language in something else that is not language itself, nor do we wish to explain other things than language as it is by means of language.[5]

Woke Marxism is an insurgency against Western culture: an ignorant, arrogant, and immoral attack on what the Greek philosophers and the apostle John identify as *the logos*. This is the heart of Woke Marxism's social experimentation on human subjects, utterly without their informed consent. This is what Eliot identifies poetically as the "Endless invention, endless experiment, / [which] Brings ... / Knowledge of words, and ignorance of the Word." That is, in Latin, ignorance of Christ the Incarnate *Verbum* (John 1:1 & 14).

---

[5] Martin Heidegger, Albert Hofstadter, translator, *Poetry, Language, Thought* (New York: Harper & Row, 1971), 190–91.

Unethical human experimentation. One more thing before we get to the winning and powerful response of the incarnate *Verbum* and His very *verba* of Holy Scripture, which is the means–by–which Lutheran education is Lutheran and educational. I deal with this biblically and logically, as an intellectual and professional heir of Martin Luther. There are at least three fallacies at work in the compromising of Lutheran— and indeed of all Christian education by the *anarchic* or "anti-first principle" ideology of Woke Marxism, and without the informed consent of parents of school age children and of young adult students of higher education.

Woke Marxism is human experimentation in defiance of any and every moral and ethical law but especially those of Western culture. For example, as the first proposition of the Nuremberg Code, codified in 1945 to oppose the horrors of Nazi experimentation on Jewish persons in the millions, and on other People of the Book as well, declares,

> The voluntary consent of the human subject is absolutely essential.
>
> This means that the person involved should have legal capacity to give consent; should be so situated as to be able to exercise free power of choice, without the intervention of any element of force, fraud, deceit, duress, over-reaching, or other ulterior form of constraint or coercion; and should have sufficient knowledge and comprehension of the elements of the subject matter involved as to enable him to make an understanding and enlightened decision. This latter element requires before the acceptance of an affirmative decision by the experimental subject, there should be made known to him the nature, duration, and purpose of the experiment; the method and means by which it is to be conducted; all inconveniences and hazards reasonably to be expected; and the effects upon his health or person, which may possibly come from his participation in the experiment.
>
> The duty and responsibility for ascertaining the quality of the consent rests upon each individual who initiates, directs or engages in the experiment. It is a personal duty and responsibility which may not be delegated to another with impunity.

My university's Interim President was unable to respond in a 2021 faculty meeting when, in response to his willingness to consider mandatory COVID or China Virus vaccinations, a few of us reminded him that such a mandatory vaccination of a new and untested mRNA would be unethical and against the Nuremberg Code.

There is no informed consent for the Woke Marxist's social experimentation in education. The experimentation being conducted upon our children and young adults is therefore immoral and unethical. Furthermore, it is anti-educational. Woke Marxism is arrogantly and pridefully anti-rational and anti-logical in the means–by–which it operates. It is an afront to our shared humanity, a weapon of mass destruction, the abolition of man (C.S. Lewis).

All of this is based upon the presupposition that language is inherently meaningless because it is open to endless interpretation. At every turn, Woke Marxism intends, with malice aforethought, to abolish language, the means–by–which we human beings have fellowship with one another (Aristotle, *Politics*, Book 1).

There are no other means. There is more. Language, in the case of the unsurpassable authority and verbally inerrant Word of Christ, that is, the biblical text, is the means–by–which God—that is, the *Creator* of the Declaration who has created all of us human beings equal and endowed us with unalienable rights such as Life, Liberty, and the Pursuit of Happiness—has established and still maintains His fellowship with us human beings. In Lutheran thought and education, we identify the Bible (and the Sacraments which it authorizes) as *the means of grace*. There are no other means–by–which God relates to humanity since the incarnation of the Verbum, the Word, His Son (see the Greek New Testament, including the opening paragraph of the Epistle to the Hebrews).

At the most superficial level, Woke Marxism depends upon the fallacy of equivocation. For example, Woke "justice" is not the justice of the God of the Bible who, according to the prophet, "Has told you, O man, what is good; and what does the LORD require of you but to do justice, to love kindness, and to walk humbly with your God" (Micah 6:8). It is not the justice of Plato's

Republic. It is not the justice of Western thought as recently as John Rawls. It is not justice at all. It is racialized vengeance. It is institutionalized racism.

Equivocation is Woke Marxism's stock–in–trade, its weapon of choice for its Marxist opposition to the Scriptures, opposition to the Western canon, opposition to the texts of the Hebrew and Greek Scriptures. As we read in Isaiah, "Woe to those who call evil good and good evil, who substitute darkness for light and light for darkness" (5:20). In the insurgent mantras of Woke Marxism, "Equity" means certain groups are more equal than others. "Diversity" means carving up our common humanity into manufactured, socially-constructed categories of skin color and sexual proclivities. "Inclusion" is the legitimization of the exclusion of Christ, of His words, from education and media. It seeks to normalize government persecution of Christians, in deliberate contradiction of the First Amendment.

At a more profound level, compromise with Woke Marxism is commitment to a treacherous slippery slope fallacy. The compromise with Woke Marxism is a philosophy of education that rejects the words and Person of the Way Himself (John 14:6) in favor of an increasingly cozy fellowship of appeasement with the wicked, the sinners, the scoffers of the world. In other words, compromise with Woke Marxism is a paradigm of the slippery slope depicted in Psalm 1: "How blessed is the man who does not walk in the counsel of the wicked, nor stand in the seat of sinners, nor sit in the seat of scoffers, but his delight is in the law of the LORD, and in His law he meditates day and night."

At its most fundamental level, the compromise of Lutheran education with Woke Marxism is an appeal to false authority, a shameful *ad Verecundiam* of biblical proportions. (The Latin name of this fallacy means "shameful.") Jesus of Nazareth, God in our human flesh, says in Matthew 28, "All authority has been given to Me in heaven and on earth." Woke Marxism scoffs at Him and His words at every turn. Woke Marxism is social experimentation conducted on the flesh and the souls of uneducated and vulnerable people to see if anything will happen when you teach them to "throw off the fetters," the words and the divine authority, of the Messiah Himself. For the guaranteed outcome of this dehumanizing experiment, see Psalm 2.

I am not simply making an argument here in favor of believing the biblical faith—although I believe, teach, and confess the Bible and the Christian creeds without qualification as a confessional Lutheran pastor and professor. So far, I have been offering for your consideration an analysis of Woke Marxism as an assault on the founding proposition in the opening words of the sacrosanct text of our American Declaration of Independence. Because of Woke Marxism, as President Lincoln said, "We are engaged in a great civil war, testing whether that nation, or any nation so conceived and so dedicated, can long endure." I have also explained that Woke Marxism is opposed to the canonical texts of Western culture. In both cases, it is more than plausible to conclude that Woke Marxist education in media and especially in our American schools and universities is an attack on the God of the founding proposition and of the canonical Scriptures.

The failure of Lutheran higher education. In the following paragraphs, I offer for your consideration this diagnosis: We in the LCMS, my Lutheran church body, are failing to hold the line against Woke Marxism in our universities. Following that diagnosis, I offer a prescription for what we need to do if we are to remain faithful to the God of Scripture, the God who has spoken to us by His Son, the God who created us all and gave us the divine gift of language for fellowship first with Him and then with one another. So, I turn now to my church body with a heavy heart because of its (a) impotence to address the Social/Racial Justice aspect of Woke Marxism and (b) growing failure to adhere to the first principle of Universal Justification, which is the heart and core of confessional Lutheranism.

Can we hope for a bright future for Lutheran education in the middle of this Woke Marxist insurgency against nation and culture, logic and language in our churches and schools? In the June 2023 *Reporter* our Synod President stated, "[Our remaining Lutheran] universities have the strongest theological and administrative presidents we've had in decades." That is not saying much, given the lightweight pastors who recently led these institutions, and given the current class of lay presidents we have in our (rapidly diminishing number of) Concordia universities.

He goes on to say, "Concordia Wisconsin and Ann Arbor's future is bright. My only goal is that we ... confess and live the authority of inerrant Scriptures and our confessions. *This precludes Wokeism*" [my italics]. His statement against Wokeism is on target. Praise the Lord. But on the one hand, neither Concordia University Wisconsin (CUW or CUWAA) nor any other Concordia, to my knowledge, has repudiated Woke Marxism.

On the other hand, the comment of bright optimism misses the point. The reality is that we must address the *conditions* at our Lutheran universities that allowed Woke Marxism to take root in the first place, otherwise this exceptionally evil ideology will continue to fester.

The pressure to Go Woke or Go Broke is immense socially. It is immense financially. There is a predictable consequence for a religious university's dependency on government funding—funding from a federal administration that is maniacally imposing Woke Marxism on every institution in our constitutional republic.

The Synod President's visits to investigate Wokeism at Mequon and Ann Arbor were helpful as far as they went, but there has not been the repentance he called for in May 2022. It also seems that no one is willing or capable of acknowledging the elephant on campus, namely, government funding. This is funding leveraged by a federal government that is striking at the heart of Christianity, the authority of the written Word of the Word made flesh. Just look at the White House's declaration of transgendered surgeries and experimental hormones for all, made the week before Holy Week in 2022, and its plans for reconfiguring Title IX in 2023 (Title IX is a Federal civil rights law that prohibits discrimination on the basis of sex in education programs and activities.)

With or without the elephant of federal funding (again, no Concordia University President has announced a plan to dislodge our religious universities from federal or state funding) it is the case that our Lutheran universities which promulgate Woke Marxism, DIE, and so-called social justice are "hitting at the inmost nature of biblical Christianity. The written Word is about the Incarnate Word and is of a piece with Him." Social Justice is neither social nor is it justice. It shuns Christ. It diminishes human nature. It is also at home in many of our churches and ecclesiastical institutions.

All this is because Woke Marxism deplores the Incarnate Word and His personal, authoritative, biblical words to us human beings but we cannot bring ourselves to reject and condemn this damnable ideology and philosophy of life. For a Lutheran institution of higher learning such as CUW to become vulnerable to such an antithetical, anti-Christ ideology as Wokeism or Critical Social Justice is outrageous and mind-boggling. How could this have happened? *This* is the question.

Due respect, when our church body President says, "Concordia Wisconsin and Ann Arbor's future is bright"—this is a naive and unwarranted assertion. He has failed to provide (or even to acknowledge the need for) a diagnosis. Here is one: A Lutheran or other religious university that goes Woke has a compromised theological immune system. The question is, "How did we wear down our immune system?" *The missing ingredient* in our universities—and in our church body as a whole—*is Lutheran disputation*.

Lutheran disputation. The Administration and Board at my LCMS university, for example, *will not have it*. They abhor it. They are actively censoring, prohibiting, and attacking it for all to see, in the church and far beyond. Their ongoing attack on academic freedom is a public scandal. It is also a Lutheran scandal.

3.4 Universal justification...is delivered *nisi per Verbum* except via the Word of God...

Let me bring this to a sharp, sharp focus in Justification. The *justice* of Justification is Jesus Himself, His person as God and human being, His work. You remember how Derrida demanded the right to reinterpret the Bible and the prophets endlessly, as well as the right to reduce the Messiah of the Jews and Christians to a messianic abstraction? Here, to spite Derrida and demolish all his *derridadaisms*, is a passage from the prophet Jeremiah, who lived and preached about 600 B.C.

> "Behold, the days are coming," says the Lord,
> "That I will raise to David a Branch of righteousness;
> A King shall reign and prosper,
> And execute judgment and righteousness in the earth.
> In His days Judah will be saved,

And Israel will dwell safely;
Now this is His name by which He will be called:
THE LORD OUR RIGHTEOUSNESS …"
(Jeremiah 23:5–6).

Religious Jewish persons who have learned from the Scriptures that Jesus is indeed the promised Messiah sometimes refer to this name, The Lord Our Righteousness, in Hebrew as *Jehovah Tsidkenu*. Jeremiah's Hebrew word, TsDK, is *righteousness* and *justice* simultaneously. Lutheran commentaries and translations tend to prefer *righteousness* to emphasize what Luther called "the Great Exchange," that "God made Jesus, who had no sin to become sin for us so that in Him we might become the righteousness of God" (2 Corinthians 5:21). Roman Catholic Bible translations tend to translate *justice* whenever TsDK shows up in the Old Testament. *The Jerusalem Bible*, which J.R.R. Tolkien had a hand in translating, translates *justice* every time this Hebrew word occurs in the psalms that I regularly pray.

The Lord Jesus is Justice and Righteousness in the flesh. Jesus is just because He is God incarnate. He credits people with His own righteousness or justice because He is God incarnate. Who Jesus is and how He "executes judgment and righteousness in the earth" has everything to do with the delivery of His justification to people. Jesus is THE LORD OUR JUSTICE.

The other part of this central article of Justification—the reason that we Lutherans call this Universal Justification—is the logical question, "To whom has He credited His own divine righteousness, His own divine justice?"

The answer is "Every human being, without exception—by grace alone, faith alone, via Scripture alone. It's all because He is who He is, namely, the Messiah, the one and only Christ!" The written text, the universal Declaration of Independence from the total and damnable corruption taught in the first part of the *Formula* (the Lutheran text being suppressed by my Lutheran university) is the following passage from Paul's epistle to the Romans.

The thesis of Romans. All human beings are, since the Insurgency against God in Eden, blind, dead, and enemies of God. The problem is this: God is righteous/just; we are unrighteous/unjust.[6] Everyone who believes has God's approval through faith in Jesus Christ. There is no difference between people. Because **all people** have sinned, they have fallen short of God's glory. **They** [that is, all people] receive God's approval freely by an act of his kindness through the price Christ Jesus paid to set us free.

> God showed that Christ is the throne of mercy where God's approval is given through faith in Christ's blood. In his patience God waited to deal with sins committed in the past. He waited so that he could display his approval at the present time. ***This shows that he is a God of justice***, a God who approves of people who believe in Jesus (Romans 3:22–26, GW).

This is Universal Justification. Believers do not believe in order to get justified. Believers are called "believers" because they believe the Gospel that everyone has been justified. This is the meaning of justice. The Gospel of Jesus the Christ is the alpha and the omega of justice for all—whether in the Constitution of the United States or in the proclamation of the Gospel. "The reason why Christ died for sins once for all, the just/righteous Man for the sake of the unjust/unrighteous people, was that He might lead you to God" (1 Peter 3:18, NAB).

Do not miss the point that Woke Marxism is so intent on revolt against God, the Bible, and language that everything they touch turns out to be, as Luther said, "an aping or mocking of God." The Social Justice/Racial Justice Movement and the DIE ideology advertised in my Concordia's search for a new university President are "fake views." As you can tell from reading the articles about Concordia's war on academic freedom in my case in *The Federalist,* DIE is not anti-racist; it is racism. Social/Racial Justice is not about righteousness and justice; it is about unrighteousness/injustice for all—as we have seen from Scripture and the Lutheran Confessions (the Apology to the Augsburg's article on Justification, for example).

Worst of all, Social/Racial Justice proponents, including, lamentably, those who identify as Christians and Lutherans, are not "demolishing sophistries and every proud pretention that

---

[6] Anders Nygren, *Commentary on Romans* (Philadelphia: Muhlenberg Press,1949), 101ff.

raises itself against the knowledge of God" (2 Corinthians 10:5). Instead, they are demolishing the knowledge God provides in the Gospel, the true knowledge of righteousness/justice in Christ alone.

Objection and reply. It is time to share a piece of instructive Marquartian sarcasm. "But, of course, it is all a matter of interpretation: 'In the beginning was the Flesh...'" In other words, it turns out that the racial justice/social justice crowd is all about outward appearances and Marxist mythology. Universal Justification by Christ alone is not enough for them. At this point someone obsessed with the Social Sciences and racial justice is likely to object, "Aha! I see that you are an unloving racist!"

I reply by recommending that you read Appendix C, a sermon I preached on the First Sunday in Lent, 2022. There I explained why students from my university went on television to accuse me of being racist. It was because of the deficient, Social Justice education they had been receiving at CUW, and in the secular corporate media. As to the accusation that by speaking so directly I am being unloving, perhaps you could hold on until the next chapter, when I explain that Professor Marquart predicted your criticism. Or you could read Appendix N right now. My love is, in fact, the kind of love that you should expect to see in the pastors and teachers with which the ascended Lord blessed His churches (Ephesians 4:7–16). Incidentally, this Ephesians passage is being aped or mocked by the Woke Marxist value of diversity. Diversity in God's universe is not about racial divisions; it is about the diversity of gifts He gives us, especially the various gifts in connection with the Gospel of Justification in Christ.

Black and white is not a real divide. Meanwhile, please read your Bible for *what God says* about justice and justification instead of importing the Social Justice ideology and cherry-picking verses which you interpret as if they confirm the lies of Woke Marxism. As Baucham says in his in-person and online sermons and lectures, "Black and white is not a real divide... The Social Justice Movement is like a train with a long string of boxcars, the lead boxcar of Marxist racism, then LGBTQ, and so on—all rooted and grounded in critical theory, cultural Marxism, and identity Marxism."

> I have heard a mantra lately that rings hollow in my ears: "There can be no reconciliation without justice." When I hear that, I want to scream, "YES! AND THE DEATH OF CHRIST IS THAT JUSTICE!" All other justice is proximate and insufficient.[7]

Universal justification is the point of the spear, that is, it is exactly the point of everything that Jesus has commanded us to believe, teach, confess for the sake of miseducated university students and other lost souls. It is also the sharp, diamond hard point of the spear for taking captive every thought to Christ the Lord of all.

> I beg you that when I come, I may not need to be as bold as I expect toward those who presume that we live according to the flesh.
>
> For though we live in the flesh, we do not wage war according to the flesh. The weapons of our warfare are not the weapons of the world. Instead, they have divine power to demolish strongholds. We tear down arguments and every presumption set up against the knowledge of God; and we take captive every thought to make it obedient to Christ. And we will be ready to punish every act of disobedience, as soon as your obedience is complete.
>
> You are looking at outward appearances. If anyone is confident that he belongs to Christ, he should remind himself that we belong to Christ just as much as he does. (2 Corinthians 10:2–7, Berean Study Bible)

The next logical question is about how God delivers universal justification to people. It is another means–by–which moment.

The problem at the root of Social/Racial Justice, as Baucham has told us, is *Marxist identity*; the solution that we confessional Lutherans bring to the table is *Baptismal identity*. The way to see this in context, in the apostle Paul's line of thought, is to read his Epistle to the Romans in its entirety, as it was inspired and written.

Observe that Saint Paul first sets out his absolute commitment to the Gospel as the means–by–which people are justified: "I am not ashamed of the Gospel. It is the power of God

---

[7] *Fault Lines*, 229.

leading everyone who believes in it to salvation, the Jew first, then the Greek" (Romans 1:16). Then follows his argument based on Scripture that all are corrupt and deserving of eternal damnation and that all are justified by God in Christ Jesus because we are all unrighteous/unjust (Romans 1–3). After the declaration of universal, by–Christ–alone justification, Paul teaches the external efficacious character of baptism: "Are you not aware that we who were baptized into Christ Jesus were baptized into His death? Through baptism into His death we were buried with Him, so that, just as Christ was raised from the dead by the glory of the Father, we too might live a new life. If we have been united with Him through likeness to His death, so shall we be through a like resurrection" (Romans 6:3–5, NAB).

Marxist identity means identifying others either as oppressor or oppressed; as L(esbian) or G(ay) or B(isexual) or T(ransgender) or Q(ueer) or whatever, against the others (by definition, there is no such thing as "the LGBTQ community"); as someone in conflict with others whose skin contains more or less melanin than mine; and on and on in endless, violent Marxist opposition and rebellion—even rebellion and disgust against our own bodies.

Baptismal identity means to be united through the external efficacious sacrament of Baptism with Christ in His death and with Him in His resurrection as well. This is not a metaphor; it is the metaphysical reality of what my Baptist acquaintances derisively refer to as "water baptism." In, with, and under the water of Baptism combined with the words of the Word is the place where God delivers His universal justice/righteousness in person, personally.

3.5 The...efficacious Word delivers universal justification ...establishes *Baptismal identity*...

To paraphrase Psalm 118, "The stone the builders of Social/Justice Theory rejected has become the cornerstone. By the LORD has this been done; it is wonderful in our eyes."

Weighed and found wanting. Without the "Lutheran 'Controls'" (*Anatomy of an Explosion*, 130) of Universal Justification and Baptismal identity, our Concordia universities have been imploding, crumbling before Social Justice and Racial

Justice—crumbling before the Marxist equivocations and repurposing of trustworthy old biblical, doctrinal, and cultural terms such as *justice*.

To maintain, as Concordia Texas has done very recently, in the spring semester of 2023, "Our Lutheran identity is central to all we do, including our Diversity, Equity, and Inclusion (DEI) work. We recognize that DEI is an important issue and believe that our efforts in this area align with Lutheran theology" is to say, "We are not Lutheran or biblical; our identity is not based on the Word and on our Baptismal identity alone, but on Marxist identity theory."

What you are hearing in those words from their university President and Board is the sound of another Concordia-class university submarine imploding. It is the sound of Lutheran higher education imploding, with great loss of life.

Lamentably, this is not an isolated implosion. According to investigative reporting by *The Federalist*, "Concordia–Wisconsin is considered one of the denomination's better universities. Another LCMS university [Concordia University Texas] recently attempted to leave the denomination to pursue identity politics more freely, a move the church rejected. The denomination has closed three of its nine universities since 2018, all of which endorsed identity politics (Appendix Q).

At Concordia Wisconsin, the Marxist identity implosion is still underway, nearly two years after the explosion over the Presidential search parameters.

> Concordia–Wisconsin maintains a Black Student Union and amid Schulz's suspension added a Hispanic Student Union. Concordia's accreditation agency requires that its "processes and activities demonstrate inclusive and equitable treatment of diverse populations." The university also maintains a "bias reporting system." Those are widely known to enable attacks against students or colleagues. Campus trainings on the system led by CUW Administrators under the previous President … allege "unconscious bias" as a cause for filing such a report (Appendix Q).

If our Concordias cannot hold the Line against Woke Marxism and Marxist identity at the point of Justification, it is time to acknowledge that our LCMS universities are no longer Lutheran institutions of higher education but have become Harvard franchises (with a blessed number of confessional Lutheran professors still on faculty)—lesser Harvards that did not invent, but nonetheless tolerate and model CRT, Marxist ideology, Social Justice, and more. Like Harvard, CUW is on track to become just another secular university with a Christian origin story.

There are confessional Lutheran professors at CUW. There are many devoutly Christian professors who would believe, teach, and confess as confessional professors do, who would love to have the opportunity to be formed by the life-changing content and the integrous teaching methodology of the *Formula*—except that Concordia broke fellowship with them by suppressing the biblical content and teaching methodology of the *Formula* and instead subjected all of us to Social Justice and racist anti-racism sessions for faculty development. Not to mention the Marxist bias-reporting apparatus hanging over their heads.

Staring these confessional Lutheran professors and all my other colleagues in the face is the university's mistreatment of one pastor–professor who followed the *Formula* (as confessional Lutherans do) in rejecting and condemning the false dogma of this damnable Woke Marxism.

What you may not realize, though, is that CUW's scandalous two-year (and counting) assault on academic freedom has also been an assault on the Lutheran and biblical article of Church and Ministry within the LCMS, to which one pastor–professor has had a front row seat. This assault on doctrine is the topic of the next, concluding chapter of *Anatomy of an Implosion*.

Chapter Four

Cringing toward Woke Marxism and away from the Lutheran/biblical Understanding of Church and Ministry

What is divinely instituted, according to Scripture and the Confessions is ... the glorious and permanent (2 Corinthians 3:11) ministry of life and justification. The Gospel and sacraments themselves—not organizational chains of command—are the content, nature, task, and power of the office... the evangelical ministry is not manipulative. It relies totally on **God's working through His holy means** *"when and where He pleases"* (Augsburg Confession, 5, 20)—*not when and where human surveys, strategies, and "goal-settings" may predict or prescribe* (Kurt Marquart, *The Church and Her Fellowship, Ministry, and Governance*, 122–123).

Concordia University Wisconsin (CUW) broke its confessional covenant by campaigning for a Woke President. The university culture—a culture in which the *Formula of* [and for] *Concord* has long been suppressed, while at the same time the hollow and deceptive postmodern philosophy of language has been embraced—this is what accounts for what Kurt Marquart would call CUW's *cringe* toward Social/Racial Justice and away from Universal Justification, the doctrinal center of gravity for confessional Lutherans.

There is another doctrinal drift of momentous consequence at my Concordia, that is, its mission or *Missio Dei* drift away from the Lutheran and biblical understanding of Church and Ministry. Church and Ministry is the area of biblical doctrine which answers the question, "How exactly does God deliver the Gospel of Christ and His accomplishment of Universal Justification to human beings?" It is in the work of the Gospel ministry, which we refer to as *"the office* of the ministry" because of its rootedness in the Latin word *officium*. *Officium* is a compound Latin word meaning "dutiful doing" or "divine doing."

4.1 Lutheran teaching of Church and Ministry...how does God deliver Universal Justification?

This is why Professor Marquart writes, "The Gospel and sacraments themselves—not organizational chains of command—are the content, nature, task, and power of the office... the evangelical ministry is not manipulative. It relies totally on **God's working through His holy means** "when and where He pleases *(Augsburg Confession,* 5, 20)."

Church and Ministry is another means–by–which matter, wherein we discover whether the university's Administration and Board of Regents are operating on the authority of texts and the External Efficacious Means of Grace view of language—or whether they have jettisoned it. Remember, Woke Marxism rejects authoritative texts and disdains the External Efficacious Means of Grace philosophy of language just as Jacques Derrida did: "I reserve the right to interpret these texts [the biblical text and other, lesser sacrosanct or authoritative texts too] as I see fit. And no one has the right to tell me that I am wrong!"

The Lutheran teaching of Church and Ministry follows from that practical question about universal justification: "But how does God deliver the reality of universal justification into the lives of human beings who are, as we confess in the first section of the *Formula,* fountainheads of corruption?" This is the question of the only means–by–which we exist as Concordia universities. That is, it is the question of the office or work of the Gospel ministry and spiritual leadership written in the requirements, for example, of who may serve as the university President.

As with its move away from Justification because of its acceptance of Social or Racial Justice, so too CUW has moved away from the Lutheran teaching of Church and Ministry in its assault on academic freedom. It is the same two-step movement that Derrida and postmodernism made popular. As I will explain in this chapter, my university's Board of Regents and its Administration have been saying in effect, "We reserve the right to interpret authoritative texts the way we want to, and no one has the right to tell us that we are wrong!"

Let me first explain (1) what academic freedom is and why it is vital for Lutheran teaching, for example, in relation to the article of Church and Ministry. After that, I will explain (2) how the so-called "reconciliation processes" of the university and its church body hierarchy contradict the ministry of reconciliation (2 Corinthians 5:11–21). I will also show (3) how the Board of Regents' process for electing the new university President contradicted the expectation of pastoral leadership at CUW (a) first in its putsch for a Woke president, and (b) then in its election of a lay administrator instead of a "compassionate theologian" as the university's new president.

4.2 ...a studied ignorance of sacrosanct texts regarding Christ's Church and its Gospel ministry...

My published essay, "Woke Dysphoria at Concordia," brought to light the adulterous affair with Woke/Social Justice/Marxist ideology on the part of the previous and Interim Administration, the Executive Committee of the Board of Regents, and various professors and staff at my Lutheran Christian university. This was most notable in the Regents' publicly posted search for a new university president who "believes in and is committed to inclusion and equity" as well as "diversity in all its myriad forms." In other words, for a president who supports Woke/Social Justice/Liberation Theology/Marxist ideology instead of staking everything on Christ and the text of the Bible.

When the university's leadership suspended me, banished me from campus, and sought my termination for criticizing them, national groups raised their voices over CUW's attack on academic freedom. The Wisconsin Institute for Law and Liberty, for one example. *The Federalist* for another. Concordia's attack on academic freedom by CUW's Administration has been publicly denounced in letters from the Academic Freedom Alliance (AFA) and from the Foundation for Individual Rights in Education (FIRE). See Appendices D–G.

Who cares? Stubborn as sin, closemouthed as a grave, our Administration and Board have not responded to censure. Nor, to this day have they responded to the nearly 7,000 pastors and laity online or to the scores of students on campus who have petitioned them to respect academic freedom and reinstate me.

There is, by the way, no question that CUW's Interim President and his Board were punishing me for that essay. "The Christian university is punishing him for obeying the Bible's commandment to publicly rebuke church leaders for public sins. Multiple regents and denomination officials *The Federalist* spoke to on the condition of anonymity said the case against Schulz is based on him criticizing the university in public" (Appendix Q).

The Faculty has been deathly silent about this widely reported transgression against academic freedom. Not one statement on academic freedom from the church authorities in The Lutheran Church—Missouri Synod (LCMS) responsible for safeguarding the rights of church workers and pastors such as me. Not a whisper about the national scandal of CUW's frontal assault on academic freedom, as far as I can tell, from administrations and faculties of other Concordias that make up the Concordia University System of the LCMS.

So why should anyone care? Let me sketch out for you a skeleton of what academic freedom should mean. I will identify this problem as a moral failure. All this, using just five sentences from Ronald Dworkin's book *Freedom's Law*. In his obituary Dworkin was acknowledged as "the most important and powerful philosopher of law in the English-speaking world."

Our five sentences are from Chapter 7, "Why Academic Freedom?" First, there is the urgent need for academic freedom in our modern cultural context. As Dworkin puts it in the first two of our five sentences:

> Academic freedom ... is often defended on the ground that scholars must be free if they are to discover objective truth. But the very possibility of objective truth is now itself under attack from an anti-truth–squad of relativists, subjectivists, neo-Pragmatists, post-modernists, and similar critics now powerful in the unconfident departments of American universities."[1]

Deeply confused administrators. Dworkin is not saying that we should give up the search for absolute truth; rather, he is saying that today we must reckon with an overwhelmingly

---

[1] Ronald Dworkin, *Freedom's Law: The Moral Reading of the American Constitution* (Cambridge, Massachusetts, Harvard University Press, 1996), 246.

dominant assumption of relativism in higher education. He also says in this context that relativism provides a pervasive but "deeply confused" challenge to academics and freedom.

The foundation for this profound and deeply confusing relativism is what I identified as the postmodern Expressionist Semiotics philosophy of language. You can see this hollow and deceptive philosophy of language at work in the Interim President's words on Woke Marxism's diversity/inclusion/equity in the town hall interview I quoted. Not incidentally, what neither the Interim President nor anyone else in power has said about *equity* in the Marxist mantra is that the Woke Marxist use of equity is in direct opposition to equity in Scripture. For example, God's people have for 3,000 years been praying,

> O Most High, You have rebuked the nations,
> You have destroyed the wicked;
> You have blotted out their name forever and ever.
> The enemies have vanished in everlasting ruins;
> Their cities You have rooted out;
> The very memory of them has perished.
> But the Lord sits enthroned forever,
> He has established His throne for judgment;
> And He judges the world with righteousness,
> *He judges the people with equity.*
> (Psalm 9:5–8; italics added).

In God's Word *equity* is a synonym for *righteousness*, which is a synonym for *justice,* as in the article of justification. As I explained in our second chapter on language and then in our third chapter on Justification, the Expressionist Semiotics of the Social/Racial Justice Movement is depleting the atmosphere of the university or submarine. Relativism provides a pervasive and "deeply confused" challenge to academic work. Therefore, those of us who are doing academic work deserve to be protected from the vindictive and "*deeply* confused" words and actions of administrators so that the university can be a university—and not an indoctrination center.

Free speech, a necessary ingredient. In the case of free speech at a Lutheran institution of higher learning, free speech is a necessary condition—a *necessary condition* is an ingredient that must be there for a lump of dough to become our daily bread—for dialog, debate, and disputation. In short, free speech for a Lutheran university is necessary if we are to have a prayer of eliminating the leaven of false, anti-Scriptural, anti-Christ, anti-Lutheran leaven of false dogma from the bakery.

Wokeism is a case in point. In "Woke Dysphoria at Concordia" I describe Wokeism as "a potent cocktail of Progressivism, Neo-Pragmatism, and Marxism," an ideology that replaces Christ and biblical authority with an "alien politics." For others it is educational foolishness, but in Lutheran circles it is educational heresy, a denial of Christ and His authority by professors, Administrators, Board members who are trading the priceless inheritance of the Lutheran Reformation for the Soylent Green of Marxist ideology.

Dworkin's observation that the relativist challenge which is assumed and taught by most professors at most Western universities in our day "is deeply confused," is illustrated by the deeply confused way Concordia's Interim President speaks about Wokeism and its ideological terms of diversity, inclusion, and equity.

As painful and embarrassing as it may be, read his response in Chapter 2 closely a second time, and notice what he clearly is determined *not* to talk about. You'll notice that Christ and His authoritative Word is clearly not part of his daily, working, administrator's vocabulary. His thinking and speaking are not framed by the text of the Bible, or any other canonical texts. Consequently, it is deeply confused. But Jesus tells us in no uncertain terms, "Whoever is not with me is against me, and whoever does not gather with me scatters" (Matthew 12:30).

Professors profess; administrators quash. Professors profess, but CUW administrators quash our pro-fessing. It's all they can think of doing. What is more, they cannot abide confessional professors who profess confessionally. Remember the confessional method of teaching prescribed in the *Formula* which bundles "reject and condemn" with "believe, teach, and confess."

In times of persecution and intense cultural pressure, as the Lutheran pastor–professor Dietrich Bonhoeffer taught during the Holocaust, Christians must speak up regarding the universal authority of Jesus in every area of life. Otherwise, they are manifestly against Him and are responsible for scattering the flock.

In dramatic contrast to the Interim President speaking confusedly about the terms of Woke Marxist ideology, and the new President and current Provost demanding my retirement and my slavish obedience to whatever teaching and writing suits them "at their sole discretion," I have been pro-fessing and providing numerous online interviews and elaborations, publishing and posting articles, teaching pastors in the United States about the biblical philosophy of language, as well as speaking, arguing, consulting overseas with Christian faculty members and undergraduate students who are hungry for help against Woke Marxism.

I must point out an obvious conclusion: considering the university's very public commitment to racial diversity, queer inclusion, and anti-Justification equity as essential characteristics of our next President, their response to my essay calling for the Board and Administration to repent of Wokeism, is just what you would expect from a Woke Marxist university.

Their response of equivocating, and then threatening any pastor–professor who says to them, "No, you're wrong!" is dialectically opposed to *The Formula of Concord*, which mandates that a Lutheran pastor and professor must "reject and condemn false dogma." The Interim President's response, quoted in Chapter 2, is precisely the kind of ambivalent non-response (sentence fragments that both say and don't say what Wokeism is, that gesture toward what the LCMS does or doesn't do, should or shouldn't teach, and so on) that a Board intent on installing a President at the university "with a demonstrated belief in and commitment to inclusion and equity" and to "diversity in all its myriad forms" would want to hear from its very own, self-appointed Interim President.

At the everyday level, academic freedom should insulate professors from administrators who speak and behave like this. You begin to see why confessional professors like me should be insulated from administrators and regents, don't you? In brief, professors pro-fess based on textual authority; however, administrators administer based on institutional, financial, hire–

and–fire power. The new President is continuing this attack on academic freedom and on the Lutheran teaching methodology laid out in the *Formula* (Appendix R).

Two levels of academic freedom. This leads into the third and fourth sentences from Dworkin. He points out that there are two levels to academic freedom, historically and conceptually speaking: "First, it insulates universities, colleges, and other institutions of higher learning from political institutions... Second, academic freedom insulates scholars from the administrators of their universities."[2]

Academic freedom is a way to ensure that administrators and entire universities act morally and that they do no harm to those of us doing the academic heavy lifting to protect our students and institution from political harm. For example, from the political harm being visited upon our curriculum, our co-curriculars, and the bodies and souls of our students, by the federal government with its imposition of DIE, transgenderism, Marxist identity, LGBTQetceteraism, Woke Marxist accreditation methods, and so on. The first level, the foundational level, is *the institutional level*. I will explain that shortly. But first, two major points regarding *the everyday level* as we transition to the level of the institution as a protection against alien politics.

Major Point #1. With rare exceptions, administrators are long–out–of–practice former professors, or "deanlets" (Benjamin Ginsberg), that is, persons ambitious to be in charge at universities who put in their time as professors purely as a means to an end, not as an end in itself.

> Until very recently, American universities were led mainly by their faculties, which viewed intellectual production and pedagogy as the core missions of higher education. Today, as Benjamin Ginsberg warns in this eye-opening, controversial book, "deanlets"— administrators and staffers often without serious academic backgrounds or experience—are setting the educational agenda.[3]

---

[2] *Freedom's Law: The Moral Reading of the American Constitution*, 256.
[3] From an anonymous Johns Hopkins review of Benjamin Ginsberg, *The Fall of the Faculty: The Rise of the All–Administrative University and Why It Matters* (New York: Oxford University Press, 2011).

Deanlet administrators. Deanlets are people who *used to be* professors, "professors" whose plan was to be professors only long enough to become administrators. This deanlet mindset is another reason why genuine professors should be insulated from administrators.

For example, at my previous Lutheran college, since I was senior faculty (*senior faculty* differentiates full professors from lesser ranks such as assistant or associate professors) I served on the Rank and Promotions Committee. In his application to us, an associate professor lied about publishing a book. When we called him out on it and then denied his promotion request, he went to the college administration and threatened a lawsuit if the college would not grant his promotion. Against the unanimous recommendation of the Rank and Promotions Committee, the college gave him a promotion to full professor. The next thing we knew, the college made him an administrator, and he has been an administrator ever since. The moral of the story is this: Professors should be insulated from administrators for the good of all concerned—especially for the sake of academic and confessional integrity at the university. Back to Dworkin on academic freedom.

The second, everyday level of academic freedom provides a kind of force field around professors so that administrators cannot overpower genuine, practicing professors and silence our teaching and preaching, our talking and writing, with censorship, suspensions, terminations, or other power moves of intimidation and retribution.

If a university president has the intellectual horsepower and academic wherewithal to take on a professor's argument, this is noble and good. Let him write a book, publish an article in a refereed journal, provide a lecture or debate the issue. Let there be sacred and lesser canonical texts, passionately and painstakingly unpacked for the good of all! But, to paraphrase Wittgenstein's *Tractatus*, Proposition 7, "Whatever can be said with academic authority should be said clearly; whatever cannot be said authoritatively by an administrator, of such matters administrators ought to remain silent."

Major Point # 2. Academic freedom is not a legal right; it's more than that: It's a moral imperative. It's actually the first principle of morality, "First, do no harm!" applied to Western universities from their founding by the church in the Medieval period.

A first principle, remember, is a feature of natural law along the lines of that T-shirt slogan about gravity: ACADEMIC FREEDOM IS NOT JUST A NICE IDEA; IT'S A MORAL LAW! You can assault academic freedom, but then you will be doing immoral things. Also, you will be making academia—at your university and beyond—inaccessible, unfathomable, and undoable.

You will be making the case for potential students and parents, and for taxpayers and pundits who already suspect that higher education is a sham, that universities are in fact irrelevant, a waste of time and money, and thus harmful to everyone. What my administration is doing to me—and, by extension what it is doing to my students, to my academic colleagues in every Concordia university and beyond—is being visited upon me contrary to such written procedures as they had available to them, without reason, and without appeal to any legitimate authority or Authority, but purely on the basis of administrative power.

Like former U.S. President Bill Clinton, they are doing it because they can. Remember, they are also violating the first principle of morality. At the foundational level, academic freedom should insulate universities from political influence.

The foundational level of academic freedom. Finally, think about the *foundational* level of academic freedom. This first, foundational level, insulation from political institutions, has everything to do with being a religious institution. Without this foundational protection from illegitimate and unconstitutional government policies such as those that characterize the forty-sixth President of the United States, a Lutheran university becomes a government school.

In 1987, President Ronald Reagan called for tearing down the Berlin Wall, "If you seek peace, if you seek prosperity for the Soviet Union and Eastern Europe, if you seek liberalization: Come here to this gate! Mr. Gorbachev, open this gate! Mr. Gorbachev, tear down this wall!" From the beginning of its attack on academic freedom in February 2021 and to this day Concordia University Wisconsin has been tearing down the wall of academic freedom and opening the gate to Woke Marxism for everyone to see. See Appendices E–G and R.

At this first, foundational level of academic freedom, this is what is happening. The exercise of our institutional academic freedom, a moral imperative, intersects in the United States with the exercise of our Constitutional rights of free exercise of religion and free speech, legal rights articulated in an authoritative American text, the First Amendment. I expect that the legal minds at WILL, AFA, and FIRE may have something to say about this regarding my case. But at this point, I must conclude.

Look at it this way: Time and again we hear about some educational entrepreneur or other who promotes his new school in the community as a public government school to receive government funding and perks, while at the same time promoting his new school in churches as a religious school to receive funding and students from churches. This is what CUW appears to be doing. They are playing both sides against the middle.

Think of CUW's accreditation and financial entanglement with the political institution of the federal government and its Woke attacks on our children's education and sexuality. Here is the second reason that academic integrity and genuine academic freedom matter. The university's administration and Board of Regents' sustained and immoral attack on academic freedom is an effective way simultaneously to disintegrate Concordia internally (by not insulating professors from administrative power plays) and externally, as a religious institution of higher learning (by making CUW a *de facto* place of political indoctrination).

Academic freedom and university culture. Hence, our fifth and final sentence. Dworkin concludes: "Academic freedom and a right to free speech—are closely related in a different way: they form important parts of a system of ideas and institutions that creates a culture of individual intellectual responsibility, and that protects it from disintegrating into a culture of intellectual conformity."[4]

A religious university exists to take a stand against a political culture of intellectual (or anti-intellectual) conformity. This is why people pay for their sons and daughters to attend religious universities, rather than more affordable state universities. Maybe it's already too late. Likely their addiction to government funding and perks and to the alien politics of Caesar that come along with that funding, is not something they even want to recover from. Thus, there is good reason to fear that all of us are beginning to feel the full effects of the Administration's assault on Academic Freedom in real time. It's as Jesus told us, "Whoever is not with Me ... scatters" (Matthew 12:30).

This is why academic freedom matters. This is why national organizations have been taking my university to task for its assault on academic freedom.

1. I write on behalf of the Academic Freedom Alliance to express our firm view that Professor Schulz should suffer no formal consequences as the result of this published article.

   For Concordia University Wisconsin to punish Professor Schulz for engaging in a public discussion of matters of church principles and university governance would have a profound chilling effect on open discourse by professors on this campus and through the Concordia University system.

   There is no question that such public speech is fully protected by traditional principles of academic freedom and professorial free speech widely recognized by American universities and elaborated by the American Association of University Professors.

   It is true that Concordia University has not chosen to fully embrace those principles in its relationship to its own faculty, but *punishing Professor Schulz for this speech would represent a narrowing of protected free speech for faculty that would go far beyond what is necessary to render academic freedom compatible with*

---

[4] *Freedom's Law*, 247–248.

"the reality of the scriptural Lutheran faith" and would damage the university's ability to operate as an institution of higher education (Appendix E, paragraph breaks and italics added).

2. As CUW recognizes, due process is "fundamental" to protecting faculty members' academic freedom. ***Schulz's academic freedom, including the freedom to criticize university governance, is exactly what is at stake here***, as CUW purports to "value the individuality of each faculty member and respect the right of faculty to hold diverse opinions" and to maintain that "pursuit of knowledge through intellectual inquiry and research is highly valued as a mark of institutional excellence"—including recognition of the right of faculty members even to "present and discuss concepts that conflict with Synodical teachings."

   To the extent CUW alleges that Schulz's *Christian News* article falls within any of the university's express "limitations" on academic freedom or violates any other university policy, CUW must provide Schulz with a meaningful opportunity to respond to those allegations before imposing any sanctions (Appendix F, paragraph break added).

3. Interim suspension may be warranted in rare circumstances where, for instance, an individual's continued presence on campus presents a safety threat. That rationale obviously has no relevance in this case. Suspension is a punishment, and not a light one, entitling Schulz to due process before it is imposed.

   Schulz is unable to teach his classes or even communicate with his students or other faculty members. Each day of the suspension that goes by is a further disruption to Schulz's career as an educator and to his relationships with his students and colleagues... CUW has failed to adhere to its due process obligations.

   Schulz's suspension also raises serious concerns about his academic freedom, which traditionally encompasses the freedom to criticize institutional governance. While CUW is a private religious institution, it makes promises of academic freedom in Schulz's contract and the faculty handbook, including "the right of faculty to hold diverse opinions" and to "present and discuss concepts that conflict with Synodical teachings." Granted, *the university also purports to limit academic freedom in certain ways. For instance, a faculty member "acknowledges that in certain situations he/she will voluntarily limit his/her expression of opinions and convictions ... so that the mission of the institution and of the church is supported rather than hindered." But CUW cannot treat this as a license to suppress all criticism of the administration*, or else its affirmative promises of academic freedom are rendered meaningless (Appendix G, paragraph breaks and italics added).

Objection and reply. Someone may object by saying, "But in the case of a religious university such as Concordia, the President and Board must have control over academic freedom. It's the only way they can deal with false doctrine by a professor!"

I respond this way. First, the reason you imagine academic freedom must be different in the case of a religious university such as CUW is irrelevant. This is not a case of a professor teaching false doctrine or doing anything wrong. The inconvenient truth is that these authorities on academic freedom point out that my essay was not merely a protected exercise of academic freedom, but *a fulfilment of my contractual and pastoral obligation to criticize the university for it false doctrine.*

Of course, Professor Schulz has a responsibility not to "advocate a position contrary to that of the Synod," but here he is participating in a public debate *on what the implications of the Synod's positions might be for the university.*

If faculty at the university must refrain from speaking in public about the future of the university and the fidelity of the university's activities to the positions of the Synod, then the university's commitment to the faculty to value their individuality and to engage in intellectual inquiry will be an empty promise (Appendix E, paragraph break and italics added).

The second part of my response is that I am not just a professor; in fact, I am also a pastor, a pastor–professor called into the ministry by the Lord working through His church (Acts 20:28, for example). This reality of Church and Ministry—this is what my Lutheran university, with the collusion of two District Presidents on its Board of Regents, has been working to rewrite by their so-called "reconciliation processes."

The cringe toward Woke Marxism at my Concordia university has included a studied ignorance of sacrosanct texts regarding Christ's Church and its Gospel ministry. For example, there appears to be a studied ignorance of Saint Paul's apostolic texts on the office of the ministry in Ephesians 4 and in his pastoral epistles such as 1 Timothy 2 and 5 as well as of the *Formula*. This cringe–and–drift maneuvering is a lamentable mission drift from what the *Formula* calls "our public common writings" (*Formula*, Of the Comprehensive Summary, Foundation, Rule, and Standard, paragraph 1).

Keep in mind that I am being threatened, disciplined, and have been forced to undergo several "processes"—all because of my essay critical of the university's introduction of Woke Marxism by way of the search for a Woke Marxist President. "The Christian university is punishing him for obeying the Bible's commandment to publicly rebuke church leaders for public sins. Multiple regents and denomination officials *The Federalist* spoke to on the condition of anonymity said the case against Schulz is based on him criticizing the university in public" (Appendix Q).

In other words, *I am being punished for believing, teaching, and confessing in line with Christ's authoritative Word and also for rejecting and condemning the false dogma of Woke Marxism in line with our authoritative Formula of Concord.* You have heard it said, "The process is the punishment," but I am telling you that the processes at my university are proof that the Administration and Regents are messing around with biblical doctrine and confessional statements regarding Church and Ministry.

To "deal with me" for rejecting the university's flirtation and adultery with the false doctrine of Woke Marxism, there have been two reconciliation processes. I will address the first one briefly and will provide a slightly longer explanation of the second, allegedly Top Secret reconciliation process. First, though, I will point out that these new-fangled reconciliation processes are a mockery of the ministry of reconciliation taught by the apostles in the first century church.

Biblical, apostolic reconciliation. The ministry of reconciliation, as taught by the apostles such as Saint Paul, who is the author of 2 Corinthians, is not an ecclesiastical mechanism for church officials to suppress criticism of false doctrine or to manipulate the Gospel ministry (as Marquart cautions). On the contrary, the ministry of reconciliation cannot be conducted *nisi per Verbum* or without pastoral fear and trembling. The apostle begins by writing, "Standing in awe of the Lord we [apostles] try to persuade men..." Here, then, is the heart of the apostolic concept of ministry and reconciliation.

> Standing in awe of the Lord we [apostles] try to persuade men, but what we are is known to God. I hope that it is also known to you in your consciences... The love of Christ impels us who reached the conviction that *since one died for all, all died*.
>
> He died for all so that those who live might live no longer for themselves, but for Him who for their sakes died and was raised up.
>
> *Because of this we no longer look on anyone in terms of mere human judgment.* If at one time we so regarded Christ, we no longer know Him by this standard. This means that if anyone is in Christ, he is a new creation. The old order has passed away; now all is new! All this has been done by God, who has reconciled us to Himself through Christ and has given us *the ministry of reconciliation*. I mean that God, in Christ, was reconciling the world to Himself, not counting men's transgressions against them, and that He has entrusted *the message of reconciliation to us*.
>
> This makes us ambassadors for Christ, God appealing through us [apostles]. We implore you in Christ's name: **be reconciled to God!** For our sakes God made Him who did not know sin, to be sin, so that in Him we might become the very holiness of God (2 Corinthians 5:11–21, author's translation).

You can see from the text that reconciliation is not about compromise, but about the application of universal justification in the fear of the Lord. The biblical and confessional ministry of reconciliation is the application of God's justice, universal justification—which has nothing to do with Social or Racial Justice—exclusively through the means of grace (the Gospel in Word and Sacrament). This biblical ministry of reconciliation cannot take place except through the Word, that is *nisi per Verbum*, the first principle tied in with Justification, as we saw in the previous chapter.

Reconciliation CUW style, first process. In opposition to the biblical teaching of justification, which is what Gospel ministers deliver exclusively by using the means of grace, the Bible, the Word of Christ and the sacraments; the so-called "reconciliation processes" in connection with Concordia University Wisconsin are programs conducted by regents or by regents who are District officials to enforce their point of view. At CUW, reconciliation processes are a mockery of the biblical ministry of reconciliation.

The first reconciliation process was a hasty meeting put together by the District President responsible for CUW (District Presidents are responsible for supervising doctrine and practice in the Concordia universities that fall within their Districts). The assumption was that he would establish a compromise between one pastor–professor's published position that the university should repent of the false dogma or ideology of Woke Marxism and the university's (largely unexplained) position that this professor should be ~~executed~~ punished for questioning them.

For the record. Two points of clarification and then we can move on to the second reconciliation process. First, the District President was confused about the issue, as I tried to explain to him before and during his meeting. This was not and is not a matter of compromise. According to 1 Timothy 5:20 and the Lutheran Confessions (see Luther's Explanation of the Eighth Commandment in his Large Catechism, especially the last two pages, Appendix M), men in positions of authority in the church who sin doctrinally and publicly must be rebuked publicly for the good of everyone concerned.

As Marquart said of the critical theory at Saint Louis

Seminary in the 1970s, "It is important to see that the uncompromising supremacy of 'scientific' human reasoning ... is not an excess or an abuse which can somehow be tempered. On the contrary, it is of the essence of the method; indeed it is its basic point (*Anatomy of an Explosion*, 120)." As explained in our two opening chapters, Marquart was referring to the Social and Political Sciences which created and supported the heretical method of biblical interpretation taught by the Seminex crowd. The critical—remember that *critical* refers to "secular atheist Marxist thinking"—ideology of Woke Marxism cannot be compromised with. What does Marx have to do with Martin Luther, or with the apostles and evangelists? So, this reconciliation process was seeking Chamberlain-like appeasement in doctrine. Such appeasement is contrary to 1 Timothy 5.

> First Timothy 5:19–20 instructs us in dealing with the sin or doctrinal error of such an office-bearer: "Do not receive an accusation against an elder except from two or three witnesses. Those who are sinning [i.e., are subsequently proved to be sinning, and persist in that sin] rebuke in the presence of all, that the rest also may fear." We need to note several things in this passage:
> 1. It clearly deals with "the elders who rule" (*proestotes presbuteroi*, verse 17), not simply older men.
> 2. The word translated "accusation" is *kategoria*, which means "a formal accusation before a tribunal." ***If a ruling elder is to be accused of wrongdoing or false teaching, it is to be done in a formal way, because it is a serious matter for the church...***
> 3. The word translated "rebuke" in verse 20 is *elegcho*, which... has both an investigative and an adjudicative sense. This is in keeping with the formality of the handling of the accusation indicated in point two above. *Elegcho* means both "to call to account and demand an explanation" and also "to convict and refute if found culpable, and thus put to shame."[5]

---

[5] From the Teaching the Word Bible Knowledgebase online.

As a pastor–professor I am acutely aware from Paul's inspired wording in 1 Timothy 5, that the Greek word for *rebuke* is in the present imperative voice, meaning "*keep on* rebuking." I am not off the hook just because I once rebuked the Administration and Board for their public Woke Marxism. I am obliged to keep on rebuking until they repent or until I am put out of action. This explains this little book. It is part of my continuing responsibility as a pastor–professor to rebuke false doctrine, an exercise of pastoral love and faithfulness. See Appendix N.

Secondly, as reported in *The Federalist*, the takeaway from that first reconciliation meeting was that I was expected to do all the compromising even though I had obviously done nothing wrong. Further, I had done nothing contrary to Scripture or Lutheran doctrine, but was the target of non-serious accusations from the university's Maoist bias reporting system.

Reconciliation CUW style, second process. The second "reconciliation process" is where you can see that the university is taking the opportunity to interpret authoritative texts in any way they see fit, while insisting that no professor is going to tell them that they are wrong. Just like Derrida.

For details on this second reconciliation process, please read Appendix L for a quick overview and Appendix K for the details. Overall, it will help to see that the charges against me are charges contradicting what first I and then our LCMS President told the Board and Administration about their Woke Marxism in terms of the presidential search. Here is a narrative of one chart (pages 7–10) from Appendix K.

> **What *is* the case: A Comparison of the Complaint with what Schulz and Harrison have Written** (in chronological order).
>
> 1. **Schulz's Letters and Essay**: "Woke–ism at CUW, exacerbated by the BoR committees' handling of the presidential search, is burdening the consciences of my students and my religious colleagues on faculty."
>
>   **Harrison's Letter to the Board**: "As the result of these very serious concerns [over Wokeism, mission drift, faculty frustrations] many pious

laypeople and congregations have lost trust in the university's faithfulness to genuine Lutheranism and her mission..."

[Interim President]'s Complaint: "Over the last several months, Concordia University has contended with a difficult and, sadly, public personnel issue regarding Dr. Gregory Schulz."

2. **Schulz's Letters and Essay**: "As I have been arguing, Woke–ism is afflicting the consciences of students, faculty, and supporters of Concordia. Therefore, programmatic, systemic Woke–ism merits reconsideration. It also merits personal and institutional repentance."

"...the Woke–ness or Progressivism that these committees are promulgating is educational heresy."

Harrison's Letter to the Board: "[the Board must] demonstrate repentance for Bylaw violations and adoption of secular worldviews and agendas."

"This philosophy [secular Wokeism] is laden with ideas antagonistic to the sacred Scriptures."

[Interim President]'s Complaint: [no repentance] "...the effect of Dr Schulz's campaign to discredit the presidential search process caused immense strife at Concordia."

3. **Schulz's Letters and Essay**: "...kindly stop manipulating our university's presidential search process... Apparently, you have preemptively 'removed from further consideration' every divinely called pastor on the university faculty who had accepted nominations from our church body and the CUWAA (Concordia University Wisconsin and Ann Arbor) constituency for the office and work of the next president."

Harrison's Letter to the Board: "The Search Committee took it upon itself to engage in a screening and notification process that was in direct contravention to the Bylaws ... This act gravely dishonored the 11 candidates officially approved ... and precipitated the Schultz (sic) matter."

"CUW has enjoyed the strongest of theological and philosophy faculties."

"To this very hour, board leadership has refused to interview ANY candidate approved…"

[Interim President]'s Complaint: "As an evident consequence of the Board's decision to pursue other candidates, Dr. Schulz has engaged in a campaign challenging the presidential search process."

4. **Schulz's Letters and Essay**: "Not incidentally, the BoR committees' posted announcements are unsurprisingly Woke in their cavalier altering of texts. True to the Woke mindset of the Presidential Search postings, someone or some committee presumed to alter the pronouns in their posted version of our LCMS bylaws."

"While there is no systemic racism at Concordia because we are committed to Christ incarnate and His universal justification of all human beings without exception, there certainly is systemic Woke–ism."

"Whether the BoR committees alter their posted, online statements, or not—without a detailed and equally widely published retraction of their Woke desires and commitments, the Woke dysphoria at Concordia will continue. After all, this is not a PR issue but a matter of repentance and showing the fruit of faith."

Harrison's Letter to the Board: "July 2021 changes to the faculty handbook include referring to the president with the pronouns "he or she" and "his or her" in violation of the teaching of Scripture that spiritual oversight in the church and its universities is given to qualified men."

"Secular ideas involving critical theory, inclusion, and equity have fond harbor on campus… Acknowledge uncritical haste that occurred in adopting language of secular diversity, equity, and inclusion initiatives."

"I fear you will continue to reject my advice, to the continued detriment of Concordia and our life together."

[Interim President]'s Complaint: "Dr Schulz called for readers to 'deluge' the search committee and LCMS leadership with feedback."

5. **Schulz's Letters and Essay**: "...it is the administration and senior administrators of CUW who bear day–to–day responsibility for the regularizing and normalizing of Woke–ness at the university. As we on the faculty bear day–to–day responsibility for what we teach or fail to teach our students."

   Harrison's Letter to the Board: "With no overall clarity and scriptural critique, secular ideas involving critical theory, inclusion, and equity have found harbor on campus."

   [Interim President]'s Complaint: "The emails [urging pre-sem students to 'speak up' regarding Wokeness in the published texts of the board's search committee] violated Dr. Schulz's ethical obligations as an academic to avoid the exploitation and harassment of students."

6. **Schulz's Letters and Essay**: "For our present situation with our Board of Regents Chairman and search Committee, we may consider as well 1 Timothy 5:20. Actually, the chairman and his committee must take to heart the authority of our Lord and His Word, including all of the apostle Paul's first letter to Timothy... I think this means that, for our part, we must pray mightily and deluge the search committee and our LCMS leadership with our input on the side of confessional, classical, Lutheran education and leadership."

   Harrison's Letter to the Board: "The Search Committee took it upon itself to engage in a screening and notification process that was in direct contravention to the Bylaws."

   "[In violation of the Bylaws] the Search Committee was ... [in] breach of fiduciary responsibility to comingle its authority ... with a body that included a majority of non-elected board members.... delegating responsibility for preparing the Presidential Search Process... The Committee took it upon itself to engage in a screening and notification process that was in direct contravention to the Bylaws."

[Interim President]'s Complaint: "... a member of the Search Committee—had expressed to the Board of Regents that Dr. Schulz had unfairly impugned the capability of her and the rest of the committee."

7. **Schulz's Letters and Essay**: "In response to my first open letter to the Chairman of the Board, copied to my ecclesiastical supervisor, our district president responded with 'Thank you!'"

In response to his December email to "cease and desist" from further open letters I ceased and desisted my open letters.

To the best of my knowledge, there was no directive from him at all regarding a total gag order—nor would he do something so inappropriate—but I have been denied access to those emails since February by the interim president.

Harrison's Letter to the Board: "The Regents reject the advice of the South Wisconsin District President [my representative], who is a voting member of the BOR and is likewise concerned about mission drift. I fear you will continue to reject my advice, to the continued detriment of Concordia and our life together."

[Interim President]'s Complaint: "Dr. Schulz's violation of Dr. Wille's order, as well as with section 1.3 of the MOP constitutes 'insubordination' ..."

It will also help to see, side–by–side the authoritative text used against me, the MOPM (Model Operating Procedures Manual). The MOPM is the Operating Procedures Manual for the entire Concordia University System. By reinterpreting this manual—studiously ignoring parts of the texts that were not what they wanted to follow; reinterpreting other texts in order to reinterpret the process as they wanted to, the Interim President and two District Presidents from the Board of Regents worked to undercut the biblical and confessional article of Church and Ministry.

I. MOPM text regarding CUW's violation of the MOPM process:

<u>3.3 Possible limitation on activities of respondent</u>

If **the board decides** that the matter is of such a nature that the interests of the college or university will best be served, it may limit the activities of the respondent. It may do so by relieving the respondent of teaching and/or administrative duties pending final resolution of the conflict. ... (November 2019 MOPM, page 13, 17. Emphasis added.)

For over six months, right after the publication of the essay critical of the Board and Administration's adoption of the false doctrine of Woke Marxism, the university was in violation of the Manual because the Interim President and another senior administrator imposed the suspension and its draconian demands without proper procedure or Board approval. Notwithstanding, the Board of Regents supported those illegitimate actions with their silence.

The Concordia University System Model Operating Procedures Manual is intended to serve as a uniform process for resolution of all complaints against faculty members and all campus disputes involving faculty and administration. All Concordia University System institutions must "have policies in place that are 'consistent with' this Model Operating Procedure Manual."

The manual specifies extensive procedures for resolving complaints against faculty members, including but not limited to allegations of insubordination and conduct unbecoming a Christian. Those procedures include an initial face–to–face meeting to attempt to resolve the matter informally; if informal reconciliation efforts fail, a "written statement" of "efforts that have been made to achieve informal reconciliation," must be forwarded to the board of regents and the respondent; an opportunity for the respondent to submit a written reply within 21 days; formation of a five-person review committee; and a formal hearing. ***Only the board of regents—not the president—may relieve a respondent of teaching*** and/or administrative duties pending final resolution of the conflict ***only if*** *the board "**decides** the matter is of such a nature that the interests of the college or university will best be served" by limiting the activities of the respondent (Appendix F. Emphasis added).*

- II. MOPM process violated by the review committee:
  - 3.2 <u>Selection of fifth committee member by Secretary of the Synod</u>
  - (2) The Secretary of the Synod shall be requested to select the fifth member by blind draw from the Synod's roster of hearing facilitators, who shall serve as chairman. ...
  - • The standard for disqualification of any review committee member shall be actual partiality or the appearance thereof. ... (November 2019 MOPM, page 13, 17.)

At least two members of the Review Committee—that is, the five-member committee to recommend to the Board of Regents whether to fire the accused—had partiality aplenty but did not recuse themselves, nor would the committee recuse them. In court cases *recuse* refers to someone who has a conflict of interest or any other bias against the person on trial and therefore should be excused.

Compromised faculty member. The faculty committee member chosen by my accuser was a close relative of the retired University President, the University President who was responsible for Woke Marxist training sessions for the faculty. This same President oversaw the Board of Regents who, after his retirement, pushed for a Woke University President.

Compromised Board member. A second biased review committee member was the recently retired LCMS District President for Michigan. Somehow he became a Board member just barely in time to qualify as the Board of Regents member to represent the Interim President, my accuser. In a February 25, 2022, email to his entire District, this District President wrote:

Brothers and Sisters of the Michigan District:

Over recent days, a very public situation has developed at our Concordia University Wisconsin and Ann

Arbor (CUWAA). As you may have read elsewhere, a professor in Wisconsin has been suspended, not for publishing a concern/complaint, but for his refusal to meet with Dr. Cario. We trust Dr. William Cario, acting President of CUWAA, to work through this appropriately.

At the same time, old complaints have also surfaced about the direction of the teaching at Concordia University Ann Arbor. These complaints and accusations were previously investigated and found to be unsubstantiated.

In other words, this retired District President brought to the table his long-held misrepresentation of the very public situation at CUW and, by extension, at Ann Arbor. Months before the second reconciliation process, the LCMS President wrote in his letter of May 9, 2022 (Appendix H), that it was *the Board* that "precipitated the Schultz (sic) matter." However, the retired District President not only did not retract his email to the Michigan District; he also refused to recuse himself as required by the November 2019 MOPM (page 13, 17.) Furthermore, the retired District President was covering up Woke Marxist problems at Ann Arbor. Ann Arbor is the daughter campus of CUW and has taken on the culture of CUW via its assimilation by CUW.

Philosophy of language. There are two outcomes of these violations of the Manual the university claimed to be following. The first outcome is further evidence of the university's (conscious or unconscious) rejection of the External Efficacious Means of Grace philosophy of language. The second outcome is further evidence of CUW's commitment to the notion that they are free to interpret authoritative and normative texts however they wish and that no one has a right to tell them that they are wrong. The process is the punishment. Their punishing process is also evidence of the university's (conscious or unconscious) acceptance of the postmodern Expressionist Semiotics philosophy of language. Just like Derrida.

It gets worse. There were two District Presidents involved in the second reconciliation process, both members of the Board of Regents, then and now. Here is a final citation from the MOPM Manual which shows that there is an innovative, entrepreneurial notion of Church and Ministry at work at my Lutheran university.

    III. The Manual's "Governing Authority" and "Governing Principles," points A and B under III. General principles and regulations were studiously ignored during the reconciliation process.

    A. Governing Authority

        The complainant and respondent, the president and board of regents of the involved college or university, and the review committee involved in the complaint resolution process ***shall be governed in all their actions by the Holy Scriptures, the Lutheran Confessions***, the Constitution and Bylaws of The Lutheran Church—Missouri Synod, and this *Model Operating Procedures Manual* (November 2019 MOPM, page 12. Emphasis added).

    B. Governing Principles

        Matthew 18 and the Eighth Commandment undergird this process for bringing and resolving complaints against members of faculty and administrations of the Synod's seminaries. While Matthew 18 provides the structure for carrying out church discipline in a local congregation, it also provides **guidance and a pattern that is to be observed in this procedure** *whenever applicable*. **And in accord with the Eighth Commandment**, everything possible should be done to protect the reputations of complainants and respondents. (November 2019 MOPM, page 12. Emphasis added.)

For a fine-grained explanation of how this works, please read Appendix K. But as our LCMS President put it in his Letter, "[Because of Bylaw violations and faculty handbook alterations, and mission drift in regard to the anti-Scriptural philosophy of Wokeism, as evidenced in deep faculty frustration] many pious laypeople and congregations of the Synod have lost trust in the university's faithfulness to Lutheran doctrine..." (Appendix K).

The above quote is from the ultimate ecclesiastical supervisor of our church university. He identifies the problem as a theological one concerning the entire church. In biblical shorthand, the issue is that one pastor–professor's published criticism of his university is <u>not</u> "a Matthew 18 matter;" on the contrary, it is "a 1 Timothy 5" matter.

It is not a matter for private reconciliation but a matter for urgent public attention by the pastors and people of the church at large. That's why President Harrison refers to *the involvement of the people and congregations [with their called pastors]* ***of the entire synod***. As the apostle Paul writes in a section of this pastoral letter concerning *elders* or the leaders in Christ's church: "Do not receive an accusation against an elder except on the basis of two or three witnesses. Those who continue to sin publicly, rebuke publicly so that the rest too will be filled with fear" (1 Timothy 5:19–20).

In the first place, then, "A. Governing Authority" states that the be–all–and–end all authority for the Manual (and therefore of our faculty handbook, and therefore the language of faculty contracts, and so on) is the Holy Scriptures and the Lutheran Confessions. My accuser's failure to acknowledge this biblical and confessional authority in practice does not license him to redefine terms such as *harassment, insubordination, or conduct unbecoming a Christian* as if these terms can be used in any way that suits his purposes as Interim President and Executive Officer of the Board.

I have not sworn fealty to the University President, nor to the Board of Regents; rather, my oath of ordination is faithfulness to Holy Scripture *per se* and to the Lutheran Confessions because they are scriptural in every doctrinal matter they address.

In the second place, as "B. Governing Principles," makes clear, the guidance and pattern of Matthew 18 is not an absolute, one–passage–fits–all portion of the Word for every conflict that might conceivably arise at our university. The text says that the administration of Matthew 18 provides "guidance and a pattern that is to be observed in this procedure [that is, concerning faculty and administration complaints and appeal of termination in our LCMS colleges and universities] *whenever applicable"* (my italics).

Since our synod President has confirmed that this incursion and promotion of Wokeness at our university is a 1 Timothy 5 matter for publicly rebuking those who have been publicly sinning by promoting "a philosophy that is anti-Scriptural," I submitted to the review committee that this is precisely the reason for the Manual's qualification "whenever applicable."

At this point let me explain what the South Wisconsin District President said in the review committee meeting as part of his testimony as the only witness against me in this so-called "reconciliation process."

I asked him if he regarded Luther's Explanation of the Eighth Commandment as authoritative. He repeatedly refused to answer the question, but again and again insisted that he had authority as District President according to Bylaws to subject me to these reconciliation processes. He said, "I have handed you over to the university to be disciplined and when they are finished, I will deal with you."

These are the concluding paragraphs of Luther's exposition of the Eighth Commandment in his *Large Catechism*:

> But if that [speaking with an offending sinner along with two or three more] do not avail, then bring it publicly before the community, whether before the civil or ecclesiastical tribunal... This is the right and regular course for checking and reforming a wicked person... All this [the earlier steps in Matthew 18] has been said regarding secret sins... For where the sin is public, the reproof must also be public, that everyone may learn to guard against it.

In the last sentence of this quotation, you will recognize that Luther is referencing 1 Timothy 5:20. For the sake of Truth, and compelled by 1 Timothy 5, I must point out that this church official (who is also a university regent) is participating in punishing a professor for following the Scriptures and the Confessions. Keep in mind the suppressed Rule and Norm at Concordia University Wisconsin, *The Formula of Concord*. A Lutheran pastor or teacher must believe, teach, and confess in faithfulness to biblical doctrine, the entirety of it; and he must "reject and condemn false dogma."

At the same time, this member of the Board of Regents seems intent on reinterpreting the Lutheran and biblical understanding of Church and Ministry. Notice how he separates the divine call of a professor who is also a pastor into two parts. He says that a pastor–professor is an entity that can be carved up, part professor and thus subject to the university's processes, but also part pastor and thus subject to his processes. He has also said that the university is not part of the church.

Instead of citing all of the Scriptures and the many Confessions and Lutheran theology in opposition to this Regent's rending asunder what God hath joined, I will contrast his claims with one passage from Holy Scripture and one passage from Kurt Marquart, of blessed memory.

According to the apostle Paul, our ascended Lord graciously and lavishly gives these particular gifts to His church: "It is He who gave apostles, prophets, evangelists, pastors and teachers in roles of ministry for the faithful to build up the body of Christ, till we become one in faith and in the knowledge of God's Son, and form that perfect man who is Christ come to full stature (Ephesians 4:11–13, NAB)." As long as you keep your eye on Paul's grammar—the use of commas in this translation is spot-on—there are four offices of the ministry here; not five. The term "pastors and teachers" refers to one office of the ministry. The pastors are men who teach the Word of God and the teachers mentioned are in fact the pastors as well. It's what we call *the explanatory "and."* This is why the term" Pastor–Professor" is in the subtitle of this book.

Mequon, we have a doctrinal problem, a problem with Church and Ministry. On the one hand, these reconciliation processes have revealed a punitive culture at the university in which a confessing pastor–professor is punished for being confessional. On the other hand, as Professor Marquart put it, there appear to be "strutting modern religious entrepreneurs" in charge who do not carry out their office in the same spirit as "the humble pastor of the famous prayer which adorns many Lutheran sacristies."[6] Instead, they regard the Gospel ministry in practice as something subject to "organizational chains of command."

---

[6] Kurt E. Marquart, Robert Preus, Editor, *The Church and Her Fellowship, Ministry, and Governance* (Fort Wayne, Indiana: The International Foundation for Lutheran Confessional Research, 1990), 123.

Objection and reply. At this point, someone may object, "So what? Those 'so called' reconciliation processes as you call them, are in the past. The university has a new President who had no part in that business. You were exonerated; time to move on."

I reply this way: First, haven't you learned anything from Seminex? Past doctrinal aberrations left unrepented will carry the false doctrine forward. Second, the new President *was* being consulted during the second reconciliation promise. The two-day hearing took place on campus and committee members were coming and going to keep him posted and, presumably, ask his advice. Third, there is a continuity, as I have been pointing out, from the Interim President to the new President. For example, as we saw in my explanation of academic freedom, they are in lockstep with one another in their assault on academic freedom. It is essentially the same Board of Regents who elected the new President and authorized the Interim President to pursue his charges against me. See Appendices E–F alongside Q–R.

4.3 ...continuing relevance of Marquart's diagnosis of Seminex and Luther's stance at Diet of Worms...

In addition, the postmodern Derrida attitude to authoritative texts that shaped the Board and Administration's reconciliation processes shaped their process for the new President. To conclude this chapter on Church and Ministry, let us turn to the entrepreneurial attitude toward Church and Ministry in the Board of Regents' selection process. *Entrepreneurial* and *innovative* are not congratulatory words in doctrine or ethics. For example, when C.S. Lewis talks about the Innovator in *Abolition of Man*, he is talking about Friederich Nietzsche whose innovation is to deny the biblical reality of good and evil to demolish the very possibility of doing ethics.

"Past is prologue," as they say. Also, the past is not very far in the past in the case of my university. In its three-year (or so) process of selecting a new University President, the CUW Board of Regents crossed the Rubicon. Twice. The phrase "crossing the Rubicon" is a reference to Julius Caesar crossing the river while in command of an army; no Roman leader was ever to cross under arms—because crossing under arms signaled Caesar's determination to disrupt the Roman Empire or to die trying. The Rubicon in this case is the ecclesiastical lines that should not be crossed by individuals in authority.

First crossing of the Rubicon. The process for electing a new President at my Concordia has been markedly anti-clerical. Early in the fall semester of 2021 the Chairman of the Board of Regents emailed all five pastor–professors who had been nominated and vetted by the LCMS, that they would not be considered for the office of University President because they "did not fit" the university's needs according to the Board of Regents.

According to the LCMS President's May 2022 letter, "First, in violation of 3.10.6.4 (g), the BOR [Board of Regents] impermissibly delegated its responsibility fully to participate in the selection of a president... [following which, the Board's illegally created] Search Committee then took upon itself to engage in a screening and notification process that was in direct contravention to the Bylaws."

It turned out that what did fit the Regents' needs were a number of unqualified men and women, including an unqualified woman who had inexplicably been put into a leadership position at the university by the retired President and his Provost, the Interim President. This is the person named by the LCMS President, who apparently prepared the Woke Presidential Prospectus (Appendix H). Without an academic degree and without college-level leadership experience, she was the person to whom they handed over the reins for faculty development and who initiated Woke racist training to the faculty and staff.

There is another reason that she was unqualified to lead the faculty development or to become President. The office of President, according to the wider context of the Bylaws cited by the LCMS President in that letter (Appendix H), is to be filled by a pastor because the President is the "spiritual authority" for the entire university. In this matter, the Bylaws simply follow the Scriptures and the apostolic authority with which Saint Paul writes, "Let a woman learn in silence with all submission. And I do not permit a woman to teach or to have authority over a man, but to be in silence. For Adam was formed first, then Eve. And Adam was not deceived, but the woman being deceived, fell into transgression" (1 Timothy 2:11–15).

This push for a Woke President was the crossing of the Rubicon, the Do Not Cross line of Church and Ministry. It was an effort, not simply to put forward women candidates that "fit" the Board's and its committee's desires, but to fulfil plans and desires that are contrary to the biblical doctrine of Church and Ministry. Moreover, it was not a one-time, isolated contradiction of 1 Timothy 2. To anticipate an objection to our Lutheran use of this passage from the pastoral Epistles, let me remind you that "teach *or* exercise authority" is much the same as "pastor *and* teacher." Both references to the ministry of the Gospel, Ephesians 4 and 1 Timothy 2, use *explaining* particles, "and" and "or." According to His Scriptures God did not give His church some people who are pastors and other people who are teachers. There is the one office or divine work of the pastor–teacher. Similarly, in the church there is not one activity of teaching and another one of exercising authority; they are the same function.

For example, the current Provost, the most senior academic officer at the university, regularly teaches and exercises authority over men. She is a woman. Is the university prepared to say, as one District President on the Board has suggested, that the university is not part of the church, but a separate entity, so that, for example, a pastor–professor can be dissected into (a) a professor who fits under the authority of the university, heedless of the authoritative texts of Scripture such as the Pastoral Epistles, and (b) a pastor who fits under the authority of a District President? Is it because the university is (allegedly) not part of the church so that 1 Timothy 2 does not apply to the university's Provost? Incidentally, I do not know if our current Provost is Lutheran or not, but this dissection model of the ministry of the Gospel must be bothering her conscience if she is. In that case, there is something disrespectful and unloving being done here, given that the University President (and perhaps the Board) has put her between a rock and a hard place.

Second crossing of the Rubicon. After the disruption, the explosion, following the criticism of the Board's disregard for the LCMS Bylaws—which included, remember, their use of the postmodern Derridean philosophy of language, "We can interpret the authoritative texts any way we choose, and no one has a right to tell us that we are wrong!"—the Board of Regents crossed the line again in their "Presidential Search, 2.0."

What they crossed this time was the LCMS President's admonition to repent and to follow specific steps. There was no repentance, still none a year and one-half later, well into the administration of the new president. Here is how the Presidential Search 2.0 process went:

> LCMS President: "[The Board Chairman and his adviser] should resign from the Board of Regents. Their demonstrated unwillingness to abide by the Bylaws and their inability to oversee the presidential search process in a manner that inspires the trust of the Synod at large, have hampered the institution too long."
>
> CUW Leadership Response: Gave the disgraced chairman's adviser an award for contributions to Christian education during the CUW graduation ceremony a week or so later.
>
> LCMS President: "The BOR should restart the presidential search with the three candidates plus additional members of the CUWAA theological faculty from the list of 11 men approved by the Prior Approval Panel."
>
> CUW Leadership Response: Search not restarted. Theological faculty not re-included.
>
> LCMS President: "CUWAA clearly needs a competent, compassionate theologian at the helm."
>
> CUW Leadership Response: Selected the only non-theologian, a front-runner at the time of the tenures of the disgraced Board leadership; announced that he had been "divinely called."

Objection and reply. Someone might object, "But the new President is a pastor and a confessional man!" My reply is, "First, the new President is not a "compassionate theologian." He is not a theologian at all. To say that he is a pastor is to disregard our article of Church and Ministry. Stop thinking of pastor and teacher as two separate but equal offices in the church. According to our Synod's or church body's doctrinal position, only pastors can be divinely called because of the apostle's wording in Ephesians 4:11, namely, that there is one office of pastor–and–teacher, and not two different offices. The clear and honest truth is that "divine calls," biblically speaking, refer to pastors (who are described as pastors–and–teachers). This text is not something that is open to endless interpretations. Keep your eyes on the men who are called *to administer the means of grace*, not on administrative titles that may pop up here or there in church history.

Anyone can say, 'I am confessional!' However, this new President has not published one article or book arguing against Woke Marxism as a false dogma. He was an Administrator at Concordia University Texas, a Concordia that is imploding from the pressures of Woke Marxism and Social/Racial Justice before our eyes. He did not stay to help them "reject and condemn" Woke Marxism or bear witness to the evils the Concordia University Texas President has been doing, as far as I can see. What he has confessed is that a confessional pastor–professor who does write and witness must be punished.

Second, while the new President may or may not complete an M.Div. degree at a seminary, what our church body intends by seeking pastors for the office of the President at our Concordias is someone who has had a decade or two of parish experience and has become a compassionate theologian because of his experience over time as a divinely called Lutheran pastor in a Lutheran congregation.

This, as we know from Luther's 1518 Heidelberg Disputation, is the way a man becomes a compassionate theologian. The other term for this is "a theologian of the cross," a pastor who calls a thing what it is, to whom everything is not transparent and thus indistinguishable as being either something of this world or something of God alone. The core of being a compassionate theologian, as Marquart says, has to do with pastoring and suffering over time with his parishioners. Marquart cites two propositions of Luther about making a theologian of the cross.

> 19. Not he deserves to be called a theologian who sees the invisible things of God as being understood through those things which have been made,
> 20. But he who understands the visible and lowlier things of God, seen through sufferings and cross.

Anyone can get away with claiming that he teaches according to the Socratic method if no one listening has spent years reading and teaching and taking to heart Plato's *Apology*. Anyone can get away with claiming he is a confessional person or a pastor if no one listening has spent years reading and pastoring and taking to heart Luther's Heidelberg Disputation.

The new president is an administrator who arrived at Concordia Wisconsin by the deanlet track; not the pastoral track. I do not want to be absolutist about this. I think it is possible that Concordia Chicago and especially Concordia Nebraska may, Lord willing, be able to turn the corner and steer their universities away from Woke Marxism and the doctrinal drift taking place at my Concordia. I do not know their universities, but I do greatly respect the president at Concordia University Chicago as a man with a Lutheran spine of iron for cutting out the cancer of Social Justice in his programs and personnel. I do know the president at Concordia Nebraska, having worked with him nearly every week for two years developing the Great Texts Pathway curriculum at CUW. I rejoice at his surefooted determination to reverse the trend of making Lutheran students an endangered minority. No one in these other universities needs my comments or anatomy of them, of course. Nor am I giving any such analysis.

Notwithstanding promising exceptions to the rule, there are good and urgent reasons for having experienced parish pastors, compassionate theologians, theologians of the cross at the helm—especially in this hour of great need. Here is what is already apparent as the result of the Board's election procedure: the new president has taken a stand against academic freedom. This is a stand against the Lutheran freedom to dispute, debate, and argue. This is also a stand against anyone who rejects and condemns the false and dehumanizing dogma of Woke Marxism.

Returning to my Concordia and our recent and ongoing experience of what Marquart identifies as *cringing* or bowing to worldly dogmas such as Woke Marxism, I know that what we need is a president as described in our LCMS President's letter. The rejection of every one of us vetted pastor–professors on faculty (my colleagues in the Theology Department), in both of their crossings of the Rubicon was cynical, not salutary. As the LCMS President wrote, "This act gravely dishonored the 11 [presidential] candidates officially approved, especially belittled candidates from the CUWAA theology and philosophy departments." See Appendix H. As our church body President wrote, this was another process that "gravely dishonored the

11 candidates officially approved, [and] especially belittled candidates from the CUWAA theology department."

Of course, the presidential election process was in keeping with the reconciliation processes against one pastor–professor, leading to my analysis of the new President and the deeply rooted powers–that–be still on site with him at Concordia University Wisconsin: "I fear you will continue to reject my advice, to the continued detriment of Concordia and our life together." Not that the powers–that–be are concerned with my advice. Indeed, they appear not to comprehend my advice.

This is because they are operating on the basis of another philosophy of language, namely, the philosophy of language coined by Derrida which is the basis for Woke Marxism: "We reserve the right to interpret the the Scriptures, the confessions, and lesser authoritative texts such as church bylaws and Concordia manuals however we want to; and no one has the right to tell us that we are wrong."

Our students and their parents, our faithful pastors and professors throughout our churches and beyond are noticing, talking, and weighing in on the implosion at CUW. Although I cannot develop this here, their attention to the cringe toward Woke Marxism at my Concordia has also affirmed for this generation *the continuing relevance of Kurt Marquart's diagnosis of the Seminex explosion and Martin Luther's Lutheran stance at the Diet of Worms* (Appendix U). You must realize by now that this book is not for the university Administrators or Regents, but for my students and my fellow confessional Lutherans.

With this in mind, I have a few after–words to share.

> You have dealt well with Your servant, O Lord, according to Your word.
> Teach me good judgment and knowledge, For I believe Your commandments.
> Before I was afflicted I went astray, But now I keep Your word.
> You are good, and do good; Teach me Your statutes.
> The proud have forged a lie against me, But I will keep Your precepts with my whole heart.
> Their heart is as fat as grease, But I delight in

Your law.
It is good for me that I have been afflicted, That I may learn Your statutes.
The law of Your mouth is better to me Than thousands of coins of gold and silver.
(Psalm 119:65–72, NKJV)

Afterword

We live in an afterword world. This has been the case, as we know only from the Word of God, ever since the insurgency in Eden (Genesis 3). Our world is not just an after–Word world but an *anti*–Word world. As Aristotle discovered and as Luther stipulated, we human beings are in our essence, *logos* or language beings. Our language essence remained after the Fall, but since we are so thoroughly corrupt (see *The Formula of Concord*, 1), left on our own we can only use language against God, against the purpose of our own human nature, and against our fellow human beings.

God was not content to leave it at that, so in the fullness of time He sent His only-begotten Son into our afterword world to save all human beings from ourselves and from His eternal judgment.

> The Word became flesh
> and made His dwelling among us,
> and we have seen his glory:
> The glory of an only Son coming from the Father
> filled with enduring love (John 1:14, NAB).

As you know, the Greek word for Word is *logos*. Fundamentally, *logos* means "language" and comes from the Greek verb *lego* which means "to gather or bring together." As we also know, Jesus the **Logos** is God's final and eternal Word to all mankind.

> In times past, God spoke in fragmentary and varied ways to our fathers through the prophets; in this, the final age, he has spoken to us through his Son, whom he has made heir of all things and through whom he first created the universe. The Son is the reflection of the Father's glory, the exact representation of the Father's being, and he sustains all things by his powerful word... (Hebrews 1:1–3, NAB).

Because God's final Word to us, His Son the *Logos* incarnate, is unknowable *nisi per Verbum* and because Woke Marxism (in terms learned and applied from Kurt Marquart) disdains "privileged authority and sacrosanct texts" we live in an aggressively after–*God's Word* world in societies or university communities where Woke Marxism has taken root.

God's Word cannot pass away (Matthew 24:35). Further, language is a divine gift of the divine *Logos* Himself, so it cannot pass away either. However, societies and university communities under the influence of Woke Marxism use and promote a philosophy of language— "a hollow and deceptive philosophy" as defined by the apostle Paul in Colossians 2:8–9—which depends exclusively on the traditions of men such as Jacques Derrida: "First, I have no stable position on the texts you mentioned, the prophets and the Bible…For me, this is an open field… I want to keep the right to read these texts in a way that has to be constantly reinvented."[7]

Woke Marxism wants, with all its heart, soul, mind, and strength to destroy language and thereby to achieve the abolition of mankind. It is a dogma and an ideology that creates vicious mockeries of language. As the *Urak–hai* are to Tolkien's Orcs, so is Woke Marxism to Communism. Proponents of Woke Marxism crave a world without Christ the *Logos*, a world in which everyone can interpret language in any way that suits him. A world without anyone, including especially God, telling them that they are wrong. This is what Derrida means by "decentering" the *Logos*.

The project is doomed to failure for the same reason that communism always fails: it does not take account of corrupt human nature. In other words, Woke Marxism and Communism disdain authoritative texts such as the Bible and the first article of the *Formula*. Keep in mind that, although the Woke Marxist Communist project will fail, it is a project that always produces incalculable loss of life. It is producing great loss of life in Christ the Life among the current generation of university students.

In the words of T.S. Eliot,

> The endless cycle of idea and action,
> Endless invention, endless experiment,
> Brings knowledge of motion, but not of stillness,
> Knowledge of speech, but not of silence;

---

[7] Deconstruction in a Nutshell, 21.

> Knowledge of words, and ignorance of the Word.
> All our knowledge brings us nearer to our ignorance,
> All our ignorance brings us nearer to death,
> But nearness to death no nearer to GOD.
> Where is the Life we have lost in living?
> Where is the wisdom we have lost in knowledge?
> Where is the knowledge we have lost in information?
> [*Where is the information we have lost in lies?*]
> The cycles of Heaven in twenty[-*one*] centuries
> Brings us farther from God and nearer to the Dust
> (Choruses from The Rock, I, 6–18, my additions in italics).

Notwithstanding its inevitable failure—or perhaps because of its impending failure (Matthew 24:35) Woke Marxism is out to create an anti-language of violence and division. This is because Woke Marxism is anti–*Logos*, opposed to Christ the *Logos* in the flesh. It is the magisterial use of reason on a globalized scale by angry and frustrated people of ill will.

Woke Marxists are frustrated and furious to find that language is not easily destroyed. This, of course, is because language is a divine gift grounded in Christ the *Logos* (John 1, Psalm 1, Psalm 119). So, the worst that Woke Marxism can do is to foist on us its hollow and deceptive philosophy of language, hoping that we will not notice while they take another run at Communism and the Holocaust of the Gulags and Communist (re-)education.

I am writing this Afterword in the immediate aftermath of the Hamas attack on Israel, which has been called "the greatest holocaust since the Holocaust." In the three weeks since the October 7, 2023, Holocaust what were we seeing in our American universities? We were seeing the fruit of Woke Marxism. Predictions of the "bursting of the college bubble" have now been drowned out by the moral implosion of our American university system. The college bubble worry was an economic worry that parents and students would bail out of colleges when it dawned on them that they were assuming staggering financial debt for the empty promise that higher education would lead to higher paying jobs. This moral implosion, though, reveals that the real threat is higher education's commitment to Woke Marxism *über alles*.

In the home state of Concordia University Wisconsin (CUW), at the University of Wisconsin Madison (UW Madison), anti-Israel students have been chanting, "Glory to the murderers!" They are praising the Hamas terrorists who murdered and decapitated Israeli children, raped Israeli women, and then celebrated their atrocities online. From California State universities to the Ivy league universities of Princeton and Harvard, thousands of students demonstrated their love and devotion for terrorists who tortured, abducted, killed, and defiled the bodies of their fellow human beings because of the anti-human ideology of Woke Marxism and Critical Race Theory (CRT), having learned from their professors the Marxist mythos that people are divisible into oppressors and the oppressed. You can hear their philosophy of language in the racist and dehumanizing slogans, which they learned in their university classrooms.

The philosophy of Harvard and the philosophy of UW Madison is the deceptive philosophy of the myth-peddling German Idealists such as Hegel and Marx, and of Derrida and the postmodern methodological disbelievers: Again, "I reserve the right to interpret the biblical texts and all other texts as I see fit because language is nothing but unending interpretation and nothing more." Woke Marxist educationists and administrators, especially in our universities, have been martialing and mutilating language to make unjust war *against* God (whether in the Founding Principle of the Declaration of Independence or in His commandment against abortion or in His announcement that all authority in Heaven and on earth belongs to Him alone, Matthew 28:18), *against* our fellow human beings, and *against* the essence of our human being.

Is Concordia University Wisconsin becoming a Harvard franchise? By their philosophy of language ye shall know them.

Woke Marxism rejects the biblical External Efficacious Means of Grace philosophy of language because that philosophy is based on Christ alone (Colossians 2:8–9). In mockery of the *Logos* incarnate, it disfigures the divine gift of language. Based on its hollow and deceptive philosophy of language, Woke Marxist educators and administrators are doing their demonic worst to mutilate the means of grace and to obliterate from all education the Bible, which teaches us by experience that language is God's external and efficacious means of communicating with humanity.

What has Concordia been teaching and tolerating? What has it been suppressing? What is it refusing to reject and condemn?

In opposition to all that is excellent and praiseworthy (Philippians 4:8–9), Woke Marxism is conducting a social science experiment. Its program of "endless invention, endless experiment" is a linguistic experiment on human beings. Wherever possible God's enemies, human and demonic, are maiming the bodies and souls of our sons and daughters and grandchildren by means of dysphoric, antihuman uses of language. Woke Marxism is the modern-day Hydra serpent with heads such as Marxist identity, CRT, LGBTQ2S+, DIE (Diversity, Inclusion, Equity), Social Justice, Racial Justice, and countless other horrors. Therefore, Woke Marxism *delenda est*. *Delenda est* is Latin for "must be utterly destroyed."

What has Concordia been teaching and tolerating? What has it been suppressing? What is it refusing to reject and condemn?

To say, "Our Lutheran identity is central to all we do, including our Diversity, Equity, and Inclusion (DEI) work. We recognize that DEI is an important issue and believe that our efforts in this area align with Lutheran theology," or to suggest that something biblical can be salvaged from Woke Marxism and that a Lutheran university can regain "its Lutheran identity and mission [in this way:] identify, define, and embrace diversity that is intentionally biblical" (Appendix H)—this is self-falsifying nonsense of biblical proportions.

What has Concordia been teaching and tolerating? What has it been suppressing? What is it refusing to reject and condemn?

As the Word says, "And what concord hath Christ with Belial? or what part hath he that believeth with an infidel? (2 Corinthians 6:15, KJV). Woke Marxism is evil. Let us not conduct gain of function experiments on our children and our children's children in the lab of our Lutheran churches and schools. As one of my LCMS (The Lutheran Church—Missouri Synod) friends puts it, "Woke Marxism is disease that corrupts the institutional host by denying the basic dignity of all human beings." Therefore, Woke Marxism must be destroyed.

What concord has Concordia been having with the infidels of Woke Marxism? Lamentably, quite a bit.

Someone is likely to object, "Well, at least the university has God's Word in its truth and purity. Whatever else may be a bit off kilter, the means of grace are still there." I reply with a true story about one stricken soul that the university cut off from pastoral care and our Lord's means of grace because of its crusade against one pastor–professor who criticized the university's sordid affair with Woke Marxism.

There has not been one ounce of concern expressed for the dysphoria afflicting our sons and daughters because of Woke Marxism. In all their fast and furious processes to silence one pastor–professor who criticized the infidelities of his Concordia university—despite their blizzard of postings and protestations, "We are confessional, we are confessional! Look at how much time and space on our website that we are devoting to Lutheran identity!"—no one has bothered to address my pastoral concern over the dysphoria, the profound and soul-deep restlessness and depression that their shenanigans have been causing to people's souls. Not a single Administrator or Regent, not one church official has in the two years since the explosion posed a solitary question or expressed one ounce of compassion for our students and faculty and staff who are suffering dysphoria at Concordia because of Woke Marxism. The LCMS President and his visitation team, to my knowledge, did not look into this pastoral concern at all. Nor has the LCMS President addressed the unrest, disquiet, and dysphoria afflicting souls throughout the LCMS because of Woke Marxism at our universities and in our publications.

I have been working very hard—or, to put it the right way: our Lord has been working on me very diligently through His means of grace—to pray in sync with our Lord Jesus, "Father, forgive them, for they do not know what they are doing" (Luke 23:34). But here is what I cannot forgive, mostly because it is not something that the powers that be have done *to me*; rather, it is something they have done *to my students*. I feel the same righteous anger that my brother pastors in parish ministry felt during the China Virus lockouts, when they were denied access to their parishioners who were suffering and dying.

When I was threatened and banished from campus in February 2022 my students were cut off from me. This caused harm to my students. For example, I was pastor–professor to a student who was in the process of transitioning. *Transitioning* does not mean just wearing the clothes of the other gender. It means going through surgeries and chemical infusions of hormones. This precious soul had taken two classes with me—a remarkable thing because most often persons who are transitioning would have no time or patience for a confessional pastor or a professor of ethics.

Here is what the Interim President has done, what his Regents have at least tacitly supported, and what the new President has normalized: Cutting off means of grace ministry at their will to justified but disquieted and dysphoric souls in order to make their irredeemable Woke Marxist point: "And no one gets to tell us that we're wrong!"

This is a student experiencing profound *dysphoria*. I gathered that the doctors assisting her to "transition" diagnosed her as experiencing gender dysphoria, something to be "treated" with amputations and experimental hormones. But according to my professional spiritual diagnosis (that is, a complete body and soul understanding informed by Scripture) I knew that she was afflicted with a profound restlessness that could only be addressed with the Word of her Lord. As Augustine knew—and as I explained at length in my essay "Woke Dysphoria," "You have made us for yourself, Lord, and we are not at rest until we find our rest in You" (Appendix B). Her dysphoria had been caused or at least it had been greatly accelerated by Woke Marxism. This is not an isolated example of suffering students.

Being a Lutheran pastor means being a *Seelsorger*, a healer of souls, as we have taught nearly one fourth of our LCMS pastors and others to date in DOXOLOGY: The Lutheran Center for Spiritual Care and Counsel. What the University Administration and Board have done in their frenzy to punish me for calling them to repent of causing Woke Dysphoria has been to deprive students of a physician of souls well qualified to bring healing by means of the Gospel of Christ, by the means of grace. What they have been doing is *magnifying Woke Dysphoria* among our university students by sidelining a Lutheran pastor–professor. Their stance toward me is, of course, a warning to anyone else, especially to any pastor–professor who has understood the times and discerned the evil of Woke Marxism (Ephesians 5:16–18), not to cross them.

You may be thinking, "Well, that is very sad, but we have people at Concordia University Wisconsin who can look after students without you." I reply this way. It is true, thanks be to God, that our children and grandchildren at CUW have Lutheran pastors to look after them. In the case of Lutheran students, these pastors are trustworthy temporary substitutes while they are away from their home pastors.

For example, our Theology Department is (for the most part) filled with world-class Lutheran pastor–professors. Several of these pastor–professors are the pastors whom the Board of Regents did not feel were a "good fit" for the pastoral office of University President. (Remember, they did not allow any of these pastor–professors even to participate in their process of electing a new President who was supposed to be a "compassionate theologian").

Here, though, is the problem at CUW. Students afflicted with dysphoria and spiritual disquiet can go to these *Seelsorgers* and receive biblical, Lutheran, and Christ-centered counsel. But before and after their time with those pastor–professors they will obviously be spending time in class and out of class with other professors and administrators as well.

- Some of their other professors may be unrepentant members of that dreadful Board of Regents Committee who pushed for a university President who would be a Woke Marxist, or a Woke-leaning woman, in defiance of 1 Timothy 2:8–15.
- Some of their professors may support the Marxist bias reporting system at the university.
- Some of their other professors may be professors who pushed for Black Lives Matter activities in place of chapel devotions or as required class activities.
- Some of their other professors may be the professors who encourage female students to imitate the "great women" of recent history who support the murder by abortion of

unborn children.
- Some of the administrators they interact with may be academic administrators who have praised and supported faculty members for participating in BIPOC organizations. BIPOC is short for Black, Indigenous, and People of Color (excluding white persons), an anti-police movement that puts its faith in CRT.
- Some of the administrators and professors may have endorsed the anti-Christian doctrine of Ibram X. Kendi taught in the university's Black Student Union.
- And so on.

In short, while a relatively small number of pastor–professors can and will minister to students suffering from spiritual dysphoria with the Gospel, many others will (consciously or unconsciously) worsen their spiritual unrest and dysphoria. These other professors and administrators may also be secondary sources of our students' spiritual unrest and sexual dysphoria based on the professors' acceptance, tolerance, and inability to reject and condemn Woke Marxism.

What are we to do, then? And who are the "we" who ought to do it? Consider that the status quo is not sustainable—not in light of God's Word, our Lutheran Confessions, and our duty to care for our students with the biblical Gospel ministry of reconciliation. Here is a blueprint, a checklist for your urgent consideration.

This list is based on the principle of subsidiarity, recommended for years by the professor and department chairman of CUW's Philosophy Department, which the university has been seeking to destroy by malignant neglect ever since my essay was published in February 2021. My chairman, by the way, is an authority on human rights and human dignity with a church-wide and worldwide reputation for confessional integrity. Now, the term *subsidiarity* comes to us from the Latin term *subsidium* which refers to soldiers who are held in reserve until they are desperately needed. Instead of rehearsing the Roman Catholic literature on subsidiarity, which they understand as an organizational method of allowing decisions to be made at the lowest level of a university, for example, I will describe and define subsidiarity as an organizational culture modeled after Roman military strategy.

What I am saying is that CUW is way out of its depth and is

in imminent danger of implosion. If it sticks with its current command and control structure, complete with the mettle fatigue I have identified in its Board of Regents, its Administration, and its church body's hierarchy, it will implode. I have also explained that, because of its suppression of Scripture and the Lutheran Confessions, especially the *Formula* of Concord–ia, the university atmosphere has been substantially depleted, so there is no time for "committee meetings," "studies," or what have you.

What I am doing is linking subsidiarity with the armor of God in Ephesians 6. (Incidentally, Ephesians 6:1–4 demolishes the educational myth that schools and not parents should determine the gender and curricula for children, while verses 5–9 demolishes the anti-biblical Marxist invention of a new caste system in which oppressed and oppressor set us all violently against one another—in studied ignorance of universal justification.) Think of the formation and tactic of *acies triplex*, the three-line way of fighting which the original wearers of the armor that Paul identifies with the sword of the Spirit, the shield of faith, and the entire panoply—think of the way of fighting carried out by the Roman centurions.

By the time of Paul's missionary journeys and his writing verbally inspired words comprising the Word of God, Roman soldiers had been fighting successfully for about three centuries according to the *acies triplex*. Three rows of soldiers fought this way: the soldiers in the first two rows did all the fighting (wearing the armor described by the apostle). With clockwork precision, soldiers in the first row were replaced by soldiers in the second row as they became tired. In turn, after repositioning to the second row, those same soldiers rested but would eventually replace those in the first row as *they* became tired, and so on.

However, when the soldiers in those first two rows were wounded, tired—or, *horribile dictu* ("horrible to say"), if they were defeated and on the brink of surrender—then the third row would stride up, fully armored, to stand their ground and beat down the enemy. They could do this because the third row in the three-row formation was made up of veterans, men who knew what means to use to kill and defeat Rome's enemies, men who would never surrender.

Subsidiarity, seen in this way, is the only strategy remaining after the weakness, the failure, the appeasement of those in the first two rows. We parents and grandparents, we pastors and professors who are confessional Lutheran veterans, you gifted donors with a heart for what Lutheran higher education ought to be doing—we are the third row. Here, on the brink of defeat, weak-kneed administrators and weak-minded Search Committee professors and deanlets must give way to us, or all will be lost. And, as the Scriptures say, "Having put on the full armor of God, we must stand firm against the tactics of the devil" articulated in the language of Woke Marxism.

These steps are interdependent. No committee compromising; only confessional, subsidiary professing.

I. Every member of the awful, illegitimate Presidential Search Committee must retire or otherwise leave the CUW faculty and administration. Seek forgiveness and receive it in the name of the Lord, but you must step aside.

II. The morbidly obese administration must be reduced by at least two-thirds. The administration must decrease so that the faculty may increase and take up its role in the curricular governance of CUW. This is the principle of subsidiarity. Further, the pastors and Senior Administrators who supported or did not stand firm against Woke Marxism must be in the first wave of the reduction in the administration. Administrators who have been out of the classroom for two years or more must be released in the first or second wave of administrative reduction. This again is warranted by the subsidiarity principle. Only faculty are competent and trustworthy in curricular matters and faculty development and decision making.

III. The university President must be tasked not just with fund-raising, but with disentangling the university from government funding. His plan must be presented to the university faculty and to all stakeholders within six months, with bi-monthly written updates posted prominently on the university website. In addition, he must lend the full authority of his office without reservation to the replacement of accreditation by the Higher Learning Commission not later than the accomplishment of its five-year plan called EVOLVE 2025, where it states that "an equity framework should permeate...all levels of institutions (e.g., students, staff, faculty and governing boards)" and then further states that "HLC will ensure that concepts of equity, diversity, access and inclusion are demonstrated in its mission and other foundational statements."

IV. The university must issue divine calls for Provosts. A divine call presupposes that the Provosts will be experienced pastors who are also credible faculty. The anti-clericalism of the Regents and Administrators must be rejected because the university is a Concordia university. There must be at least two Provosts in order to guarantee that each Provost can continue as a pastor–professor in the classroom. Further, the pastor–professors in the office of the Provost must have regular direct access to the Regents. For too long and to the harm of the university, the traditional understanding that the university President should represent the faculty to the Board of Regents has been disregarded. On principle of subsidiarity the Provosts will guarantee that the faculty, of which they are active professors and not mere administrators, have representation to the Board of Regents.

V. The faculty must be restructured away from the siloed Schools of Whatever model to a model such as that of Concordia University Irvine, with its Christ College (the home of the Theology and Philosophy Departments) at the hub of the university. Lutheran identity is never established by merely claiming Lutheran identity; it is an ongoing means of grace process. In practical terms of subsidiarity, this means that the Theology and Philosophy Departments must be well staffed with confessional professors who not only profess the dependence of theology and ethics, for example, on Christ and His Word, but who are in the thick of things, providing mentoring, being examples of Lutheran pro-fessing, and maintaining a shoulder–to–shoulder presence with colleagues young and old for the mutual conversation and consolation of the Gospel among the entire faculty in all phases of its development.

Bring every hollow and deceptive Marxist thought captive to Christ (2 Corinthians 10:5). This is what a genuine Lutheran university would find a way to do. If it is to recover its Lutheran culture, this is what Concordia University Wisconsin must do. Now.

For a last word in this Afterword, let me leave you with a word of pastoral counsel. This is how Professor Marquart, of blessed memory, spoke to the church a generation ago.

> The key to the Missouri debacle lies in the Biblical and Confessional Principles, which this little study has sought to spell out and apply. Explanations which fail to come to grips in any precise way with these principles may well be interesting, informative, and even witty, but can hardly be considered very relevant.
>
> On the other hand, all discussions leading to a further clarification of these principles should be warmly welcomed…
>
> In this time of chaos and dissolution we modern Lutherans need nothing more than a painstaking inspection of our roots. Glib 'trendiness' cannot help us (*Anatomy of an Explosion*, Epilogue, 147).

Author's Church and Academic Biography

Greg Schulz is a product of God's work through the means of grace in Lutheran churches and schools. Baptized as an infant into Christ's death and resurrection in Holy Baptism at Zion Lutheran (LCMS), Milwaukee, he was profoundly formed by 21 years of Lutheran education, from Kindergarten through Seminary (WELS). LCMS is The Lutheran Church—Missouri Synod; WELS is the Wisconsin Evangelical Lutheran Synod.

He has been in the ministry of the Gospel for over 40 years, serving in parish ministry for 14 years (in churches with Lutheran day schools and, very briefly, in a Lutheran high school); ever since, as a professor in Lutheran higher education.

With earned doctorates both in Ministry and in Philosophy, he has authored journal articles in philosophy and theology, book chapters, and books such as *The Problem of Suffering*, published in a second edition and translated for use in its Gospel ministry by the Lutheran Church of Latvia. Professor Schulz has taught and lectured at the university and seminary levels in the United States. He has also lectured and taught overseas at Cambridge University, the WELS Seminary in Hong Kong, in mainland China, and at universities in South Africa as well as the Lutheran Seminary in Tshwane (Pretoria).

After publishing an essay critical of his Lutheran university's efforts to elect a Woke Marxist president in February 2022, Dr. Schulz was suspended without due process and threatened with termination if he would not "recant" his essay. He stood his ground. For the next year he was threatened and subjected to various "reconciliation processes" by the university's administration and regents. As this book is being printed late in 2023, he remains banished from campus and from teaching at Concordia University Wisconsin (CUW). The new university president and his provost have demanded his retirement and that he sign an agreement authorizing them to fire him "at their sole discretion." Here too he has stood his ground.

Suspended and threatened with termination by two university presidents, this pastor–professor responded by writing, interviewing, and forming the popular online teaching platform Lutheran Philosopher with the support of fellow pastors, former students, and like-minded Lutherans.

He continues to teach pastors and others, for example, in DOXOLOGY: The Lutheran Center for Spiritual Care and Counsel, and in continuing education courses throughout his church body under the auspices of his alma mater, Concordia Theological Seminary, Fort Wayne, Indiana. He also presented papers, keynote addresses, and consulted with the Christian faculty of Akademia, Pretoria, and the leadership and African students at Ratio Christi, South Africa, during his month-long residency in South Africa in July 2023.

Anatomy of an Implosion—a book written in the "far louder and more academic" footsteps of Kurt Marquart's 1977 book, *Anatomy of an Explosion*—is an adaptable blueprint for use in biblical, credal, Christian universities. Above all, this book is a call to arms for individuals of Christian consciences—parents, students, supporters, besieged professors, and pastors for the courage and biblical integrity to repulse the attacks of Woke Marxism in their churches and schools with the Gospel of Jesus the Christ.

Appendices

These twenty-one appendices are **documentation** of Concordia University Wisconsin's (CUW) cringe toward Woke Marxism and its mission drift away from confessional Lutheran doctrine and practice in a mostly chronological order. They are the primary text footnotes to the four essay chapters that make up the first part of this little book.

For a **quick overview** of the *anatomy* of CUW (also known as the "culture," the "infrastructure," and the "philosophy of education" of my religious university) please read Appendices (K especially but also B, D, H, Q through R).

While there is further documentation of the university's cringe toward Woke Marxism and its drift from Lutheran doctrine and practice not included in these appendices—for example, emails and memoranda from the university's administration, past and present—these Appendices are limited to my own writings in response to the actions and procedures of CUW's administration and regents, and other relevant published essays and reports. Of course, as our Lord says, "Whatever you have said in the dark will be heard in the light, and what you have whispered in the inner rooms will be proclaimed on the housetops" (Luke 12:3).

In lockstep with agencies of our federal government, the regents and the Interim President and the current President of my Concordia have attempted to stamp their activities and declarations with a "Top Secret" classification to cover up their shenanigans.

But according to Scripture and our Lutheran Confessions, the issue at hand is a matter of public transgression against our Lord and His Gospel which must be publicly corrected, for the good of everyone involved (see 1 Timothy 5:20, and Appendices C, L and N). In Appendix H, the President of the Lutheran Church—Missouri Synod (LCMS) agrees that the CUW Board of Regents, of which the university's President is the Executive Officer, caused churchwide harm and disquiet by introducing and tolerating the anti-Scriptural ideology of Woke Marxism. He too called for their repentance.

Further, as I explain in detail in my first chapter, the university's conduct seeking to condemn and suppress my witness against the false doctrine of atheist Woke Marxism at CUW is itself in opposition to the Lutheran Confessions such as *The Formula of Concord* which calls for pastor–professors such as I am both to "believe, teach, and confess" the complete Word of Christ, the Scriptures, and to "reject and condemn false dogmas" such as Woke Marxism.

A. My response to censorship by the Provost and the Dean of the School of Arts and Sciences, January 2021....... p143

B. My essay, "Woke Dysphoria at Concordia" in Christian News, February 14, 2022. .... p148

C. Preaching on Psalm 32, one of the Seven Penitential Psalms, March 6, 2022. .... p154

D. Reporting in *The Federalist*, "Christian University Bans Professor From Campus For Critiquing Its Dive Into 'Equity' And 'Inclusion,'" March 7, 2022. .... p160

E. Letter of Censure from AFA, Academic Freedom Alliance, February 28, 2022. .... p165

F. Letter of Censure from FIRE, Freedom and Individual Rights in Education, March 4, 2022. .... p168

G. Essay from FIRE, "Concordia University Wisconsin Must Reinstate Professor Suspended without Due Process for Article Critical of the University's 'Woke Dysphoria,'" FIRE, March 8, 2022.. p173

H. Letter to the Board of Regents from LCMS President, May 9, 2022. .... p176

I. Reporting in *The Federalist*, "Christian University Still Hasn't Reinstated Professor It Kicked Out After He Criticized Identity Politics," May 16, 2022. .... p180

J. My essay "Dem Dry Bones: Can Academic Freedom Live Again at My Religious University?" *Christian News*, June 5, 2022. .... p183

K. My Response to the Interim President's Complaint seeking my termination, August 29, 2022. .... p188
L. Brief to the Review Committee hearing determining the outcome of the "reconciliation" process seeking my termination, November 29, 2022. .... p207
M. The Eighth Commandment, concluding paragraphs from Martin Luther's *Large Catechism*. p216
N. Kurt Marquart, "The Question of Procedure in Theological Controversies," in *Australian Theological Review*, April–September 1966.. p217
O. Christian Preus, "Bad Company Corrupts Good Character: The Only Way to Keep a Lutheran College Lutheran," *Christian Culture: A Journal for Lutherans*, Spring/Summer 2022. .... p226
P. Dietrich Bonhoeffer, "The Successful Man," from his unfinished *Ethics*, translated by Eberhard Bethge, 1949 .... p234
Q. Reporting in *The Federalist*, "Professor Banned For Calling Out Racism at Christian University Negotiates His Return," February 23, 2023... p236
R. Reply to the President–Provost "Agreement" Memo, March 18, 2023.. p240
S. Essay, *"Cur Verbum Verba,"* to the First Annual Convention of Luther Classical College, June 6–7, 2023...... p246
T. The Dallas Statement on Social Justice and the Gospel p256
U. Luther's 1521 Speech at the Diet of Worms. p262

Appendix A

Against Censoring or Banning Terms such as "China Virus" or "CCP Virus" at Concordia University Wisconsin

Rev. Gregory P Schulz, DMin, PhD
Professor of Philosophy, CUW

I wrote this informal essay for my CCE 120 students and posted it on our class site, where I regularly post timely resources—including my own published essays, sermons, book chapters, online courses and interviews, excerpts of books in progress, and so on—for the purpose of extending important conversations begun in class. It's also a good way to address topics proposed by students in after-class conversations. I am sharing this particular essay with students and colleagues beyond my current Western Thought and Worldview classes for reasons that will become clear as you read and think about the essay itself. You're welcome to share it as well.

Thanks again for the exhilarating conversation we had in Friday's (29 Jan 2020) class! In our discussion of Aristotle and the Three Acts of the Mind I referred very briefly to terms such such as "love," "racism," "conservative and liberal," "insurrection," and "China Virus." I said that we have a moral obligation to define and then discuss such terms in a way that everyone can understand what it is we are talking about. Then, we discussed how to be sure—together and as members of the human race, or the language species—that our judgments are true and reliable. Many of you expressed agreement before and after class when I pointed out that our inability to have honest, true, Three–Acts–of–the–Mind conversations is destroying our nation.

In light of all this, I promised you two things: (1) that you can ask about *anything you might need to discuss* as part of our growth together in our classes in Western thought and (2) that I would guarantee, beginning with clear definitions of the important terms at issue, that you would always receive from me a respectful, honest, and thoughtful response so that you can develop the capacity to think well for yourself.

In so many words, I promised to provide a safe place in your life for the intellectual and scriptural conversation that you may be unable to find anywhere else right now. Our mission is to learn how to oppose any hollow and deceptive philosophy of life by practicing truly good philosophy, namely, philosophy based on Christ the Life in His own words (Colossians 2:8; see also my online MOOC, Philosophy KATA CHRISTON). Lord willing, there is more to come on our Colossians 2:8 study in our second week, along with an engaging introduction to logical reasoning.

Sad to say, that safe space for honest conversation at our university is at risk from censorship at CUW.

Before I explain further, let me state for the record as the pastor–professor that I am that my goal here is to steer us away from foolish, ignorant controversies at our university and to correct my opponents with gentleness, leading to a knowledge of the truth (2 Timothy 2:23–26). That said, the times are evil and getting worse by the moment. Great harm is being done to our Western and Christian heritage by people in positions of leadership. Great harm is being inflicted on us all in the political realm. Great harm is being inflicted on us all in the realm of education. I do not want anyone, by censoring what you or I can or cannot talk about in light of written texts and the Scriptures, to keep professors such as me from teaching you how and why to think honestly and for yourself.

1.

Last week, the first week of our spring semester, the newly inaugurated president of the United States issued an executive order banning the use of the term "China Virus" by federal employees. See https://humanevents.com/2021/01/27/biden-v-xenophobia-new-executive-order-bans-term-china-virus/.

He clearly intends to censor all uses of this term in every corner of the country. The president decreed, "Executive departments and agencies shall take all appropriate steps to ensure that official actions, documents, and statements, including those that pertain to the COVID–19 pandemic, do not exhibit or contribute to racism, xenophobia, and intolerance...".

You will notice at least three serious problems with the president's unilateral order. First, his banning of terms such as "China Virus" is being done as if the American Scriptures (the Declaration and the Constitution) are irrelevant. This is what we will come to recognize in our study of Western logic and reasoning as *the fallacy of ignorance*. Secondly, he is rationalizing his ignoring (or his studied ignorance) of the American Scriptures that declare our God-given rights to liberty and our freedom of speech by arbitrarily declaring that anyone who uses this term is exhibiting racism and is contributing to racism. This is a *red herring* distraction as well as a demonstrable and pernicious falsehood. Thirdly, the president is begging the question by assuming that more scientific-sounding terms such as "COVID–19" are what we need for ethical or policy-making decisions.

Here is what I mean about that third problem. Science, as I have argued at length in my most recent book and elsewhere, is non-moral. In the words of Professor Kurt Marquart, "Science has neither use nor room for privileged authorities or sacrosanct texts. It recognizes only observations, experiments, logical inferences based on them, and, reluctantly, whatever axioms or assumptions are necessary to sustain these operations" (Kurt Marquart, *Anatomy of an Explosion*, 120). See my presentation made last semester both to the visiting pastors of our LCMS South Wisconsin District and to our CUW pre-seminary students at https://cuwaa.zoom.us/rec/share/IFmJaNnMFdOti8hqJ3wB4GvUzSTLKuqVjRN7yoIo1OlB8rWISr8cDz8JeZ0sS5YW.gD4cPCni s6eE0KAH.

Last week, the first week of our spring semester, and the same week that our country's president banned the use of the words "China Virus," I received an email from the university's administration banning me from using the term "China Virus." According to their email notification, they had heard second hand that I had included the term "China Virus" in one of my syllabi, alongside "Covid Virus." I was told to delete "China Virus" and not use it again because in their view "it is or could be offensive."

Now, there are similar problems with our Concordia administration's move to censor a professor's use of the term "China Virus" as there are with the president's executive order banning the term. In fact, it's the same three problems as with President Biden's order for censorship, although for our university the fallacy of ignorance involves not simply the American Scriptures but the Holy Scriptures and our Lutheran Confession commitments in addition.

There is also a fallacy of *equivocation* in our administration's rational for censoring me. The term "offense" may be a reference to biblical offense, a serious sin as explained by our Lord in Matthew 18. In this case they are saying that I am sinning or may be about to sin by so much as using the term "China Virus." Or, it may be a reference to people getting upset. Let's assume it is the latter. Think about it for a moment and you will realize that to claim that something is "offensive" in a non-biblical sense is disingenuous. Obviously, anyone can claim to be offended about anything in order to get their way for any reason or for no reason whatever.

Either way, the university's efforts to ban me as a professor from even mentioning "China Virus" is a violation of my academic freedom to teach in line with the Holy Scriptures and the Lutheran Confessions, as I have publicly promised to do as a confessional Lutheran pastor. As my department chair tried to explain to the administration, censoring anyone from using the term "Chinese or China Virus" because it is or may be offensive *is itself an uneducated and arbitrary position* since this exact term has been widely used in the very recent history of all sorts of discussions of this virus. For example, see https://www.breitbart.com/politics/2020/03/18/cnn-embraced-racist-terms-chinese-coronavirus-wuhan-coronavirus/.

I am ready, willing, and able to argue that our administration needs to repent of its readiness to censor me or any of its professors. Further, I am saddened to conclude that it is possible that my administration is on the brink of accusing me of being a racist, according to the same "reasoning" that our new president is imposing on any conversation by federal employees for so much as using the term "China Virus." Please reread the Biden quote in my previous paragraph to see this for yourself.

My concern is not far-fetched. After all, professors are being charged with racism for merely mentioning the term "Chinese Virus" in other universities. Unfounded accusations of racism—complete with tsunamis of tweets and twits calling for firings and prosecutions with no factual basis whatever—have led to university "investigations" and so on in recent months. For example, against a Syracuse University professor for doing nothing other than using the term "Chinese Virus" in an email confirming that a student had missed class because of sickness, and against a University of Cincinnati professor who simply used the term "Wuhan Flu" in a class syllabus.

So, the censoring of this particular term in any professor's syllabus or conversation is serious business. I'm happy to talk through any of these problems with censoring that I've mentioned, but I am mostly concerned right now with showing you how and why this notion that the term "China Virus" should be censored because it is "potentially offensive" (as our university administrators are saying) or because it is "racist," etc. (as President Biden is saying) is untrue and immensely harmful to us as human beings. Not to mention how harmful it is to the health of our national and educational institutions. Whether we are talking about the national conversation or about conversations inside and outside classes at our university, censorship is as anti-conversation and anti-intellectual as it is anti-textual.

2.

Because I am a pastor and a professor who adheres to the Lord's admonition to be as wise as serpents, and harmless as doves (Matthew 10:16), let me say this clearly to anyone who thinks that discussing terms such as "China Virus" or "CCP Virus," etc. is racist: You are wrong and you are being deliberately ignorant.

In my case, I love the Chinese people; therefore, I oppose the philosophy and the actions of the Chinese Communist government. I am a confessional Lutheran pastor, therefore I love every member of the human race because of the historical reality of the Incarnation for all us human beings, without exception, and because of universal justification. I am a professor; therefore, I help my students and others to love their neighbors and oppose the antihuman philosophy and actions of the Chinese Communist government. I have lectured in China at the invitation of a professor who was himself banned from saying what only a visiting scholar such as I could teach his students. (When we discuss truth theories later in our semester I will tell you about those philosophical lectures and my discussion of John 14:6 with Chinese graduate students. It's quite a story!) I have taught, preached, and talked long into the night with pastors and students in Hong Kong about lost freedoms and their hopes for their businesses, their churches, their children. I have former students in China.

Furthermore, I have taught since 2008 in the PhD Missiology program one of our LCMS seminaries, where I have come to know many ethnic pastors from the Pacific Rim, whose families and ministries are conducted under the shadow of the Communist Chinese government. I love and care for these brethren and their families and church members.

This leads me to my reason for keeping the term "China Virus" in the conversation. As I said, because I love these souls in China, because I have former students, friends, and fellow pastors and professors there, and because I am a pastor and because I am a professor educating the next generation to love their neighbors as themselves, I know a few things about censorship and its impact on teaching and ministry.

Even if my administration is unaware, I know there is much more at stake here than someone's alleged hurt feelings or claims that they are "offended" at being reminded of the historical realities. The terms "China or Chinese Virus" and "CCP Virus" are not racist; in fact, they are a learning opportunity. Here is my documentation. https://www.theepochtimes.com/the-origin-of-wuhan-coronavirus_3308349.html. If you cannot manage to view this entire one-hour documentary, please be sure to view the last twenty minutes, at least.

As I have begun to explain, there are three (fundamental ethical/moral) problems with President Biden's executive order arbitrarily banning conversations that would so much as use the term "China Virus." These same three problems are the fundamental ethical and moral problems with the administration's move to ban and censor the term "China Virus" at Concordia.

You may expect me to refer next to their censoring as a case of *slippery slope* reasoning. I am not saying that at all. That there is even any measure of censoring going on is an indication that we are already crashing and burning at the bottom of the slope.

Do you know what the surest sign is that we are at grave risk from this "little bit" of censoring? There was no conversation. The administration did not even consider that there may be solid intellectual and even theological reasons for discussing the meaning of a term such as "China Virus." The did not ask for any conversation at all. Even after my department chair recommended that they stop and think about what they were doing, they dismissed his concern over administration's studied ignorance and its censoring of faculty out of hand. At the same time, they seem to be "all in" on the scientific term "COVID," oblivious to the reality that "science has neither use nor room for privileged authorities or sacrosanct texts," such as the American Scriptures and the Holy Scriptures.

Appendix B

Woke Dysphoria at Concordia

Rev. Gregory P Schulz, DMin, PhD
Professor of Philosophy, Concordia University Wisconsin
Published in the Feb. 14, 2022 issue of Christian News
Posted on online Feb. 15, 2022 by Christian News

Dysphoria is another word for "restlessness." It doesn't mean being fidgety or ill at ease; it means being depressed, disquieted, overcome by *Angst*. Much like the term *euphoria* at the other end of the emotional spectrum, dysphoria connotes being under the influence. My Concordia university is experiencing dysphoria because it is coming under the influence of Woke–ism (that is, a potent cocktail of Progressivism, Neo-Pragmatism, and Marxism).

We are under the influence of the Woke–ness in our nation and our Western culture, of course, but Wokeness appears to be developing into a pathology at my "institution of Lutheran higher education" as it says in our mission statement. Our institutional dysphoria at Concordia University Wisconsin (CUW) has come to light—and has been exacerbated by the search for a new university president and the manner in which our Board of Regents and, in particular, its Executive Board and its Search Committee who have been pushing for a president who will be, in their own words, "disruptive" and "transformational."

It turns out that they mean disruption and transformation in the sense of installing a president who would disrupt the expectation of a pastor–president as described in the written By-laws of the Lutheran Church—Missouri Synod, and who would thus be radically different from spiritual and educational leadership as authoritatively described in the Scriptures. For example, as laid out for us in the pastoral epistles such as the apostle Paul's letters to Timothy. They mean to transform the ways and means of being Concordia.

The Cause of Our Restlessness and Dysphoria

In their own words (posted now for a second calendar year on their microsite at https://www.cuw.edu/microsites/president-search/index.html#nomi nation), committees from our Board of Regents have been publicly announcing their determination to have a president who exhibits a "demonstrated belief in and commitment to equity and inclusion" and who promotes racialized "diversity in all its myriad forms."

These are aggressive–progressive Woke mantras. *Diversity* refers to a racialized diversity with unsubstantiated assumptions of white privilege and systemic (national and institutional) racism that form the mythological basis of Harvard's Critical Race Theory and the 1619 Project. *Inclusion* is an aggressive, almost violent version of what used to be known as affirmative action, now construed as racial reparations—again, on the basis of the mythological thinking from Critical Race Theory. *Equity* is the enforcement of Diversity and Inclusion by any means necessary—excepting by means of thoughtful, reasonable, and honest writing and discussion.

The lynchpin issue is this: *The Woke agenda (*DIE, for *Diversity, Inclusion, Equity) is utterly opposed to texts and to textual authority.* In theory (such as it is) and in practice, the Woke agenda being championed by our BoR committees is literally an illiterate philosophy of education that has no place for authoritative texts. For example, Woke–ness has no place for authoritative texts such as the Constitution or the Declaration of Independence. It also has no place for the authority of the biblical text. (On this issue please see my January 2022 presentation at our LCMS Making Disciples for Life Conference, Live Not by Lies: The Self-Evident Proposition Versus Marxist Ideology, and my three-part essay, The Self-Evident Proposition, published in *Christian Culture* by Luther Classical College.)

A generation ago in response to the Seminex explosion in our church body, which was something of a foreshock to this Woke earthquake in Mequon right now, Kurt Marquart wrote this about agendas and methodologies that put themselves between Scripture and students: "Science has neither use nor room for privileged authorities or sacrosanct texts. It recognizes only observations, experiments, logical inferences based on them, and, reluctantly, whatever axioms or assumptions are necessary to sustain these operations" (*Anatomy of an Explosion*, 120).

When expressed as a universal formula Marquart's reply exposes the fundamental problem with Woke–ness. Think of his formula this way. "X has neither use nor room for privileged authorities or sacrosanct texts." You can plug in for X every element of the Woke agenda: DIE, BIPOC, LGBTQ-ism, Transgenderism, Harvard's Critical Race Theory, and so on. In each case, it comes to light that there is no room for privileged authorities or sacrosanct texts. (Please see my widely-disseminated desktop presentation, Trust, but Edify, posted on GETTR @profgschulz.)

Just look at the published wish-list for our next university president in terms of Marquart's formula. There is no room for privileged authorities—not a hint that all teaching authority at the university has been given to Christ (Matthew 28:18–20). There is no room for sacrosanct texts—not a mention of what Christ says in His verbatim Word about education, not a clue that they are seeking a president capable of articulating a philosophy of education that is based on Christ Himself (Colossians 2:8–9). Not a scintilla of a hint that they would seek a president capable of leading us in the work of "destroying arguments and all arrogance raised against the knowledge of God, and taking every thought captive to the obedience of Christ" (2 Corinthians 10:5).

In other words, the Woke–ness or Progressivism that these committees are promulgating is educational heresy. Our Lord says clearly, "Whoever is not with me is against me, and whoever does not gather with me scatters" (Matthew 12:30). During the Holocaust, the Lutheran Pastor Dietrich Bonhoeffer wrote that this passage is about those within the church who, in time of persecution and tribulation, simply will not articulate the authority of Christ in all areas of life. Those who are "not with Me" are those who neglect and refuse to confess Christ's words and His authority, particularly in time of crisis and cultural abandonment of the Gospel, such as the church is experiencing right now—nowhere more obviously than in higher education.

This Wokeness—with its dismissal and replacement of sacrosanct texts—is also anti-Lutheran inasmuch as it defies what I have been teaching and publishing as "the first principle of Lutheran thought:" "But God cannot be treated with, God cannot be apprehended, *nisi per Verbum*, except through the Word" (*Apology*, Article 4, On Justification). *Woke–ism is in point of fact a renunciation of the very means by which we "do ministry" and thus a renunciation of the means by which we "do Concordia."* (Please see my NISI PER VERBUM articles in *LOGIA* or speak with my undergrads, your sons and daughters, your grandchildren, at CUW as well as our pastors and missionaries who are my PhD students in Fort Wayne's Missiology program.)

When our BoR committees announce their intentions to install a president who exhibits a "demonstrated belief in and commitment to equity and inclusion" and promotes racialized "diversity in all its myriad forms," they are announcing their plan to disrupt the authority of the biblical text and in this way to transform our university from an institution of Lutheran higher education to ... who knows what. They are announcing their intention to transform this LCMS institution into a DIE–ing institution. See, for instance, the language and content of the Office of Multicultural Engagement on the university's website at cuw.edu.

Not incidentally, the BoR committees' posted announcements are unsurprisingly Woke in their cavalier altering of texts. True to the Woke mindset of the Presidential Search postings, someone or some committee presumed to alter the pronouns in their posted version of our LCMS bylaws. As one of my faculty colleagues pointed out, in that posting the first two sentences of the LCMS Bylaw 3.10.6.6, addressing "Concordia University System Presidents," read: "The president of the institution shall be the executive officer of the board of regents. He shall serve as the spiritual, academic, and administrative head of the institution." The first two sentences under "Role of the 9th President of Concordia University" in the Presidential Prospectus, however, read: "The president of Concordia University is the chief executive of the institution, reporting to the Board of Regents. The president serves both as academic head of the faculty and as spiritual leader of the institution."

Notice, my colleague explained, how closely the posted Presidential Prospectus follows the exact language of Bylaw 3.10.6.6. in its first sentence "The president," "executive," "of the institution," "the board of regents"—but then *avoids using the masculine pronoun "He"* at the beginning of its second sentence. One might also ask why *Presidential Prospectus* places "spiritual" *after* "academic" instead of keeping "spiritual" first as the bylaw has it, and why *Presidential Prospectus* uses the term "leader" with "spiritual," as "leader" is not found anywhere in Bylaw 3.10.6.6 when describing a Concordia University president.

Whether the BoR committees alter their posted, online statements, or not—without a detailed and equally widely published retraction of their Woke desires and commitments, the Woke dysphoria at Concordia will continue. After all, this is not a PR issue but a matter of repentance and showing the fruit of faith.

Only Rest for our Systemic Restlessness and Dysphoria

To conclude, let me return to the broader concern for Woke dysphoria among the students and parents, among the pastors and other dedicated supporters of my university. Unsurprisingly, our help comes from Christ and His authoritative words. I say "unsurprisingly" because we are officially a Lutheran institution of higher learning and I am actually one of a number of divinely called LCMS pastor–professors at CUW.

One of the most impactful sentences written in the history of Western and Christian thought after the Bible comes from Augustine of Hippo. "You have made us for Yourself, Lord, and we are restless (*inquietus* in his Latin) until we find our rest in You" (*Confessions* 1.1). This sentence is a master's class on human nature distilled from Ecclesiastes (concerning the meaninglessness of life apart from the words of the one Lord our Shepherd), and our Lord's words in Matthew 11:28 (His invitation to come to Him for the Sabbath rest for our souls)—packaged as a field kit for personal or cultural emergencies, or as a classroom thesis to save souls who are suffering from dysphoria / disquiet / *Angst* here in the trenches of Lutheran higher education.

At the same time, Augustine's master class of a sentence is a decisive indictment of every philosophy of education that refuses to form its curriculum by means of the ultimate sacrosanct text, the Hebrew and Greek Scriptures—an indictment of every educational institutional culture that neglects to re-form itself according to God's Word, that is, according to the incarnate, rest-giving Word of God Himself and according to His verbatim words to us. That is, according to the divinely instituted means of grace.

On this basis, I offer my professional diagnosis that the Woke–ism at CUW, exacerbated by the BoR committees' handling of the presidential search, is burdening the consciences of my students and my religious colleagues on faculty. (Please see my 2013 book, *Wednesday's Child: From Heidegger to Affective Neuroscience, A Field Theory of Angst*. In the first chapter I explain how conscience is founded on *Angst* in human consciousness. In the book's concluding Afterthought, I explain that there will be either a religious or a non-religious response to Augustine's sentence.)

What, then, shall we say in response to the Woke Dysphoria at Concordia? There are matters of accountability and responsibility to be attended to. **While there is no systemic racism at Concordia because we are committed to Christ incarnate and His universal justification of all human beings without exception,** there certainly is systemic Woke–ism.

As another of my faculty colleagues explains it, accrediting bodies are a major source of power driving the Woke–ness at our university. The university's commitment to securing accreditation from Higher Learning Commission (HLC) has likely led to the disquieting DIE changes in staffing, in scholarships, in programs, and in curricula at CUW. HLC criteria for accreditation include "1.C. The institution provides opportunities for civic engagement in a diverse, multicultural society and globally connected world, as appropriate within its mission and for the constituencies it serves. …1.The institution encourages curricular or cocurricular activities that prepare students for informed citizenship and workplace success. 2.The institution's processes and activities demonstrate inclusive and equitable treatment of diverse populations. 3.The institution fosters a climate of respect among all students, faculty, staff and administrators from a range of diverse backgrounds, ideas and perspectives."

A fellow professor in the sciences also pointed out to me that the ACS approval (a chemistry curriculum approval that is very important for the BS in Chemistry) mandates that "The collective expertise of the faculty should reflect the breadth of the major areas of modern chemistry. Because faculty members serve as important professional role models, an ACS-approved program should have a faculty that is diverse in gender, race, and ethnic background."

Accreditation in turn influences our university leadership and curriculum because of our financial entanglement with the government. The financial expediencies by which we are "doing Concordia" cry out for immediate, urgent reconsideration. The apostolic mandate comes to mind. "We must obey God rather than men" (Acts 5:29). Three thoughts come to mind as well.

First, given that the love of money is the root of all kinds of evil (1 Timothy 6:10), is it possible that Concordia is under the influence of inept metrics and methodologies for the assessment of its work as a Lutheran institution of higher learning? In this regard, a text that we must make a place for in our conversations is "The Successful Man" in Dietrich Bonhoeffer's *Ethics*.

This will further suggest a detailed report from, and perhaps a forensic audit of the university's Initiatives and the funding practices of Concordia University Wisconsin Foundation Board as listed on our cuw.edu website. Whence the funding for the Woke agenda at our university? Apart from the headline mentions of our Lord's name, exactly how does DIE–ing fulfil the university's churchly and Lutheran educational mission?

Secondly, it is the administration and senior administrators of CUW who bear day–to–day responsibility for the regularizing and normalizing of Woke–ness at the university. As we on the faculty bear day–to–day responsibility for what we teach or fail to teach our students. There seems to be an assumption that the DIE is cast and we are willy-nilly fully committed to Woke–ism. How the presidential search turns out will mark a watershed moment for Concordia—perhaps for all of our remaining Concordias—but I do not think we should miss this point: *There has been no suitably academic study or proper professional discussion of this looming tectonic shift in educational philosophy and university policy from Lutheranism to Woke–ism.* This is scandalous.

There are urgent academic and theological questions for our leadership in the administration and for our DIE–ing colleagues on faculty. Where are your own books, your published journal articles, your white papers, your writings and reasonings about this shift—this "disruptive" and "transformational" shift championed by our BoR committees? What exactly are you pro-fessing, dear colleagues? Come, let us reason together in the forum of God's Word (Isaiah 1:18).

As I have been arguing, Woke–ism is afflicting the consciences of students, faculty, and supporters of Concordia. Therefore, programmatic, systemic Woke–ism merits reconsideration. It also merits personal and institutional repentance.

Finally, I offer this recommendation in direct opposition to the BoR committees' postings.

- The next president must believe in and have a demonstrated commitment to Scripture and the Lutheran Confessions.
- He must be a pastor–professor with an exceptional, longstanding spiritual and intellectual / academic record of ministry and leadership in concord with his belief in and commitment to the Scripture and the Lutheran Confessions.
- He must be a pastor–professor of substantial moral authority on the basis of his commitment to bringing Christ, the Lord of Sabbath-rest to students, to faculty, to the Concordia community, and to all restless people of the world whom we can reach—this via the means that Christ has instituted and commended to us for the work of teaching in a world largely in rebel-

lion against God's authority and thus disquieted, dysphoric, and in need of a genuinely *higher* education: education in the Way, the Truth, and the Life incarnate.

Appendix C

Sermon on Psalm 32
6 March 2022 — First Sunday in Lent
Luther Memorial Chapel, Shorewood Wisconsin

Our sermon today is drawn from the words of our Lord in this penitential Psalm for the first Sunday in Lent, Psalm 32. Let me now reread the framing verses, the beginning and the end, of this Psalm from our Lord Jesus Christ.

"Blessed is the one whose transgression is forgiven, whose sin is covered." "Many are the sorrows of the wicked, but steadfast love surrounds the one who trusts in the LORD. Be glad in the LORD, and rejoice, O righteous, and shout for joy, all you upright in heart!" This is the Word of our Lord.

In the name of Jesus. Amen.

Happy Lent! A very, very merry first Sunday in Lent to each and everyone one of you! O how joyfully, O how merrily Lent-time comes with its joy divine!

That feels wrong, doesn't it? What we are going to experience this morning is Jesus, the Trinity, working through the very words of God to reeducate our feelings. It is also the case that in Psalm 32, as in all his Word, but I think especially in the Psalms, you are going to notice that Jesus is re-forming our intellect and resyncing our will with the will of God. But this morning I would like you to notice especially how the Lord addresses the emotions with which he has created us and educates them to be in line with his love for us.

1. *The means by which* we are blessed

"Blessed is." That is the start for our Psalm. You are going to find that there are three basic parts for this Psalm, at least in the way we are looking at it this morning. There is this part about blessed—and it is absolutely astonishing; just wait a second. There is the part about forgiveness and confessing—it is astonishing and will rearrange everything in your heart, soul, and mind. And then there is the Lord talking to us about instruction or teaching. And this brings us to a conclusion that, well, is going to remind you for all the world of Palm Sunday, heading right down the line to Holy Week where our Lord is surrounded by people, the righteous rejoicing in the coming of the Messiah.

But first I am going to take a half step back right now before we launch into the exact wording that God's Psalm writer brings to us this morning. I am going to take a half step back and remind you of something that is so obvious that we might be inclined to neglect it and not think twice about it, but is so very, very mission critical to the work of Christ's Church through the ages, and especially in our day today.

The thing that I want to take that half step back and point out several times during our preaching of this text is the *means* by which:

THE MEANS BY WHICH GOD WANTS US TO DO LENT

The *means* by which God teaches us to know and rejoice in that full, free, grace-alone forgiveness that he has given us. And the means by which God wants us to teach all people about him, what he has done for every soul everywhere and every when. So I have a brief story. A few years ago I had the opportunity to be teaching at our seminary in Pretoria, South Africa. It was quite a thrill let me tell you. Among other things that were going on at that time, I had the chance to teach a class at our Lutheran seminary there and interact with our pastors and future pastors for the continent of Africa and beyond. And, strange as this may sound in a sermon, I had an invitation to speak to, guess what, the theology faculty of the nearby University of Pretoria. In the meeting with that theology faculty (academic stuff) I had the opportunity to talk about the absolutely critical issue of using the Psalms for pastoral care of people who were suffering and dying. I was harping, in my paper and presentation to them, on the fact that Psalm 22 needed to be used and prayed verbatim. That our Lord, after all, had prayed that on the cross for all of us. And that he wanted us to be comforting each other, up-taking people in the midst of their suffering into the suffering of Christ in his own words.

Now, as happens at the end of that kind of presentation, there was a long question and answer, and one of the pastors (who I found out later was on the faculty) said, "I am very worried about what you just said. I am very worried because I am actually responsible for teaching the pastors in our denomination how to do hospital visits and how to minister to people who are dying. And I think I just heard you say something terrible. I am going to pass by," he said, "any mention of whether or not I think David really wrote Psalm 22. And I am not going to comment on whether I think Jesus actually prayed that Psalm on the cross or not," he said, "but I tell my pastoral students that they need to be authentic when they comfort people. They need to speak to them in their own words, not just parrot something that they got from somewhere else."

Well, I responded, "And I am very worried for you and for those pastors who are studying with you. Because what I just heard you say is that you feel that it is adequate and right just to speak off the cuff with your own feelings instead of bringing Christ to those people who are suffering and dying in his own words."

Do you see the point? The *means* by which. *The means by which.*

So here now we come to our Psalm which is part of God's Word, which is God's actual words translated for us, which is the means by which he teaches us to do Lent and life. So here is the opening. "Blessed is the one." Now we are in the book of Psalms. I know that this is not as familiar territory as it needs to be to us in the Lutheran Church frankly, but I know that we are inclined to take a look at the individual Psalms as standalone works. I think there is good reason to feel that God's providence is at work exactly the way the Psalms have been set in the order that they are, too.

So, for instance, think about that word "blessed." Quick check. What does that remind you of? Psalm 32 begins, "Blessed are." Psalm 1! Psalm 1. That is the opening of the book of Psalms. Here is a reminder: "Blessed is the man who walks not in the counsel of the wicked nor stands in the way of sinners nor sits in the seat of scoffers, but his delight is in the law of the LORD, and on his law he meditates day and night."

Some people think that this is what we would call in logic a slippery slope kind of warning: watch out that you don't start off by kind of listening to these people and end up sitting down with them and learning from them and teaching their stuff. That is not at all correct. This is actually a black ice situation. It is when there is something happening where your bearings are completely lost and everything is out of control. Just like no friction at that intersection where you come across that black ice and everything is going every which way.

You can see that from Psalm 2 actually. In Psalm 2 the Lord who speaks to us through the *means* of Scripture and works on us through the *means* of baptism and brings to us his body and blood through the *means* of Holy Communion—that God says this about those who oppose his Messiah. First, they say: "Let us burst their bonds apart and cast away their cords from us." That is the stuff of the Lord, his Word, and his Messiah. "He who sits in the heavens laughs; the Lord holds them in derision. Then he will speak to them in his wrath, and terrify them in his fury, saying, 'As for me, I have set my King on Zion, my holy hill.'" Now I don't think that God's laugh is exactly the kind of joy I was using for a dissonance with our *feelings* during the first Sunday in Lent. But you can't help but notice the sheer jubilation of it: "I mean, really? You are going to oppose Christ and my Messiah? You are—ah ha—you are seriously going to set aside all of this forgiveness, all of this stuff I have done for you in Christ (or promised in the Old Testament to do for you in the Messiah)? Really? How well do you think that is going to work out for you?"

2. *The means by which* we are forgiven

Now we are back at our Psalm. "Blessed." All right. The word blessed is actually an Old Testament–New Testament, Old Testament–New Testament, Old Testament–New Testament term. If you want to understand what blessed means in the Old Testament, you have to be listening to Jesus in Matthew 5 talking in the Sermon on the Mount: "Blessed are you when." In order to understand what Jesus is doing there (as fully as he wants us to) you have to understand how often he talks to us through his means about how blessed we are *when*. See? "Blessed is the one whose transgression is forgiven, whose sin is covered. Blessed is the man against whom the LORD counts no iniquity and in whose spirit there is no deceit."

Now we come to the second section of our Psalm where we hear about forgiveness, full, free, and by grace alone; and *con*–fessing. But I would very much like you to hear the echo of what is going on with this word *blessed* in here. Blessed does not mean a nice thing has happened to you. Blessed does not mean, "Oh, well, this is good; I really appreciate it." Blessed means that we are blessed with a happiness that is so overwhelming, so abundant, that we can't contain it. This is happiness as in joy! This is happiness as in you cannot keep it in! That is this first Sunday in Lent Psalm reading. Blessed! Blessed! Blessed! And here is why: forgiveness. Our Luther wrote this about our Psalm for today: "No one prays for these things except the one who feels the tumult of his conscience." Conscience is another word for consciousness, you know. It is not a particular little part of our consciousness; it is a particular performance of our human consciousness.

It is when, I think, in large part, when we are unsettled; when we are disquieted; when we are angst-ridden. It is that feature of our consciousness on which plausibly saint Paul is basing his explanation about conscience in Romans: "Our thoughts now defending us, now accusing us." If we are listening to and following God's means of grace there is going to be rest. If we are not even leaving room for God's means of grace in our lives, there is going to be disquiet, restlessness, and angst. This is Augustine in *Confessions* Book 1 paragraph 1: "You have made us for yourself Lord, and we are restless until we find ourselves in you." Well.

What of those things in our lives that foment restlessness? How can they hold a candle to the Sabbath rest of Christ? I ask you! And don't you see the blessedness and joy bubbling up right about here? Because actually this Psalm is the basis for part of some very familiar stuff to us as Lutherans from Romans 3 and Romans 4. Here is a quick reminder. Romans 4: "What then shall we say was gained by Abraham, our forefather according to the flesh? For if Abraham was justified by works," something he did got him justified, "he has something to boast about, but not before God. For what does the Scripture say? 'Abraham believed God, and it was counted to him as righteousness.' Now to the one who works, his wages are not counted as a gift but as his due. And to the one who does not work but believes in him who justifies the ungodly, his faith is counted as righteousness, just as David also speaks of the blessing of the one to whom God counts righteousness apart from works." Sola fide, right? And here is the quote: "'Blessed are those whose lawless deeds are forgiven, and whose sins are covered; blessed is the man against whom the Lord will not count his sin.'" This is that second part of our blessed, jubilation, overflowing–happiness Psalm. "For when I kept silent, my bones wasted away through my groaning all day long. For day and night your hand was heavy upon me; my strength was dried up as by the heat of summer. I acknowledged my sin to you, and I did not cover my iniquity; I said, 'I will confess my transgressions to the LORD,' and you forgave the iniquity of my sin. Therefore let everyone who is godly offer prayer to you at a time when you may be found; surely in the rush of great waters, they shall not reach him. You are a hiding place for me; you preserve me from trouble; you surround me with shouts of deliverance." Happy! Blessed! Lenten! Shouts!—of the blessing of deliverance.

3. *The means by which* we instruct and teach

Well, there is a third part to our Psalm. This is the part about instructions and teaching. Here is Martin Luther for another quote on his writing about this Psalm: "In the holy Scriptures," he says, "understanding takes its name from the object rather than any capacity." Can I translate that for you? He means that what the Bible talks about as understanding doesn't come from the capacities or the abilities that we have, but it comes from the object of our faith; it comes from *whom* we believe in. It comes from him to us. Do you see? This is the means by which forgiveness is delivered. This is the means by which our feelings are reeducated to realize, "I am indeed a poor miserable sinner, but in Christ, in Christ who became sin for us so that in him we might become the righteousness of God, we are filled with joy and happiness." Here is one more quote from Augustine: "There is no reason to be doing philosophy unless it is with a view toward beatific happiness." Unending, beatitudes happiness. Interesting thing: when you think about the Classic writers and also when you think about Scripture, that word "philosophy" means all learning and teaching. It doesn't just mean a particular department at a modern university. It means your philosophy of life. It means what is your learning all about. And do you see this again? The means *by which* are absolutely crucial! Are they going to be the means of grace—which are the only means through which God gives us rest, speaks to our emotions and our intellect and lines up our will with his—or something else, something inferior, something less than Christ. "Understanding takes its name from the object." In our studied Lutheran way of thinking about this we say, very joyfully I might add, that "God does not want to be apprehended, he cannot be got to, nisi per Verbum, except through the Word."

The Word is Christ and the Word of Christ is the Scripture and it is all about *the means by which*.

All right. Time to conclude. Here is a quote. This is from Voddie Baucham: "We cannot continue to send our children to Caesar for education and be surprised when they come home as Romans."

It is a matter of means by which, do you see? The joyful means, the Christian Christ-centered means; or the idols and ideologies and other things which are never, *ever* going to put people's hearts at rest. There is no joy to be found except in our Lord, our God, our Savior, Jesus Christ. The last part of this Psalm as I mentioned sounds for all the world like something that could be describing Jesus in the center of things on Palm Sunday. You have to understand that this whole talk about blessed—this whole conveyance of joy and free forgiveness and instruction in the ways of righteousness to life everlasting—this is all dependent on the means by which. The means of Word and Sacrament that God has ordained. You have heard it said, "I have a dream." I think that is a perfectly wonderful statement. I think it addresses in a powerful and winning way issues of justice in society. I respect and admire Dr. King for saying that, not for his theology. If I may just briefly note that I appreciate and teach him because of his attendance to natural law and his attention to great texts in Western thought. If you read his Letter from Birmingham Jail you are going to hear him quote more Augustine than I did in the sermon today.

"I have a dream." But I think that when it comes to the matter of education, we want to look not at the Martin Luther who was named Martin Luther King by his dad because his dad was so taken by the teachings of Martin Luther—as I said, great civic help for us, great natural law help—but for education, we Lutherans are the place to go.

Because we know the means.

Because, well, not of anything that we have done, but of everything that God has been doing among us *through the means that he has appointed*. So I say to you, with malice toward none but with Christ's Word for all: those who may espouse ideologies such as Harvard's Critical Race Theory need to hear this: We in the Lutheran Church do not teach on the basis of Marxist mythology. We teach on the basis of Christ himself and we want everyone to come and hear. We teach in line with the apostle Peter: "We did not follow cleverly invented myths when we told you about the power and coming of our Lord Jesus Christ."

To students and others who cannot seem to think of any way to talk about things that they don't quite get or think they are supposed to be angry with—can't think of any other way other than to describe people as racist, I would say with all sincerity, with malice toward none and with Christ's love toward all, that they have been woefully let down in their educations. That is the sort of thing that comes from bad educations, from the media, from society, and clearly not from Christ. I would say: come with your restlessness. Let us talk about this. Let's open the Bible and see what your Savior says.

And I tell you what. The whole key to this is the incarnation. It is *not* going "all racist" on everybody. It is looking at the God who in fact took on our human flesh and blood to charge the entire human race without exception with infinite worth and *eternal* worth to boot.

And to those who fumble around for ways to do education and attract people to Lutheran education by anything other than the Scriptures, I say this: you need to watch the means by which.

And instead of diverse-looking pictures and slogans, how about universal justification? It is in universal justification that we know, for all of our sinfulness, for all of our foibles—no doubt, for certain idiosyncrasies that we have—we know that everybody without exception: abled or disabled, whatever color, whatever socioeconomic background, whatever nation they happen to be in, whatever demographic they are—everyone, everyone has been justified freely by God's grace through the redemption that came by Christ Jesus. How is that for an educational philosophy?

So back to the conclusion of our Psalm. Please remember to *notice the means by which and take another look at how you feel about this blessedness on the first Sunday in Lent twenty twenty-two*. "I will instruct you and teach you in the way you should go; I will counsel you with my eye upon you. Be not like a horse or a mule, without understanding, which must be curbed with bit and bridle, or it will not stay near you. Many are the sorrows of the wicked, but steadfast love surrounds the one who trusts in the LORD. Be glad in the LORD, and rejoice, O righteous, and shout for joy, all you upright in heart!"

Happy Lent! A very, very merry and joyful first Sunday in Lent to you and yours. Time to share that joy. Amen.

Now the peace of God, which passes all understanding, shall keep your hearts and minds through faith in the rest given us only in Christ Jesus. Amen.

Rev. Gregory Schulz, DMin, PhD
Professor of Philosophy
Concordia University Wisconsin

Appendix D

Christian University Bans Professor From Campus For Critiquing Its Dive Into 'Equity' And 'Inclusion'

Joy Pullmann
thefederalist.com
March 7, 2022

A professor was locked out of his classes and email account without warning in apparent retaliation for criticizing his Christian university's use of "diversity" and "equity" as criteria for selecting its new president, he and several witnesses told The Federalist.

The Rev. Dr. Greg Schulz was immediately and indefinitely suspended from his classes at Concordia University Wisconsin and banned from campus by interim college President William Cario on Feb. 18, a Friday. That was not formally conveyed to Schulz, however, until his lawyer obtained the suspension letter on Feb. 22, Schulz's Wisconsin Institute for Law and Liberty attorney Dan Lennington told The Federalist.

"They told him to 'recant' in a memo that they never gave him," Lennington said in a phone call. Lennington also noted his public interest law firm, which won a high-profile 2016 academic freedom case in Wisconsin's Supreme Court, has "never heard of something like this" swift ejection of a professor from campus for publicly expressing his views.

Schulz found out about his suspension and campus ban from colleagues after he couldn't log into his work email on the weekend, said Schulz and his department chair, Dr. Angus Menuge. Menuge said Schulz's suspension meant that colleagues, several already teaching double courseloads amid a hiring freeze, had to suddenly pick up all of Schulz's classes.

"I have since contacted the president and asked him to reconsider and I have received no response whatsoever," Menuge told The Federalist by phone on March 4. Menuge described the suspension as "extraordinarily draconian" and "Kafka-esque" because of not only the reasons Schulz was suspended but also how it was managed.

"Are we being told that you have to mute your Christianity so that it conforms to these ideologies of niceness and all of it? If so, that has a chilling effect on not only academic freedom but also on the Christian conscience," Menuge said. Especially in a time when many Christians are feeling increasing pressure from cultural Marxism, and amid current efforts to encourage Concordia faculty to stay bold in their Christian scholarship, he said, "This is such an own goal, it really sets us back."

Christians Not Happy About Their Institution Endorsing Racism

Concordia Wisconsin is a university of the Lutheran Church—Missouri Synod, one of the United States's largest Christian denominations, with approximately 1.8 million U.S. members. It has approximately 8,000 students, the majority of whom are not Lutherans. The university is located in Mequon, Wis., an upscale suburb of Milwaukee.

The institution with a $107 million annual budget gets significant income from federal student loans. Accepting those loans requires accreditation, which mandates racial policies at odds with Christian teachings about the equal and priceless value of all humans, who are created in God's image.

Concordia Wisconsin has come under fire from many of its own pastors and members after instituting a Black Student Union and hiring a "director of multicultural engagement" in 2019. The Office of Multicultural Engagement that diversity officer oversees "strives to advance Concordia's efforts to embed diversity as a transformational force," according to its web page. That page also states the office trains faculty, staff, and students in "social identities, microaggressions, and implicit bias" and in being "culturally competent."

The university's Black Student Union recommends the fact-challenged and racially biased 1619 Project to students, as well as making purchases based on a vendor's skin color. It also recommended author Ibram X. Kendi's work. Kendi has stated, "The only remedy to racist discrimination is antiracist discrimination. The only remedy to past discrimination is present discrimination. The only remedy to present discrimination is future discrimination."

Following Schulz's suspension, a local Lutheran congregation held a service praying and calling for repentance for the university's departure from Christian teaching about racial equality.

A public petition to university leaders to reinstate Schulz and repent of publicly endorsing the "diversity, equity, and inclusion" ideology that encourages racial segregation had garnered more than 5,500 signatures as of March 6. Students also delivered their own petition of support for Schulz to Cario, although some are concerned that expressing such support could get them blacklisted and ostracized, Menuge said.

Free Speech Advocates With Lawyers Are Watching

Schulz's suspension also prompted letters of support from the Academic Freedom Alliance on Feb. 28 and, on March 4, the Foundation for Individual Rights in Education. Both organizations, which raise funds and pursue lawsuits on behalf of free speech in higher education, called for the university to reinstate Schulz immediately.

"For Concordia University Wisconsin to punish Professor Schulz for engaging in a public discussion of matters of church principles and university governance would have a profound chilling effect on open discourse by professors on this campus and through the Concordia University system," wrote Princeton University professor Keith Whittington in the AFA letter.

"CUW's apparent suspension of Schulz without any semblance of due process violates university policy and the terms of Schulz's contract. FIRE accordingly calls on CUW to immediately reinstate Schulz and ensure any misconduct investigation adheres to CUW's binding commitments to due process and academic freedom," wrote FIRE's Aaron Terr, requesting a response from Cario by March 11.

Controversy Flares Amid Presidential Search

Schulz is a retired U.S. Air Force lieutenant colonel who has two PhDs and teaches for a seminary PhD program. Awarded for his teaching prowess, Schulz has also presented his academic work in universities from England to Hong Kong. The 40th anniversary of his ordination as a minister, he said, will occur this coming summer.

"It's a wonderful responsibility teaching immortal souls in this age group," he told The Federalist of his work at Concordia.

Schulz was selected as one of 11 candidates the synod gave Concordia Wisconsin from which to pick a new president. The synod is the ultimate authority over the university. Yet the university's board of regents decided to dump the synod's candidate list and start a new search, adding social justice commitments.

Schulz's article that preceded his suspension focused on the university's use of racially charged language in its criteria for a new president. That article, which came out in

Christian News four days before Schulz's suspension and was cited in his suspension letter, criticizes the university's Board of Regents for "publicly announcing their determination to have a president who exhibits a 'demonstrated belief in and commitment to equity and inclusion' and who promotes racialized 'diversity in all its myriad forms.'" These criteria are in the university's "Presidential Prospectus."

"While there is no systemic racism at Concordia because we are committed to Christ incarnate and His universal justification of all human beings without exception, there certainly is systemic Woke–ism," Schulz writes in the article.

In the Feb. 18 letter to Schulz suspending him, obtained by The Federalist, Cario accuses Schulz of "Insubordination; lying to administration about actions taken," "Conduct unbecoming a Christian," and "Not following faculty grievance or dispute process." The letter also refers to "several complaints from students and at least one from a faculty member" apparently through the university's bias and harassment reporting system.

Bias Reports Instead of Repentance

While Cario declined through a university spokeswoman Federalist requests for comment, he wrote of the situation to students and faculty on Feb. 24: "Despite my effort to meet with the individual outside of class time to discuss the situation using biblical principles as outlined in Matthew 18, my request was rejected."

Menuge and Schulz said this, and claims Schulz did not bring his concerns to the administration before his Christian News article, are false. It was amid his attempts to schedule a meeting with Cario to discuss the article that Schulz was suddenly suspended, Schulz and Menuge said. Menuge said he was copied on multiple emails verifying this.

Schulz said he also offered several times—via verifiable emails—to meet with the university's Board of Regents and with Cario to discuss his concerns about the university's dive into "woke" policies and language. He said these attempts were ignored. So, because his university's endorsement of racism has been public, Schulz said, his criticism has also been public, in line with the

Bible's command in 1 Timothy 5.

"You don't practice woke procedures against people who are bringing up issues of urgent discussion," Schulz said. "I suppose that maybe to make a point what I should have done was just kept entering complaints on that God-awful bias reporting system on the website. But that's not the way real people should operate."

The Reconciliation That Wasn't

Schulz and Cario attended a Feb. 25 "reconciliation" meeting moderated by the most immediate church authority over the situation, Rev. Dr. John Wille. At the meeting, "There was no engagement with scripture nor was there any engagement with the arguments in my essay. In fact there was no discussion at all except this discussion of privileging and hurt feelings," Schulz said.

Rev. Dr. Peter Scaer, a seminary professor who attended as Schulz's witness, told The Federalist that while the meeting did not resolve the conflict, it "clarified things for me. It became patently obvious that the charges against Schulz are ridiculous. And by the end of the meeting I said, 'Is this all you guys got? I'm not angry about these things, but when the church sees this, nobody's going to take this seriously.'"

Scaer described the charges against Schulz as "petty," based on "feelings," and most importantly ignoring the core issue of Concordia's apparent indulgence of anti-Christian racial separatism.

"Our goal is to make every effort to encourage and gain repentance from the other side," Schulz said. "I don't accept this notion that everybody is at fault. That's a patronizing notion at this point. I don't think that I've done anything wrong. I'm still willing to accept correction if somebody can point something out scripturally, but I don't think that's going to be forthcoming."

A 'Dispute Resolution Process' Nobody Can Find

The university administration and leaders of its Board of Regents declined to comment to The Federalist for this article, referring inquiries to Lisa Liljegren, the university's assistant vice president for communications. Liljegren sent this statement: "Regarding the suspension of Rev. Dr. Greg Schulz, Concordia University is currently abiding by the Lutheran Church—Missouri Synod dispute resolution process, under the direction of Rev. Dr. John Wille, president of the South Wisconsin District of the LCMS. In conformity with the dispute resolution process, we can share no more information at this time."

Asked for further details about that "process," Liljegren could not provide any information, instead referring The Federalist to the LCMS. Two LCMS spokesmen contacted last week referred The Federalist back to the university and Wille. A voicemail requesting comment left on Wille's cell phone last week was not returned.

LCMS President Rev. Matthew Harrison "is well aware of the challenges the 'woke' culture poses to the church's very valuable institutions. He is deeply committed to the fact that CUW belongs to the congregations of the Synod, and these congregations have entrusted theological supervision of the Universities to the President of the Synod," an LCMS spokesman wrote in a Friday email to The Federalist. "This controversy erupted when the Board of Regents rejected the very capable, theologically competent candidates given to it by the Prior Approval committee. Under Harrison's leadership, the Church has elected similar, highly competent, theologically astute leaders at many of our beloved Concordias, and he intends to see the same at CUW."

None of these entities responsible for the university's governance provided any information about the next steps for resolving Schulz's suspension. So far, a lawsuit has not been filed.

"I hope they figure it out soon because everybody's thinking if that's all it takes—to disagree with the direction of the university—to suspend somebody, then academic freedom means nothing because you can't use it to robustly disagree when you think there's a problem," Menuge said.

Appendix E

Letter of Censure
Academic Freedom Alliance
28 February, 2022

Dear President Cario,

The Academic Freedom Alliance (AFA) is a coalition of faculty members from across the country and across the ideological spectrum who are committed to upholding the principles of academic freedom and professorial free speech.

Principles of free speech include the right of professors to speak in public on matters of public concern without the threat of sanctions by their university employer. We call upon Concordia University Wisconsin to live up to its free speech commitments in the case of Professor Gregory P. Schulz.

Gregory Schulz is a tenured professor of philosophy at Concordia University Wisconsin. He is also a frequent public speaker and writes for a public audience. On February 14, 2022, he published an article at the *Christian News* website on "Woke Dysphoria at Concordia." The article is critical of the general "influence of Woke–ism (that is, a potent cocktail of Progressivism, Neo-Pragmatism, and Marxism)" and is critical in particular of the presidential search for a "disruptive" candidate at Concordia University Wisconsin and the potential conflict between "the Woke agenda" and Lutheran traditions and commitments. On February 19, Professor Schulz was notified by his department chair that he had been suspended. He was subsequently prohibited from entering campus. He has now received notice from your office that he has been suspended pending an investigation into violations of university policy, notably for conduct unbecoming of a Christian and for not acting as a responsible colleague.

I write on behalf of the Academic Freedom Alliance to express our firm view that Professor Schulz should suffer no formal consequences as the result of this published article. For Concordia University Wisconsin to punish Professor Schulz for engaging in a public discussion of matters of church principles and university governance would have a profound chilling effect on open discourse by professors on this campus and through the Concordia University system. There is no question that such public speech is fully protected by traditional principles of academic freedom and professorial free speech widely recognized by American universities and elaborated by the American Association of University Professors. It is true that Concordia University has not chosen to fully embrace those principles in its relationship to its own faculty, but punishing Professor Schulz for this speech would represent a narrowing of protected free speech for faculty that would go far beyond what is necessary to render academic freedom compatible with "the reality of the scriptural Lutheran faith" and would damage the university's ability to operate as an institution of higher education.

The Faculty Handbook explicitly sets out policies respecting academic freedom. The Bylaws of the Lutheran Church—Missouri Synod specifies at 3.10.5.7.3 that appointments of university faculty should be made only with such "limitations of academic freedom" that are necessary to "the religious and confessional nature and aims of the seminary." The Faculty Handbook in Section 4.5 specifically recognizes "individuality of each faculty member and respects the right of faculty to hold diverse opinions," while noting that that the university has "specific expectations regarding the presentation of doctrinal teachings." It expects the faculty to engage in "the pursuit of knowledge through intellectual inquiry," and recognizes the right of faculty even to "present and discuss concepts that conflict with Synodical teachings."

Your letter of suspension points out that the Faculty Handbook also states that "as a responsible colleague, the faculty member has a clear awareness of the position of respect and responsibility that those communities confer upon faculty members" and a responsibility to "limit his/her expression of opinions and convictions" so as to support rather than to hinder "the mission of the institution and of the church." It is likewise true, according to 4.2.C of the Faculty Handbook, that faculty can be terminated for "conduct unbecoming a Christian."

It is a basic component of academic freedom that professors have the right to express themselves on matters of university policy and governance. In its 1994 statement On the Relationship of Faculty Governance to Academic Freedom, the American Association of University Professors stated that the "academic freedom of faculty members includes the freedom to express their views (1) on academic matters in the classroom and in the conduct of research, (2) on matters having to do with their institutions and its policies, and (3) on issues of public interest generally." As the AAUP emphasized in a 2009 report, professors are "institutional citizens," and as such professors should "not be made subject to retribution because the position he or she has advanced on matters relating to governance displeases those in power" nor should they suffer "institutional retaliation" for "expressing a lack of confidence in the institution's trustees or president" or communicating informally by e-mail messages or other channels criticism of institutional policies or governance.

If robust criticism of university governance and policies is understood in itself to be a hindrance to the mission of the university or that participating in an ongoing public debate over the social commitments of the Lutheran church and Lutheran educational institutions is inconsistent with responsibilities of members of the faculty, then the university will have dramatically departed from ordinary understandings of the duties and responsibilities of professors in American universities, including American universities dedicated to a Christian mission. Of course, Professor Schulz has a responsibility not to "advocate a position contrary to that of the Synod," but here he is participating in a public debate on what the implications of the Synod's positions might be for the university. If faculty at the university must refrain from speaking in public about the future of the university and the fidelity of the university's activities to the positions of the Synod, then the university's commitment to the faculty to value their individuality and to engage in intellectual inquiry will be an empty promise.

Speech on such controversial social and political topics can sometimes be heated and disruptive, but universities should be places where scholars can in good faith engage in a robust debate over the principles and commitments of the community. If university leaders are willing to sanction faculty members for such speech, particularly when such speech involves criticisms of university administration, then free intellectual inquiry will be stifled rather than encouraged and the university will not be able to perform its charge of supplying "the higher education services needed to accomplish the mission of the church."

The Academic Freedom Alliance calls on Concordia University Wisconsin to reaffirm and adhere to its principles of academic freedom by making clear that Professor Schulz will not be sanctioned in any way for the publication of his views in this article.

Sincerely,
Keith Whittington
Chair, Academic Committee, Academic Freedom Alliance
William Nelson Cromwell Professor of Politics, Princeton University

Appendix F

Letter of Censure

FIRE—Freedom and Individual Rights in Education
March 4, 2022

Dear President Cario:
The Foundation for Individual Rights in Education (FIRE), a nonpartisan nonprofit dedicated to defending liberty, freedom of speech, due process, academic freedom, legal equality, and freedom of conscience on America's college campuses, is concerned that Concordia University Wisconsin (CUW) has suspended Professor Gregory Schulz without prior notice or adequate opportunity to respond to the alleged misconduct, for an article in which he criticized CUW for actions inconsistent with its religious purpose.

CUW's apparent suspension of Schulz without any semblance of due process violates university policy and the terms of Schulz's contract. FIRE accordingly calls on CUW to immediately reinstate Schulz and ensure any misconduct investigation adheres to CUW's binding commitments to due process and academic freedom.

I. CUW Suspends Schulz for Article Critical of University Administration

The following is our understanding of the pertinent facts. We appreciate you may have additional information to offer and invite you to share it with us. Gregory Schulz is a full professor of philosophy at CUW. In its February 14, 2022 issue, Christian News published an article by Schulz entitled "Woke Dysphoria at Concordia," which was posted on its website the following day.1 In the article, Schulz criticized CUW for "coming under the influence of Wokeism (that is, a potent cocktail of Progressivism, Neo-Pragmatism, and Marxism)," which Schulz argued is antithetical to the university's Lutheran foundation. In particular, Schulz criticized the university's presidential search, expressing concern the board of regents seeks to install a "disruptive" and "transformational" president who would be "radically different from spiritual and educational leadership as authoritatively described in the Scriptures."[1]

In the early afternoon of Friday, February 18, you emailed Schulz requesting that he attend a meeting that afternoon to discuss the article. Schulz responded at 3:15 PM, noting he had not seen the email until then because he had been teaching classes and visiting with students scheduled to meet during his posted office hours.[2] Schulz further noted he was on his way to teach his third class of the day, but said he would be available for a meeting the following Monday. In response, you told Schulz his "request" was denied, and that you would see him at 4:00 PM.[3] That meeting did not happen because Schulz was

---

[1] *Id.*

[2] Email from Rev. Gregory Schulz, Professor of Philosophy, Concordia Univ. Wisc., to Dr. William Cario, Interim President, Concordia Univ. Wisc. (Feb. 18, 2022, 3:15 PM) (on file with author).

not able to access that email until after his final class of the day and after speaking with a student who asked to speak with him immediately after that class. That student visit lasted until 4:30.

That same day, you and Executive Vice President and Chief Operating Officer Allen Prochnow sent Schulz a memorandum notifying him he was suspended pending an investigation into multiple allegations of misconduct, including insubordination, conduct unbecoming a Christian, disclosure of confidential information, and not following various limitations on academic freedom.[4] The memo directed Schulz to stay off campus, to refrain from contacting any other employees, students, or individuals associated with CUW without your permission, and to immediately and publicly recant the article or face further sanctions including the possibility of termination.

Since Schulz was locked out of the university's online system thereafter, it was not until his lawyer formally requested any documentation of suspension on Monday, February 20, 2022, that Schulz received access to the memorandum.

II. CUW's Suspension of Schulz Violates His Right to Due Process

CUW imposed severe sanctions on Schulz—removing him from the classroom and campus—before providing sufficient notice or adequate opportunity to respond to your allegations.

CUW's actions represent an unacceptable departure from its commitment to due process.

A. CUW promises faculty due process.

Schulz's contract with CUW incorporates language from the faculty handbook stating the "fundamental purpose of due process regarding academic freedom responsibilities is to protect the academic freedom of the faculty member and to uphold the policies and positions of the institution."[5] The contract further provides CUW is "responsible for maintaining clearly stated procedures for due process that include the process described in the most current [Lutheran Church Missouri Synod] handbook."[6]

The Concordia University System Model Operating Procedures Manual is intended to serve as a uniform process for resolution of all complaints against faculty members and all campus disputes involving faculty and administration.[7] All Concordia University System institutions must "have policies in place that are 'consistent with' this Model Operating Procedure Manual."[8]

The manual specifies extensive procedures for resolving complaints against faculty members, including but not limited to allegations of insubordination

---

[3] Email from Cario to Schulz (Feb. 18, 2022, 3:31 PM) (on file with author).

[4] Memorandum from Cario and Allen Prochnow, Exec. Vice President and Chief Operating Officer, Concordia Univ., to Schulz, Feb. 18, 2022 (on file with author).

[5] Concordia Univ. Wisc. & Ann Arbor, Agreement Between Concordia University and Gregory Schulz (2020) (on file with author).

[6] *Id.*

[7] CONCORDIA UNIV. SYS., MODEL OPERATING PROCEDURES MANUAL § I.B (2019) ["MOPM"] (on file with author).

[8] MOPM § I.A. Neither the faculty handbook nor documents available on CUW's website set forth CUW's specific procedures, but whatever procedures CUW uses must at least be consistent with those in the model policy, as well as the ordinary understanding of "due process." [10] MOPM § V.

and conduct unbecoming a Christian.[10] Those procedures include an initial face-to-face meeting to attempt to resolve the matter informally; if informal reconciliation efforts fail, a "written statement" of "efforts that have been made to achieve informal reconciliation," must be forwarded to the board of regents and the respondent; an opportunity for the respondent to submit a written reply within 21 days; formation of a five-person review committee; and a formal hearing.[9] Only the board of regents—not the president—may relieve a respondent of teaching and/or administrative duties pending final resolution of the conflict only if the board "decides the matter is of such a nature that the interests of the college or university will best be served" by limiting the activities of the respondent.[10]

Beyond this, the term "due process" generally refers to the legal suite of significant procedural protections to which individuals are entitled when government authorities, including public universities, subject them to adjudicatory proceedings.[11] Thus, while CUW is a private institution, its invocation of the term "due process" in Schulz's contract and the faculty handbook[12] reflects its promise to provide more than the minimal—or no—process generally owed by private institutions, and places its faculty on par with their counterparts at public institutions. The United States Supreme Court has held that a "tenured public employee is entitled to oral or written notice of the charges against him, an explanation of the employer's evidence, and an opportunity to present his side of the story."[13] Notice and a meaningful opportunity to be heard are the most basic requirements of due process.[14]

Before suspending or imposing any other sanction on Schulz, CUW must at least afford him these elementary procedures; otherwise, CUW's contractual promise of due process is meaningless and contrary to basic legal principles of contract interpretation.[15]

---

[9] MOPM §§ V.1.2, V.2.1, V.2.2, V.3, V.4.

[10] MOPM § V.3.3.

[11] *Due Process,* MERRIAM-WEBSTER, https://www.merriam-webster.com/dictionary/due%20process (last visited Mar. 2, 2022) [https://perma.cc/GKP5-3DT5] ("A course of formal proceedings (such as legal proceedings) carried out regularly and in accordance with established rules and principles — called also *procedural due process.*"); *see also Mathews v. Eldridge,* 424 U.S. 319, 334–35 (1976).

[12] CONCORDIA UNIV., FACULTY HANDBOOK § 4.5.E (2021-2022).

[13] *Cleveland Bd. of Educ. v. Loudermill,* 470 U.S. 532, 546 (1985). While, again, CUW is a private institution, the Constitution's guarantee of due process to individuals facing governmental deprivation of a liberty or property interest sets a baseline for what faculty would reasonably expect from a university, such as CUW, that promises due process.

[14] *Mullane v. Cent. Hanover Bank & Trust Co.,* 339 U.S. 306, 314 (1950) (notice is "[a]n elementary and fundamental requirement of due process"); *Mathews,* 424 U.S. at 333 ("The right to be heard before being condemned to suffer grievous loss of any kind, even though it may not involve the stigma and hardships of a criminal conviction, is a principle basic to our society. The fundamental requirement of due process is the opportunity to be heard at a meaningful time and in a meaningful manner.") (cleaned up); *see also Joint AntiFascist Refugee Comm. v. McGrath,* 341 U.S. 123, 171 (1951) (Frankfurter, J., concurring) ("The validity and moral authority of a conclusion largely depend on the mode by which it was reached.... No better instrument has been devised for arriving at truth than to give a person in jeopardy of serious loss notice of the case against him and opportunity to meet it.").

[15] *See Stubbe v. Guidant Mut. Ins. Co.,* 651 N.W.2d 318, 323 (Wis. Ct. App. 2022) ("contract should be construed whenever possible so that ... none of the language is discarded as superfluous or meaningless") (cleaned up).

B. CUW failed to provide Schulz sufficient notice or an adequate opportunity to respond to the charges.

CUW's suspension of Schulz is inconsistent with the procedures in the Model Operating Procedure Manual and with commonly understood principles of due process reflected in decades of judicial decisions.

Suspension is a punishment, and not a light one, entitling Schulz to due process *before* it is imposed.[16] Schulz is unable to teach his classes or even communicate with his students or other faculty members. Each day of the suspension that goes by is a further disruption to Schulz's career as an educator and to his relationships with his students and colleagues.

Before suspending Schulz, CUW failed to give him proper notice of the charges—including an explanation of how his speech or conduct violated university policies—and an adequate opportunity to respond to them, let alone anything resembling the process outlined in the Model Operating Procedures Manual.

Your February 18 email to Schulz requesting that he meet with you that same day to discuss the *Christian News* article did not constitute sufficient notice or provide Schulz a meaningful opportunity to respond to the charges, nor was it a reasonable attempt to resolve the matter through an informal face-to-face meeting. By notifying Schulz of allegations of misconduct and giving him mere hours to meet in person to address them—amid a busy schedule of teaching classes and fulfilling other professional obligations—then abruptly suspending Schulz instead of accepting his offer to meet the next business day, CUW has failed to adhere to its due process obligations.

There also is no credible argument that Schulz's presence on campus would pose any type of threat or danger justifying an interim suspension, as the allegations against him arise merely from his authorship of an article critical of the university.[17] There is no reason why Schulz cannot continue to teach and perform his other job duties while CUW investigates his alleged wrongdoing. Moreover, the Model Operating Procedures Manual places authority in the board of regents—not the president—to decide whether to remove a faculty member from teaching or administrative duties pending an investigation.

III. Conclusion

As CUW recognizes, due process is "fundamental" to protecting faculty members' academic freedom. Schulz's academic freedom, including the freedom to criticize university governance, is exactly what is at stake here, as CUW purports to "value[] the individuality of each faculty member and respect[] the right of faculty to hold diverse opinions" and to maintain that "pursuit of knowledge through intellectual inquiry and research is highly valued as a mark of institutional excellence"—including recognition of the right of faculty members even to "present and discuss concepts that conflict with Synodical teachings."[18] To

---

[16] *See Goss v. Lopez*, 419 U.S. 565, 579 (1975) ("[T]here can be no doubt that at a minimum [the words of the Due Process Clause] require that deprivation of life, liberty, or property by adjudication be preceded by notice and opportunity for a hearing appropriate to the nature of the case.").

[17] FACULTY HANDBOOK, *supra* note 14, §§ 4.5.B, 4.5.C; *see also* AM. ASS'N OF UNIV. PROFESSORS, ON THE RELATIONSHIP OF FACULTY GOVERNANCE TO ACADEMIC FREEDOM (1994), *available at* https://www.aaup.org/report/relation ship-faculty-governance-academic-freedom

[18] [https://perma.cc/UF66-7EDJ] (recognizing that in matters of institutional governance, it is "essential that faculty members have the academic freedom to express

the extent CUW alleges that Schulz's *Christian News* article falls within any of the university's express "limitations" on academic freedom or violates any other university policy, CUW must provide Schulz with a meaningful opportunity to respond to those allegations before imposing any sanctions.[19]

Given the urgent nature of this matter, we request receipt of a response to this letter no later than the close of business on March 11, 2022, confirming that CUW will immediately lift all sanctions placed on Schulz, return him to the classroom, and ensure that any investigation of alleged wrongdoing fully complies with CUW policy and its contractually binding commitments to due process and academic freedom.

Sincerely,
Aaron Terr
Senior Program Officer, Individual Rights Defense Program

---

their professional opinions without fear of reprisal" and that "grounds for thinking an institutional policy desirable or undesirable must be heard and assessed if the community is to have confidence that its policies are appropriate"). We further note that Concordia is accredited by the Higher Learning Commission, whose standards require that each accredited institution be "committed to academic freedom and freedom of expression in the pursuit of truth in teaching and learning." HIGHER LEARNING COMM'N, CRITERIA FOR ACCREDITATION (rev. June 2014), *available at* https://www.hlcom mission.org/Policies/criteria-and-core-components.html [https://perma.cc/3JBF2TJC]; *see also* Peter Bonilla, *An accreditor tells an institution to do better on academic freedom. Will more follow?*, FIRE (Nov. 12, 2021), https://www.the fire.org/an-accreditor-tells-an-institution-to-do-better-onacademic-freedom-will-more-follow (discussing the Higher Learning Commission's decision to place Southwest Baptist University on probation in part because the meaning of the university's stated commitment to academic freedom was unclear).

[19] While notice and an opportunity to respond generally must precede a suspension, courts have recognized an exception to this rule in exigent circumstances, where the presence of the accused "poses a continuing danger to persons or property or an ongoing threat of disrupting the academic process." *Haidak v. Univ. of Massachusetts-Amherst*, 933 F.3d 56, 72 (1st Cir. 2019) (citing *Goss*, 419 U.S. at 582–83).

Appendix G

Concordia University Wisconsin must reinstate professor suspended without due process for article critical of university's 'woke dysphoria'

Aaron Terr
thefire.org
8 March 2022

Add Concordia University Wisconsin to the list of universities that use the backward and unjust tactic of "punish now, investigate later."

CUW abruptly suspended professor Gregory Schulz days after he wrote an article critical of the university, without giving him a meaningful opportunity to answer university allegations of misconduct. FIRE wrote to CUW on March 4, calling on the university to immediately reinstate Schulz and adhere to its binding commitments to due process and academic freedom.

In the Feb. 14 issue of Christian News, Schulz wrote an article entitled "Woke Dysphoria at Concordia." Schulz's article criticized CUW for "coming under the influence of Woke–ism (that is, a potent cocktail of Progressivism, NeoPragmatism, and Marxism)," which he argued is a departure from the university's Lutheran foundation.

On Friday, Feb. 18, CUW President William Cario emailed Schulz requesting that he attend a meeting that afternoon to discuss the article. Schulz responded at 3:15 p.m., noting he had not seen the email until then because he was teaching classes and visiting with students during his posted office hours. Schulz said he was on his way to teach his third class of the day and offered to meet the following Monday. Cario responded, "Request denied. I will see you at 4pm, Greg." Schulz did not see Cario's response until after that time because he was teaching.

That same day, Cario sent Schulz notice that he was suspended pending an investigation into multiple allegations of misconduct stemming from the article, including "conduct unbecoming a Christian," disclosure of confidential information, and failure to adhere to various limitations on academic freedom.

Not only did CUW relieve Schulz of his teaching duties, it barred him from campus, prohibited him from contacting any faculty, students, or other members of the CUW community without Cario's permission, and demanded that he publicly "recant" the article or face potential further sanctions, including termination.

All this because Schulz wrote an article expressing disappointment with his university. If that doesn't seem like the type of thing that justifies immediately booting a professor off campus and imposing a gag order without even giving him an opportunity to defend himself, that's because it isn't.

As FIRE's letter explains, CUW abdicated its commitment to due process, which is memorialized in Schulz's contract and the faculty handbook. As we wrote (footnote omitted):

Suspension is a punishment, and not a light one, entitling Schulz to due process *before* it is imposed. Schulz is unable to teach his classes or even communicate with his students or other faculty members. Each day of the suspension that goes by is a further disruption to Schulz's career as an educator and to his relationships with his students and colleagues.

Before suspending Schulz, CUW failed to honor the basic elements of due process, including proper notice of the charges and adequate opportunity to respond to them, let alone anything resembling the extensive procedures (such as formation of a review committee and a formal hearing) that are outlined in the university's policies for handling complaints and campus disputes.

The president's emails to Schulz on the day he was suspended fall far short of what due process requires. As FIRE told CUW:

> By notifying Schulz of allegations of misconduct and giving him mere hours to meet in person to address them—amid a busy schedule of teaching classes and fulfilling other professional obligations—then abruptly suspending Schulz instead of accepting his offer to meet the next business day, CUW has failed to adhere to its due process obligations.

Interim suspensions may be warranted in rare circumstances where, for instance, an individual's continued presence on campus presents a safety threat. That rationale obviously has no relevance in this case.

Schulz's suspension also raises serious concerns about his academic freedom, which traditionally encompasses the freedom to criticize institutional governance. While CUW is a private religious institution, it makes promises of academic freedom in Schulz's contract and the faculty handbook, including "the right of faculty to hold diverse opinions" and to "present and discuss concepts that conflict with Synodical teachings." Granted, the university also purports to limit academic freedom in certain ways. For instance, a faculty member "acknowledges that in certain situations he/she will voluntarily limit his/her expression of opinions and convictions ... so that the mission of the institution and of the church is supported rather than hindered." But CUW cannot treat this as a license to suppress all criticism of the administration, or else its affirmative promises of academic freedom are rendered meaningless.

At a minimum, given CUW's commitment to due process, which the university states has a "fundamental purpose" of protecting academic freedom, it is incumbent on CUW to explain to Schulz how his speech allegedly violated any institutional policies and to allow him to respond *before* imposing any sanctions. Instead, CUW has put the cart of punishment before the horse of investigation.

This is part of an unfortunate trend. Author John K. Wilson recently inveighed against "preemptive suspensions" and the damage they cause:

> Over and over again, universities respond to allegations of misconduct with a routine practice that violates due process, endangers academic freedom, and all too often punishes the innocent: The preemptive suspension made before any hearing. For any accusation of wrongdoing, the knee-jerk response of many administrators seems to be to suspend the alleged culprits first and figure out the facts later. It's a practice that inherently violates basic concepts of justice, and it's particularly

alarming in higher education when the suspension is a response to the expression of controversial views.

FIRE agrees wholeheartedly.

Wilson suggests that administrators "love suspensions because they take the heat off: They allow the university to 'do something' about a public embarrassment while still maintaining the facade of academic freedom and due process." Administrators may be concerned about their public image or frustrated by harsh criticism, but they have no excuse for abdicating their responsibility to protect student and faculty rights.

FIRE calls on CUW to immediately lift all sanctions placed on Schulz, return him to the classroom, and adhere to its contractually binding commitments to due process and academic freedom.

Appendix H

Letter to the Board of Regents from LCMS President

May 9, 2022
Monday of Easter IV, A.D. 2022

Dear members of the CUWAA Board of Regents,

Grace and peace to you in this holy Eastertide, where the joy and hope of resurrection and restoration pervades all that we do! It is in this resurrection confidence that I write this letter. Before I write some hard things, I want to note that Dr. Cario and his team were very accommodating and cordial to our visitation team of 10. We were granted access and treated well, and there was no effort to restrict staff, student, and faculty access to our interviews. There are many truly great things going on at CUWAA. A full report of the findings and conclusions of the visitation team are forthcoming, but I wanted to send you this letter in advance of your May 12 Board of Regents (BOR) meeting, previewing some of our findings and giving you a clear path forward. My primary concerns are fourfold: Bylaw violations, mission drift, faculty frustrations, and loss of trust from the Synod.

Bylaw violations

In addition to the concerns about Bylaw violations that I expressed to you in my Oct. 13, 2021, email— further expressed in my March 9, 2022, letter to Dr. Cario outlining the reasons and purpose of my visit—the visitation team uncovered the following concerns.

- First, in violation of 3.10.6.4 (g), the BOR impermissibly delegated its responsibility fully to participate in the selection of a president. The selection of a search committee is specifically required by the Bylaws in 3.10.6.6.2 (b)(1), but it must be done in a manner consistent with 3.10.6.4 (g).
- The BOR violated 3.10.6.6.2 (b)(1). The Search Committee was comprised of 15 members of which only six members of the Search Committee were Regents. The rest were advisors, faculty, and staff. This created a situation where Search Committee votes could be determined without a single Regent voting in favor of a proposed action. It was a breach of fiduciary duty to commingle its authority in this way with a body that included a majority of non-board members. (Bylaw 3.10.6.5: "under no circumstances shall a board delegate its authority to, nor commingle its authority with, any other body that includes non-board members.")
- In violation of Bylaw 3.10.6.6.2 (b)(2), the BOR delegated all responsibility for preparing the Presidential Prospectus to Gretchen Jameson. Input from the BOR was not sought.
- In violation of Bylaw 3.10.6.6.2 (b)(3), the Search Committee delegated the development of written criteria to screen candidates to the executive board of the Search Committee, without input or approval of the BOR. The visitation team found that the screening criteria were created by Kimberly Masenthin based on the Presidential Prospectus

prepared by Gretchen Jameson.
- The Search Committee then took upon itself to engage in a screening and notification process that was in direct contravention to the Bylaws. Polzin has been clear that he doesn't like the current process set forth in the Bylaws. He prefers a process from an older version of the Bylaws that allowed the Search Committee to prescreen nominees before sending them on to the Prior Approval Panel. The direction he gave to the Search Committee throughout this process seems to be in line with his stated preference instead of with the current Bylaws.
- On Oct. 4, 2021, in an email to Gerhard Mundinger, Richard Laabs informed him that he believed they were following the Bylaws, that Polzin was used to interpret the Bylaws, and that a package of information would be sent to all Regents that included the full list of 38 nominees and the 11 men approved by the Prior Approval Panel. It seems that, at no time, was Laabs or Polzin willing to admit that only those nominees approved by the Prior Approval Panel were the only names the BOR could consider. They continued to push forward the names of men and women who had not been approved and desired to choose a man from the pool of the 38 names, not the 11. Most of the 11 were informed they would, in fact, not be considered. And to this very hour, board leadership has refused to interview ANY candidate approved, including the three candidates both on the Prior Approval Panel's list AND the Regents-preferred short list. This act gravely dishonored the 11 candidates officially approved, especially belittled candidates from the CUWAA theology and philosophy departments, and precipitated the Schultz matter.
- July 2021 changes to the faculty handbook include referring to the president with the pronouns "he or she" and "his or her," in violation of the teaching of Holy Scripture that spiritual and doctrinal oversight in the church and its universities is given to qualified men. Accordingly, Commission on Constitutional Matter rulings have consistently ruled that presidents of CUS schools must be qualified men. Mr. Polzin's errant council to the Regents, even after I spoke at length with the Regents in person, about this matter, is unacceptable.

Mission drift

CUWAA is a tremendous institution. The positives are many. But throughout our visit, concerned faculty, staff, and students expressed concern over the introduction of secular diversity, equity, and inclusion language and initiatives into the mission of the university. This philosophy is laden with ideas antagonistic to the sacred Scriptures, including great lies about human sexuality and race. Much of this seems to have been promoted and pushed by administrators and faculty who are no longer at the school. This, along with the presidential search, pose a unique opportunity for the university to reassert its Lutheran identity and mission; identify, define, and embrace diversity that is intentionally biblical (all are created in the very image of God, and each worth the very blood of Christ); and give the theological faculty a greater role and responsibility in shaping the Lutheran ethos of the institution and catechizing new faculty in a Lutheran worldview.

Consider the example of Grove City College in Grove City, Penn., formerly affiliated with the Presbyterian church, now a self-described conservative Christian college with a Christ-centered mission. When concerns about the infiltration of Critical Race Theory into the mission and instruction of the college became public last year, the college owned up to ways in which it had drifted from its mission, appointed a committee to investigate concerns, and developed a plan to move back to its institutional Christo-centricity. Concordia University Wisconsin and Ann Arbor has such an opportunity right now, in the midst of a presidential search, to acknowledge past mistakes and move intentionally back to its clear Lutheran mission.

The Regents have consistently rejected the input of the elected pastors on the BOR and of my representative. They are seasoned men. They know the Scriptures and they are all deeply concerned about mission drift. The Regents reject the advice of the South Wisconsin District president, who is a voting member of the BOR and is likewise concerned about mission drift. I fear you will continue to reject my advice, to the continued detriment of Concordia and our life together.

Faculty frustrations

Our visitation team included educational, legal, corporate, and ecclesiastical experts. We interviewed some 80 individuals. It has become very apparent to the visitation team that many of the faculty of CUWAA are deeply frustrated. The theological faculty feels marginalized. Two prominent members of the theology department have left for other institutions; there may be other departures soon. LCMS Lutherans in other departments have expressed similar concerns. Recently, several faculty members have reached out to the CUS board and members of the visitation team to voice their concerns over new language in the updated faculty contracts, which they feel makes them more disposable and susceptible to firing without due process. As the premier university in the Concordia system, CUWAA has enjoyed the strongest of theological and philosophy faculties. The science faculty is also very strong and faithful.

Loss of trust from the Synod

As a result of these very significant concerns, some of which have been made public across the Synod and in news reports beyond the church, many pious laypeople and congregations of the Synod have lost trust in the university's faithfulness to genuine Lutheranism and her mission to raise up both church workers and faithful citizens in other vocations, all while reaching the lost with the Gospel of Christ.

A Path Forward

1 Here is my proposal for a clear path forward—from confusion and uncertainty back to the proudly confessional Lutheran mission for which the university was once known.

2 Richard Laabs and Mark Polzin should resign from the Board of Regents. Their demonstrated unwillingness to abide by the Bylaws and their inability to oversee the presidential search process in a manner that inspires the trust of the Synod at large, have hampered the institution too long.

3 The BOR should restart the presidential search with the three

candidates plus additional members of the CUWAA theological faculty from the list of 11 men approved by the Prior Approval Panel. CUWAA clearly needs a competent, compassionate theologian at the helm. My time interviewing faculty and staff made this painfully obvious to me. With no overall clarity and scriptural critique, secular ideas involving critical theory, inclusion, and equity have found harbor on campus. The new president can add to his staff those who are capable of assisting him with administering the $100 million budget of the institution. However, to prioritize demonstrated competence in managing a budget of this size at the cost of eliminating from consideration for the CUWAA presidency very competent theologians is unwise and at odds with the mission of the university.

4 Demonstrate repentance for Bylaw violations and adoption of secular worldviews and agendas. Acknowledge uncritical haste that occurred in adopting language of secular diversity, equity, and inclusion initiatives. Assemble a team from within to assess the pervasiveness of this secular influence. Invite the participation of theologians from CUWAA and the Synod at large. Make use of the considerable abilities of the Synod's Commission on Theology and Church Relations. Use this unique opportunity to craft diversity resources based upon the inerrant Scriptures, without the additional baggage of secular inclusivity initiatives. Produce something of value—for all our universities—that will help us all to be and remain solid, biblically conservative institutions serving the church and her mission, and training young people to have meaningful lives. I stand ready to assist. The Synod stands ready to help.

Jesus is risen from the dead. This is certain. The gates of hell cannot prevail against His church. This, too, is certain. What we do as stewards of His gifts in the interim we do with this confidence. As long as this Synod remains and the people and congregations entrust me with this leadership, I will work to ensure that the Synod and her institutions remain faithful to Scripture and the Confessions; labor toward unity in our stewardship of Christ's gifts; and fight those who oppose our clear and confident proclamation of the crucified and risen Christ. For decades, Concordia has been an ally in this work and fight and an invaluable asset to the church's mission and ministry. I pray that this continues.

In Christ,
Rev. Dr. Matthew C. Harrison,
President The Lutheran Church—Missouri Synod

Appendix I

University Won't Hear Professor It Kicked Out After Criticizing Wokeness

Gregory Schulz
thefederalist.com
16 May 2022

The administration and board of regents at Concordia University Wisconsin has been deathly silent about this widely reported transgression against academic freedom.

Today's academic landscape is littered with the dry bones of academic freedom. This is true of my own religious university, Concordia University Wisconsin (CUW), from which I have been suspended and put under threat of termination for publishing an academic essay critiquing identity politics.

As reported by The Federalist in March, soon after I published that essay, I was banned from campus and put on administrative leave. There I remain three months later, with no clear path to restoration to my post.

This brings to light the adulterous affair with cultural Marxism by CUW's interim president, its Executive Committee of the Board of Regents (BoR), and various professors and staff at my Lutheran Christian university. The presence of this ideology is most notable in the publicly posted desires of the regents' search for a new university president who "believes in and is committed to inclusion and equity" as well as "diversity in all its myriad forms." In other words, they seek a president who supports or is willing to compromise with woke ideology instead of staking everything on Christ and the text of the Bible.

Refusal to Answer Calls for Repentance

Concordia's attack on academic freedom has been publicly denounced in letters from the
Academic Freedom Alliance (AFA) and from the Foundation for Individual Rights in Education (FIRE). It's also been put on alert by The Wisconsin Institute for Law and Liberty and The Federalist.

Stubborn as sin, closemouthed as a grave, our administration and regents have not responded. Nor have they responded to 6,000 pastors and laity online or to the scores of students on campus who have petitioned them to respect academic freedom and reinstate me.

The faculty as a whole has also been deathly silent about this widely reported transgression against academic freedom. There's also been no statement on academic freedom from the church authorities in the Lutheran Church—Missouri Synod (LCMS) responsible for safeguarding the rights of church workers and pastors such as me. There's not been a whisper about the national scandal of CUW's frontal assault on academic freedom, as far as I can tell, from the faculties of other universities of the LCMS. No rattlin' bones.

So why should anyone care? Let me sketch out for you what academic freedom *should* mean. I will identify this problem of dry, silent bones as a moral failure, using Ronald Dworkin's book "Freedom's Law." In his obituary, Dworkin was acknowledged as "the most important and powerful philosopher of law in the English-speaking world."

Academic Freedom in Context

First, there is the urgent need for academic freedom in our context. As Dworkin puts it: "*Academic freedom ... is often defended on the ground that scholars must be free if they are to discover objective truth. But the very possibility of objective truth is now itself under attack from an anti–truth–squad of relativists, subjectivists, neo-Pragmatists, postmodernists, and similar critics now powerful in the unconfident departments of American universities.*"

Dworkin is not saying we should give up the search for absolute truth. Rather, he means that we today have to reckon with the dominance of relativism in higher education. He says relativism provides a pervasive but "deeply confused" challenge to academics and freedom.

Wokeism is a case in point. In my essay that triggered my suspension, "Woke Dysphoria at Concordia," I describe wokeism as "a potent cocktail of Progressivism, Neo-Pragmatism, and Marxism," an ideology that replaces Christ and biblical authority with an "alien politics." For others it is educational foolishness, but in Lutheran circles it is educational heresy, a denial of Christ and his authority by professors, administrators, and board members who heretically trade the priceless inheritance of the Lutheran Reformation for the Soylent Green of Marxist ideology.

Dworkin's observation that the relativism most professors at most Western universities teach and assume today "is deeply confused" is illustrated by the deeply confused manner in which Concordia's interim president speaks about the ideological terms of diversity, inclusion, and equity. You'll notice that Christ and His authoritative Word is simply not part of his daily administrator's vocabulary. His thinking and speaking are not framed by the text of the Bible, nor any other texts. As a consequence, it is deeply confused.

Jesus tells us in no uncertain terms, "Whoever is not with me is against me, and whoever does not gather with me scatters" (Matthew 12:30). In times of persecution and intense cultural pressure, as the Lutheran pastor–professor Dietrich Bonhoeffer taught during the Holocaust, Christians must speak up regarding the universal authority of Jesus in every area of life. Otherwise, they are manifestly against Him and are responsible for scattering the flock.

I regret to point out an obvious conclusion: This administrator's manner of responding to serious questions about my case is just what you would expect if my call for the regents and administration to repent of wokism is on target.

Why Professors Must Have Academic Freedom

Dworkin points out that there are two levels to academic freedom, historically and conceptually speaking: "First, it insulates universities, colleges, and other institutions of higher learning from political institutions… Second, academic freedom insulates scholars from the administrators of their universities."

Academic freedom is a way to ensure that administrators and entire universities act morally and do no harm to academic work. The everyday level of academic freedom keeps administrators from silencing genuine, practicing professors from teaching and preaching with censorship, suspensions, terminations, or other power moves of intimidation and retribution. To paraphrase Wittgenstein's *Tractatus*, Proposition 7, "Whatever can be said authoritatively can be said clearly; whatever cannot be said authoritatively by an administrator, of such matters administrators ought to remain silent."

You can assault academic freedom, but then you will be doing immoral things. Also, you will be making academia—at your university and beyond—inaccessible, unfathomable, and undoable. You will be making the case for potential students and parents, and for taxpayers and pundits who already suspect that higher education is a sham, that universities are in fact irrelevant, a waste of time and money, and thus harmful to everyone.

What my administration is doing to me—and, by extension what it is doing to my students, to my academic colleagues in every Concordia university and beyond—is being visited upon me contrary to the written procedures available to them, without reason, and without appeal to any legitimate authority, but purely on the basis of administrative *power*. They are doing it because they can.

Free Speech Is Tied to Free Consciences

The first level of academic freedom, insulation from political institutions, has everything to do with what we are as a religious institution. The exercise of our institutional academic freedom, a moral imperative, intersects with the exercise of our constitutional right of free exercise of religion, a legal right articulated in an authoritative American text, the First Amendment.

As Dworkin concludes: "Academic freedom and a right to free speech—are closely related in a different way: they form important parts of a system of ideas and institutions that creates a culture of individual intellectual responsibility, and that protects it from disintegrating into a culture of intellectual conformity."

A religious university exists to take a stand *against* a culture of intellectual conformity. The executive committee's fond wishes for a woke *diversity* to take the place of our Concordia Lutheran *University* will come to pass if the administration keeps this up.

Maybe it's already too late. Likely their addiction to government funding and perks, and to the alien politics of Caesar that come along with that funding, is not something they even want to recover from.

Appendix J

Dem Dry Bones: Can Academic Freedom Live Again at My Religious University?

Gregory Schulz

Published in 5 June 2022 Issue of Christian News and The Federalist, 16 May 2022 (in an abbreviated version).

Today's academic landscape is littered with the dry bones of academic freedom—desiccated and disjointed bones. This is true of the landscape at my own religious university, Concordia University Wisconsin (CUW), from which I have been suspended and put under threat of termination for publishing an academic essay. My essay brings to light the adulterous affair with Woke / Social Justice / Marxist ideology on the part of the Interim Administration (Admin), the Executive Committee of the Board of Regents (BoR), and various professors and staff at my Lutheran Christian university, most notably in the publicly posted desires of the BoR's search for a new university president who "believes in and is committed to inclusion and equity" as well as "diversity in all its myriad forms." In other words, for a president who supports or is willing to compromise with Woke / Social Justice / Liberation Theology / Marxist ideology instead of staking everything on Christ and the text of the Bible.

At this moment, there are no rattling sounds about academic freedom; nothing but dry bones at my university. National groups have raised their voices. The Wisconsin Institute for Law and Liberty, for one example. The Federalist for another. Concordia's attack on academic freedom by CUW's Admin and BoR has been publicly denounced in letters from the Academic Freedom Alliance (AFA) and from the Foundation for Individual Rights in Education (FIRE).

Stubborn as sin, closemouthed as a grave, our Admin and BoR have not responded. Nor have they responded to 6000 pastors and laity online or to the scores of students on campus who have petitioned them to respect academic freedom and reinstate me.

The Faculty as a whole has been deathly silent about this widely reported transgression against academic freedom. Not one statement on academic freedom from the church authorities in the Lutheran Church—Missouri Synod (LCMS) responsible for safeguarding the rights of church workers and pastors such as me. Not a whisper about the national scandal of CUW's frontal assault on academic freedom, as far as I can tell, from faculties of other Concordias that make up the Concordia University System of the LCMS. No rattlin' bones.

So why should anyone care? Let me sketch out for you a skeleton of what academic freedom *should* mean. I will identify this problem of dry, silent bones as a moral failure.

All this, using just five sentences from Ronald Dworkin's book *Freedom's Law*. In his obituary Dworkin was acknowledged as "the most important and powerful philosopher of law in the Englishspeaking world." Our five sentences are from Chapter 7, Why Academic Freedom?

Academic freedom in context

First, there is the urgent need for academic freedom in our modern cultural context. As Dworkin puts it in the first two of our five sentences:

"*Academic freedom* ... is often defended on the ground that scholars must be free if they are to discover objective truth. But the very possibility of objective truth is now itself under attack from an anti–truth–squad of relativists, subjectivists, neo-Pragmatists, post-modernists, and similar critics now powerful in the unconfident departments of American universities" (246).

Dworkin is not saying that we should give up the search for absolute truth; rather, he means that we today have to reckon with an overwhelmingly dominant assumption of relativism in higher education.

He also says that relativism provides a pervasive but "deeply confused" challenge to academics and freedom.

Wokeism is a case in point. In my essay Woke Dysphoria at Concordia I describe Wokeism as "a potent cocktail of Progressivism, Neo-Pragmatism, and Marxism," an ideology that replaces Christ and biblical authority with an "alien politics."

For others it is educational foolishness, but in Lutheran circles it is educational heresy, a denial of Christ and His authority by professors, administrators, board members who are being heretical by trading the priceless inheritance of the Lutheran Reformation for the Soylent Green of Marxist ideology.

Dworkin's observation that the relativist challenge which is assumed and taught by most professors at most Western universities in our day "is deeply confused," is illustrated by the deeply confused manner in which Concordia's Interim President speaks about Wokeism and its ideological terms of diversity, inclusion and equity.

As painful and embarrassing as it may be, listen closely to his response a second time and notice what he clearly is *not* talking about. You'll notice that Christ and His authoritative Word is simply not part of his daily, working, administrator's vocabulary. His thinking and speaking are not framed by the text of the Bible, or any other texts. As a consequence, it is deeply confused.

Jesus tells us in no uncertain terms, "Whoever is not with me is against me, and whoever does not gather with me scatters" (Matthew 12:30). In times of persecution and intense cultural pressure, as the Lutheran pastor–professor Dietrich Bonhoeffer taught during the Holocaust, Christians must speak up regarding the universal authority of Jesus in every area of life. Otherwise, they are manifestly against Him and are responsible for scattering the flock.

In dramatic contrast to the Interim President speaking confusedly about the terms of Woke / Marxist ideology, I have been pro-fessing and providing numerous online interviews and elaborations including a three-part series "What Is DIE–versity?" at Luther Classical College.

I regret to point out an obvious conclusion: This administrator's manner of responding to serious questions about my case in light of the university's very public commitment to diversity, inclusion, and equity as essential characteristics of our next President is just what you would expect if my call for the BoR and Admin to repent of Wokism is on target. It is dialectically (and I do mean *dialectically*) opposed to my professorial and pastoral thinking and speaking.

The Interim President's response is precisely the kind of ambivalent non-response (sentence fragments that both say and don't say what Wokeism is, that gesture toward what the LCMS does or doesn't, should or shouldn't teach, and so on) that a BoR intent on installing a president at the university "with a demonstrated belief in and commitment to inclusion and equity" and to "diversity in all its myriad forms" would want to hear from its very own, self-appointed Interim President. It has little to do with teaching and learning at a religious institution of higher education.

At the everyday level, academic freedom should insulate professors from administrators

You begin to see why professors like me should be insulated from administrators, don't you? *In a nutshell, professors pro-fess on the basis of textual authority;* however, *administrators administer on the basis of institutional, financial, hire–and–fire power.*

This leads into my third and fourth sentences from Dworkin. He points out that there are two levels to academic freedom, historically and conceptually speaking:

"First, it insulates universities, colleges, and other institutions of higher learning from political institutions… Second, academic freedom insulates scholars from the administrators of their universities" (246).

Academic freedom is a way to ensure that administrators and entire universities act morally and that they do no harm to those of us doing academic work. The first level, the foundational level, is the institutional level. I will explain that shortly. But first two major points regarding the everyday level.

Major Point #1. With rare exceptions, administrators are long–out–of–practice former professors, or even "deanlets" (Benjamin Ginsberg), that is, persons ambitious to be in charge at universities who put in their time as professors as a means to an end, not as an end in itself.

The second, everyday level of academic freedom provides a kind of force field around professors so that administrators cannot overpower genuine, practicing professors and silence our teaching and preaching, our talking and writing, with censorship, suspensions, terminations, or other power moves of intimidation and retribution.

If a university president has the intellectual horsepower and academic wherewithal to take on a professor's argument, this is noble and good. Let him write a book, publish an article in a refereed journal, provide a lecture or debate the issue. Let there be sacred and lesser canonical texts, passionately and painstakingly unpacked for the good of all! But, to paraphrase Wittgenstein's *Tractatus*, Proposition 7, "Whatever can be said authoritatively can be said clearly; whatever cannot be said authoritatively by an administrator, of such matters administrators ought to remain silent."

Major Point #2. Academic freedom is not a legal right; it's *more* than that: It's a moral imperative.

It's actually the first principle of morality, "First, do no harm!" applied to Western universities from their founding by the church in the Medieval period.

A first principle is a feature of natural law along the lines of that T-shirt slogan about gravity: ACADEMIC FREEDOM IS NOT JUST A NICE IDEA; IT'S A MORAL LAW!

You can assault academic freedom, but then you will be doing immoral things. Also, you will be making academia—at your university and beyond—inaccessible, unfathomable, and undoable. You will be making the case for potential students and parents, and for taxpayers and pundits who already suspect that higher education is a sham, that universities are in fact irrelevant, a waste of time and money, and thus harmful to everyone.

What my administration is doing to me—and, by extension what it is doing to my students, to my academic colleagues in every Concordia university and beyond—is being visited upon me contrary to such written procedures as they had available to them, without reason, and without appeal to any legitimate authority or Authority, but purely on the basis of administrative *power*. Like President Clinton, they are doing it because they can. They are also violating the first principle of morality, remember.

At the foundational level, academic freedom should insulate universities from political institutions

Finally, recall the foundational level of academic freedom. *The first level of academic freedom, insulation from political institutions, has everything to do with what we are as a religious institution.* At this level, it becomes apparent that the exercise of our institutional academic freedom, a moral imperative, intersects with the exercise of our Constitutional rights of free exercise of religion and free speech, legal rights articulated in an authoritative American text, the First Amendment. I expect that the legal minds at WILL, AFA, and FIRE may have something to say about this in regard to my case. But at this point, I must conclude. Look at it this way: Time and again we hear about some educational entrepreneur or other who promotes his new school in the community as a public government school in order to receive government funding and perks, while at the same time promoting his new school in churches as a religious school in order to receive funding and students from them. This is what CUW appears to be doing. For more, see "Lent and Anti-Lent 2022" regarding CUW's entanglement with the political institution of the federal government and its Woke attacks on our children's education and sexuality.

Here is the second reason that academic integrity matters. The university's Admin and BoR's sustained and immoral attack on academic freedom is an effective way simultaneously to disintegrate Concordia internally (by not insulating professors from administrative power plays) and externally, as a religious institution of higher learning (by making CUW a de facto place of political indoctrination).

Hence, our fifth and final sentence. Dworkin concludes:

"Academic freedom and a right to free speech—are closely related in a different way: they form important parts of a system of ideas and institutions that creates a culture of individual intellectual responsibility, and that protects it from disintegrating into a culture of intellectual conformity" (247–248).

A religious university exists to take a stand *against* a culture of intellectual conformity. The Executive Committee's fond wishes for a Woke *Diversity* to take the place of our Concordia Lutheran *University* will come to pass if the Administration keeps this up. Maybe it's already too late. Likely their addiction to government funding and perks—and to the alien politics of Caesar that come along with that funding, is not something they even want to recover from.

Thus, there is good reason to fear that all of us are beginning to feel the full effects of the Administration's assault on Academic Freedom in real time. It's as Jesus told us, "Whoever is not with Me ... scatters." Dem dry bones are not even rattlin'; but this is why *academic freedom matters*.

Appendix K

Response to President's Complaint Seeking My Termination

Rev Gregory P Schulz, DMin, PhD
31 August 2022
The Week of the Eleventh Sunday after Trinity

Dear members of the review committee (and regents who have oversight of this process),

May our Lord grant the five of you and all of us involved in this process the knowledge and wisdom that flows from the fear of the Lord (Prov 1:7 and 9:10). This is my written response to the claim submitted against me and already filed with the secretary of the board of regents by the Interim President of my university, Concordia University Wisconsin (CUW) in his August 11, 2022, document.

Before I begin, let me first express my concern for my onetime colleague who is now taking on the role of my accuser. I am worried for his physical and spiritual health. While I have been offering to talk with the regents since my first open letter to the board chair nearly a year ago, and while I have been writing and publishing and submitting my call for doctrinal repentance to the entire church for its consideration and critique, as necessary—making myself available for the church to question and to cross examine my theology and assertions that the secular and Marxist, etc. dalliance with Wokeism at our university is contrary to biblical and Lutheran doctrine and practice—he has not been able to respond, but only to silence and to threaten. This is not a good sign.

It is also unhealthy for anyone to refuse to repent when he is called on to repent for public, doctrinal transgressions (1 Timothy 5:20). But this is exactly what my former colleague and brother in Christ is doing right now, while at the same time instituting this process of termination of one of his own professors because he cannot come up with any other way to relate to me except on the basis of institutional, financial, hire–and–fire power.

In my essay published in February I called for "personal and institutional repentance" for the secular Wokeism afflicting the consciences of students, faculty, and supporters of Concordia. In his letter published in May our synod president called on the board of regents and Dr. Cario to "demonstrate repentance for ... adoption of secular worldviews and repentance." In June, summarizing the resolutions and prayers of the South Wisconsin District Convention our district president said in his sermon in our university's chapel, "This week the church has come for its university."

At the time I am writing this response there has been no repentance whatever expressed by the board. "The board" includes our interim president, my accuser, who has an executive role. As our LCMS Handbook says of our Concordia presidents, "The president of the institution shall be *the executive officer of the board of regents*. He shall serve as the spiritual, academic, and administrative head of the institution" (3.10.6.6, my italics).

Bill and I are of a similar vintage, I believe, so we are probably both keeping an eye out for the health concerns that befall us as we approach the "threescore years and ten" mark. I gather (although I cannot know for certain) that the stress of this Woke business may have already led to serious health problems for two board members, so I am urging the board members who are reviewing my response to have some urgent and prayerful conversation among yourselves. Lean on the called and ordained pastors in your midst. Show genuine Christian care and love for your executive officer. The problem here is not politics or even reconciliation; actually, it's repentance: Law and Gospel, contrition–plus–faith–in–Christ–plus–fruit–of–faith *repentance* (Apology, 12). This is what the majority of the board and your executive officer are refusing to do. This refusal is not healthy. Some of us are thinking of 1 Corinthians 11:30 in this regard.

One more thing. If the board determines to move forward with Dr. Cario's complaint by establishing a review committee, there is a priority of concerns which you on the committee will need to address. While it is true that my livelihood is on the line, let me urge the members of the committee to keep in mind the two even more important dimensions of your work: First, there is the real matter at hand which is the *doctrinal matter* of replacing the means of grace with the alien politics and ideology of Wokeism. Second, there is the chilling effect that terminating me will have on professors and their teaching here at CUW as well as at our few remaining Concordia universities. There is reason to think that, because of the interim president's treatment of me, already the fear of the Lord in faculty members is being replaced with fear of the administration and its God-awful bias reporting apparatus. These two matters, doctrine and the chilling effect on faculty, are more important than my status.

For my part, I am good to go. I certainly am no Martin Luther, but I am a well-trained and experienced confessional Lutheran pastor and professor. I recognize a "Here I stand" moment for standing on God's Word alone when I see one. I have dedicated myself to being a faithful theologian of the cross. As Luther says in his 1517 Heidelberg Disputation, "a theologian of the cross calls a thing what it is."

As I said in the February reconciliation meeting, "It means very little to me that you or any human court should cross-examine me. I don't even ask myself questions. I have a clear conscience, but that doesn't mean I have God's approval. It is the Lord who cross-examines me…" (1 Co 4:3ff). I do not know what vow, if any, the interim president has taken as a certified religious teacher. For my part, I know that I have been fulfilling my vow publicly as a divinely called pastor: to preach, teach, and confess according to the Holy Scriptures and the Lutheran Confessions. The church with her pastors and pious laypeople, and those in leadership have already expressed their agreement with my confession against Wokeism at our Concordia university.

It is because I have been faithfully teaching and confessing in line with the Holy Scriptures and the Lutheran Confessions that I am now facing termination—in a procedure to be overseen by an unrepentant board of regents under the leadership of an unrepentant interim president who was selected for his position by that same board.

Precis / Preview

As my response below shows, the complaint that the interim president / executive officer of the board has filed seeking my termination is, in its very essence, *disingenuous*. It is disingenuous in the way it is framed, and it is disingenuous in its particulars. It is *the text of the complaint* that I am referring to, not the complainant's heart, of course (1 Sam 16:17)

The complaint is *disingenuous* in both senses of the term: it withholds relevant information, and it gives a false impression concerning the claimant's own actions, the university's governing policies, and Holy Scripture, including Matthew 18.

As I illustrate in graphic detail in my response and analysis below, the complaint disingenuously omits to mention the 9 May Letter to members of the CUWAA Board of Regents (the Letter) from the president of the university's church body. This Letter urges the board and its executive officer, my accuser, to repent of their adulterous affair with the secular ideology of Wokeism and to take appropriate and specific action to bring forth the fruit of repentance. As I write, it is nearly four months now that the board with its executive officer, our interim president, has failed to repent. You may ask, "Why is the complaint's omission of the Letter relevant?"

Here is one example, which I elaborate in my response: On the first page of his documentation dated August 11, 2022, my accuser frames his charges against me as the unavoidable consequences of "a difficult and, sadly, public personnel issue regarding Dr Gregory Schulz" which "over the last several months, Concordia University has had to contend with." But this directly contradicts the Letter in which our synod's president points out that it is the board and its rogue search committee who are responsible for the matter that Concordia university has had to contend with over the last several months. The uncritical promotion of secular Wokeism is responsible for the university's difficulties. From the Letter: "The Search Committee took it upon itself to engage in a screening and notification process that was in direct contravention to the Bylaws ... This act gravely dishonored the 11 candidates officially approved ... and precipitated the Schultz (sic) matter."

There are two fundamental problems with the complaint, according to the printed words and previous and current actions of my accuser. As my response shows, (1) the complaint exhibits a fundamental and persistent disregard for authoritative texts. It is disingenuous in its offhanded use of, or rather its failure, to submit to the greater authoritative texts: Holy Scripture (for example, Mat 18) and the Lutheran Confessions (for example, Luther's teaching on the Eighth Commandment in his *Large Catechism*).

True to form, the complaint is disingenuous in its selective use of the lesser authoritative texts (that is, the governed–by–Scripture–and–the–Confessions texts) as well, such as The Manual, The Faculty Handbook, and my Faculty Contract, which depend on the authority of Scripture and the Lutheran Confessions for their proper definitions, interpretation, and application at the university.

In addition to its disregard for authoritative texts, my response shows that (2) the complaint proceeds as if what is the case is not really the case. According to the correspondence understanding of truth, which is the understanding of truth held by the Scriptures and our Lutheran Confessions alike, "To say that what is the case is not the case, or to say that what is not the case is the case, is to speak a lie, (*pseudos* in Greek)" (Aristotle, *Metaphysics*, 1011b25). A theologian of the cross calls a thing what it is, but the complaint against me denies what is already the case. For example, it denies the reality of what really is the case with the presidential search at CUW. The complaint pretends that the words and actions of a disgraced chairman of the board, a second disgraced member, and an errant search committee are true, *months after this fiction has been publicly and definitively debunked by church leadership.*

The interim president's complaint proceeds *disingenuously*, that is, on a misleading as-if basis:

- *As if* he is addressing my actions and not my writing, but this is not the case;
- *as if* he were seeking my termination in line with the policies and procedures of the university and the Manual, but this is not the case;
- *as if* the issue at hand were merely a matter for reconciliation between two aggrieved parties, but this is not the case;
- *as if* the synod president has not already called for repentance on the part of the board of which he is the executive officer over the very matters I brought to the attention of the church in my writings, but this is not the case;
- *as if* I am not still a viable presidential candidate, vetted by district, CUS, and synodical leadership, but this is not the case;
- *as if* the synodical district in which the university resides has not weighed in against the secular Wokeism championed by the board and interim administration at CUW and which I brought to the attention of the Board and then to the church in my writings, but this is not the case;
- *as if* Dr. Cario has been following Mt 18 all along in his relationship to me and can do nothing more but move for termination, but this is not the case.

According to the biblical text, the complaint appears to be a clear case of a religious teacher, Dr. Cario, "both deceiving others and being deceived himself" (2 Tim 3:13).

I begin my response by explaining that the interim president's claim that he "is *not* seeking discipline because of the content" of my public writings (Complaint, III. Grounds for Termination) is disingenuous. Among other reasons, it is disingenuous in the context of President Harrison's Letter to Dr. Cario and the board. While refusing to repent as our university's ultimate ecclesiastical supervisor has told him to do, my accuser engages instead in a largescale ad hominem fallacy of irrelevance against me. Further, his accusations are manifestly about the content of my writings, culminating in my February essay for which his demand that I "recant" or be terminated continues in effect to this day.

To amplify the inappropriateness of the claim against me, I turn next to the text of the 2020 Model Operating Manual, Faculty and Administration Complaints and Appeal of Termination: Colleges and Universities (the Manual), III. A. Governing Authority and B. Governing Principles Authority, with special reference to Luther's *Large Catechism* on the Eighth Commandment. The issue at hand, I explain, is a *doctrinal matter concerning the whole church*; not a matter for reconciliation between a professor on the one hand and the interim president / executive director of the board on the other. I argue that the complaint is again depending on a fallacy of irrelevance in its opposition to the clear and appropriate scriptural and confessional texts, as well as to the lesser authoritative text of the Manual.

With the text of the Manual regarding the Governing Authority and Governing Principles in hand—a text from our Concordia University System (CUS) which establishes that the governing authorities of Scripture and the Lutheran Confessions are normative for the particulars of the Faculty Handbook and my Faculty Contract, for example—I challenge my accuser's idiosyncratic and disingenuous renderings of *unethical exploitation/harassment of students, insubordination,* and *conduct unbecoming a Christian* (Complaint III. Grounds for Termination, a–e) as bases for termination, or indeed for any other sort of discipline. Along the way I address several (but not all) of the complaint's numerous and disingenuous assertions in this regard.

Far from committing any offense against CUW, much less against CUS and LCMS policy, I argue throughout that I have been fulfilling my obligations under contract not to contradict the doctrinal teachings of my church body, the confessional Lutheran Church—Missouri Synod. I have been acting as the church expects a confessional Lutheran pastor and professor to act under the circumstances of the university's mission drift toward the secularism of Wokeness. Proof of this is found in the synod president's Letter. Another indication is found in the resolutions by, and the district president's closing sermon for, the South Wisconsin District Convention in June 2022 which I have mentioned.

What is more, contrary to Dr. Cario's statements and insinuations in his complaint, I am at the present time one of the 11 candidates for president of the university. I have been all along. Nominated both at the congregational and faculty levels, vetted by the prior approval panel of my district president, the CUS president, and the synod president, I am one of the 11 still-viable candidates for the office of university president. According to the synod president's letter, "The Search Committee [of the CUW board of regents] ... took it upon itself to engage in a screening and notification process that was in direct contravention of the Bylaws... This act gravely dishonored the 11 candidates officially approved, especially belittled candidates from the CUW theology and philosophy departments, and precipitated the Schultz (sic) matter."

Now, in his proposal for a path forward, the synod president says, "Richard Laabs and Mark Polzin should resign from the board of regents... The BOR should restart the presidential search ... from the list of 11 approved by the Prior Approval Panel... [and] demonstrate repentance for Bylaw violations and adoption of secular worldviews and agendas" (Letter). This letter was written and delivered *after my accuser had suspended me.* In his document, written more than three months after receipt of this Letter, Dr. Cario's complaint (a) omits to mention that I am (as the synod president states) a candidate for the office of president, and further maintains (b) "Concordia considered Dr. Schulz as a candidate for appointment as President of Concordia, but the Board determined in late September 2021 that Dr. Schulz's qualifications and experiences did not match the [search] committee's requirements for the open position" (complaint, first page). This is a flagrant contradiction of the synod president's Letter and a continuation of the Laabs / Polzin / search committee defiance of

Bylaws and Scripture.

My accuser justifies his complaint and his move for my termination by suggesting that he has done everything that he could do to bring things to a God-pleasing resolution. But on this issue too, his complaint is disingenuous in both senses of that term.

As a concluding example of this, I explain that my accuser has not been applying our Lord's words in Matthew 18 to the "Schultz matter" at all—except for his attempts to turn our Lord's words into a gag order to provide cover for his actions and his impenitence. What his words and actions indicate, as brought to a focus in this very belated, unwarranted, and disingenuous complaint, is that he is unwilling to heed our synod president's Letter to repent, and that he is either unwilling or unable (or both) to lead his board to repent, to put it mildly.

Instead, Dr. Cario has chosen to move to fire the pastor–professor who followed 1 Timothy 5 and, in so doing, assisted the president of the LCMS in calling the board and the senior administration to account for CUW's uncritical promotion of the secular religion and Marxist ideology of Wokeism, under the Ferry–Cario administration. Our synod's president has unequivocally identified Wokeism as "a philosophy that is laden with ideas antagonistic to the sacred Scriptures" (Letter).

1.

The complaint asserts, "I am not seeking discipline because of the contents of Dr. Schulz's messages and opinions. I am seeking discipline because of Dr. Schulz's actions in conveying his opinions" (5), but this is not the case. For example, eighteen pages of his twenty-five-page complaint consist almost entirely of my writings.

What the complaint refers to derisively as my "messages and opinions" *are* my actions. I am not an administrator whose actions to fire and hire at will may or may not be justified in words; I teach, preach, admonish, and instruct with words. I am a minister of the Word. As one of the Eleven—one of the 11 current candidates referred to (and named) in the Letter, one could even say that I had an obligation as part of the selection and interviewing process, to articulate my CHRISTian and Lutheran philosophy of education and weigh in on matters of theology and policy that are threatening the university.

Further, it is disingenuous at this point in time to dismiss my letters and other writing against Wokeness at the university as mere "messages and opinions." My words on this subject have been vetted by the church and her pastors in numerous interviews, for example, and have been validated by our church's synod president in his Letter to the board of regents. Regarding the extensive vetting of my writing by the church and her pastors, please refer to Appendix A, *A Professor Confessing Christ and the Scriptures Over and Against Woke-Ism at His Lutheran University* (21–28 below). This is the beginning of my response to the complaint's accusations of student harassment, insubordination, and so on in the complaint, III. a–e.

Another part of my response to his disagreement with my actions–in–words is to cite at some length the Letter from the LCMS President provided by Pr Joshua Sheer, editor of The Brothers of John the Steadfast, under the title President Harrison Faithfully Addresses CUW Regents.

Here, for your consideration, are relevant quotations of what I have written in my open letters and essays, together with similar quotations from President Harrison's Letter, which has been suppressed in the complaint—showing our shared concerns in contrast to Dr. Cario's complaint.

What is the case: A Comparison of the Complaint with what Schulz and Harrison Have Written
(In Chronological order, 1a 1b 1c etc.)

1a Schulz's Letters and Essay
"Woke–ism at CUW, exacerbated by the BoR committees' handling of the presidential search, is burdening the consciences of my students and my religious colleagues on faculty."

1b Harrison's Letter to the Board "As the result of these very serious concerns [over Wokeism, mission drift, faculty frustrations] many pious laypeople and congregations have lost trust in the university's faithfulness to genuine Lutheranism and her mission..."

1c Cario's Complaint
"Over the last several months, Concordia University has contended with a difficult and, sadly, public personnel issue regarding Dr. Gregory Schulz."

2a (Schulz)
"As I have been arguing, Woke–ism is afflicting the consciences of students, faculty, and supporters of Concordia. Therefore, programmatic, systemic Woke–ism merits reconsideration. It also merits personal and institutional repentance." "...the Woke–ness or Progressivism that these committees are promulgating is educational heresy."

2b (Harrison)
"[the Board must] demonstrate repentance for Bylaw violations and adoption of secular worldviews and agendas."
"This philosophy [secular Wokeism] is laden with ideas antagonistic to the sacred Scriptures."

2c (Cario)
[no repentance] "...the effect of Dr Schulz's campaign to discredit the presidential search process caused immense strife at Concordia.'

3a (Schulz)
"...kindly stop manipulating our university's presidential search process... Apparently, you have preemptively "removed from further consideration" every divinely called pastor on the university faculty who had accepted nominations from our church body and the CUWAA constituency for the office and work of the next president."

3b (Harrison)
"The Search Committee took it upon itself to engage in a screening and notification process that was in direct contravention to the Bylaws ... This act

gravely dishonored the 11 candidates officially approved ... and precipitated the Schultz (sic) matter."
"CUW has enjoyed the strongest of theological and philosophy faculties."
"To this very hour, board leadership has refused to interview ANY candidate approved..."

3c (Cario)
"As an evident consequence of the Board's decision to pursue other candidates, Dr Schulz has engaged in a campaign challenging the presidential search process."

4a (Schulz)
"Not incidentally, the BoR committees' posted announcements are unsurprisingly Woke in their cavalier altering of texts. True to the Woke mindset of the Presidential Search postings, someone or some committee presumed to alter the pronouns in their posted version of our LCMS bylaws."
While there is no systemic racism at Concordia because we are committed to Christ incarnate and His universal justification of all human beings without exception, there certainly is systemic Woke–ism.
"Whether the BoR committees alter their posted, online statements, or not—without a detailed and equally widely published retraction of their Woke desires and commitments, the Woke dysphoria at Concordia will continue. After all, this is not a PR issue but a matter of repentance and showing the fruit of faith."

4b (Harrison)
"July 2021 changes to the faculty handbook include referring to the president with the pronouns "he or she" and "his or her" in violation of the teaching of Scripture that spiritual oversight in the church and its universities given to qualified men."
"Secular ideas involving critical theory, inclusion, and equity have fond harbor on campus... Acknowledge uncritical haste that occurred in adopting language of secular diversity, equity, and inclusion initiatives."
"I fear you will continue to reject my advice, to the continued detriment of Concordia and our life together."

4c (Cario)
"Dr Schulz called for readers to "deluge" the search committee and LCMS leadership with feedback."

5a (Schulz)
"...it is the administration and senior administrators of CUW who bear day–to–day responsibility for the regularizing and normalizing of Woke–ness at the university. As we on the faculty bear day–to–day responsibility for what we teach or fail to teach our students."

5b (Harrison)
"With no overall clarity and scriptural critique, secular ideas involving critical theory, inclusion, and equity have found harbor on campus."

5c (Cairo)
"The emails [urging pre-sem students to 'speak up' regarding Wokeness in the published texts of the board's search committee] violated Dr. Schulz's ethical obligations as an academic to avoid the exploitation and harassment of students."

6a (Schulz)
"For our present situation with our Board of Regents Chairman and search Committee, we may consider as well 1 Timothy 5:20. Actually, the chairman and his committee must take to heart the authority of our Lord and His Word, including all of the apostle Paul's first letter to Timothy… I think this means that, for our part, we must pray mightily and deluge the search committee and our LCMS leadership with our input on the side of confessional, classical, Lutheran education and leadership."

6b (Harrison)
"The Search Committee took it upon itself to engage in a screening and notification process that was in direct contravention to the Bylaws."
"[In violation of the Bylaws] the Search Committee was … [in] breach of fiduciary responsibility to comingle its authority … with a body that included a majority of non-elected board members…. delegating responsibility for preparing the Presidential Search Process… The Committee took it upon itself to engage in a screening and notification process that was in direct contravention to the Bylaws."

6c (Cairo)
"… a member of the Search Committee—had expressed to the Board of Regents that Dr. Schulz had unfairly impugned the capability of her and the rest of the committee."

7a (Schulz)
In response to my first open letter to the chairman of the board, copied to my ecclesiastical supervisor, our district president responded with "Thank you!"
In response to his December email to "cease and desist" from further open letters I ceased and desisted my open letters.
To the best of my knowledge, there was no directive from him at all regarding a total gag order—nor would he do something so inappropriate—but I have been denied access to those emails since February by the interim president.

7b (Harrison)
"The Regents reject the advice of the South Wisconsin District President [my representative], who is a voting member of the BOR and is likewise concerned about mission drift. I fear you will continue to reject my advice, to the continued
7c (Cairo)
"Dr. Schulz's violation of Dr. Wille's order, as well as with section 1.3 of the MOP constitutes 'insubordination' …"

2.

According to his official complaint, the Interim President frames his petition for my termination as the result of "a difficult and, sadly, public personnel issue regarding Dr Gregory Schulz" which "over the last several months, Concordia University has had to contend with" (1), but this is not the case. In the first place, this claim is contradicted by Pres. Harrison in his Letter, as also shown in the chart, *What is the case: A Comparison of the Complaint with what Schulz and Harrison Have Written*, just above.

Secondly, his complaint only pretends to be following university and Concordia University System policy. As I pointed out in a letter to my accuser on Ascension 2022 in anticipation of a meeting scheduled for 28 June but delayed until 3 August,

This is critical: Although you did not flag this portion of the Model Manual in your letter to me, Section 3.3 of the Detailed Model Process says that *only the Board of Regents—not the President—may (in the Manual's terminology) relieve a respondent of teaching and/or administrative duties pending final resolution of the conflict* if the Board "decides the matter is of such a nature that the interests of the college or university will be served" by limiting activities of the respondent. ... my suspension with threat of termination instituted unilaterally by you as Interim President, [is and was based upon] measures that bear no relation to any formal measures of policy or procedure of the CUS or of the University... *this is obvious from the Flowchart of the procedure in the Manual*... (my italics).

Because of the manner in which he suspended me, my accuser is under censure from The Foundation for Individual Rights and Expression (FIRE) and the Academic Freedom Alliance (ALA). Because he has suspended me unilaterally and without the board's involvement in concord with the CUW Manual, he could just as well be under censure from the Concordia University System or synod.

A noteworthy feature of the Manual that the interim president is violating right now is that, unlike the Faculty Handbook and the faculty Contract, it is not subject to "is subject to all regulations of Concordia University now in force or which the Board of Regents may enact in the future." This means that there cannot be any in-house administrative or retroactive board revisions of this policy instrument.

Based on what I have just explained about the Manual, it follows that the complaint's appeal to "process" and "confidentiality," etc. must be in line with the Concordia University System, first and last. The fungible in-house sources such as the faculty handbook and professor contracts can be read accurately and put into practice faithfully only to the extent that they meet this synodical standard in the policies that the Manual addresses.

To reiterate: There is no process underway. For a process to be underway, it would have been necessary for the board, not the interim president, to have initiated my suspension. This is according to the Manual, Section 3.3. My accuser is not entitled to do to me that which he has done and is still doing. His complaint is, so to speak, fruit of a poisoned tree, a branching, ongoing violation of a CUS document that must not be altered at will by the board or by its executive officer, the university's interim president. If my Lord and Master had not commended me to go the extra mile, I would stop right here.

To this point, I have shown that the actions that the interim president have taken and the allegations he has levelled in his complaint are both (1) disingenuous because of the complaint's suppression of the Letter from our ecclesiastic supervisor to him and the board of regents, and (2) baseless because of his violation of the steps of the process contained in the Manual of the Concordia University System, our synodical authority for the Concordias. Next, consider the complaint's representation that this termination is a "personnel matter."

3.

As is well documented in the investigative reporting of Joy Pullmann, a member of one of our LCMS congregations and managing editor for The Federalist, the complainant's assertions that Dr. Cario acted properly, that Concordia's public difficulties are due to me, that he followed Matthew 18, and so on, are simply not the case. Please refer to the following, point–for–point contrast between the investigative reporting of The Federalist and the assertions of my accuser in his complaint.

What *is* the case: A Comparison of the Complaint with What The Federalist has Reported
(In Chronological order, 1a to 1b, 2a to 2b etc.)

Reported in The Federalist
1a "They told him to 'recant' in a memo that they never gave him" [WILL atty Dan] Levington said…"

Cario's Complaint
1b "I determined that Dr. Schulz should be placed on administrative leave while Concordia resolved how to respond to his multiple episodes of insubordination and his breach of the faculty/student relationship."

Reported in The Federalist
2a "Menuge described the suspension as 'extraordinarily draconian' and 'Kafkaesque' because not only of the reasons Schulz was suspended but also how it was managed."
"Cario…wrote to students and faculty on Feb. 24: "Despite my best efforts to discuss the situation using biblical principles as outlined in Matthew 18, my request was rejected."Menuge and Schulz said [that] this and claims [that] Schulz did not bring his concerns to the administration before his Christian News article, are false. It was amid attempts to schedule a meeting with Cario that Schulz was suddenly suspended… Menuge said he was copied on multiple emails confirming this."

Cario's Complaint
2b "I informed Dr. Schulz that I needed to speak with him. Dr Schulz refused to attend."

Reported in The Federalist
3a "Rev. Dr. Peter Scaer, a seminary professor who attended [a reconciliation meeting] as Schulz's witness, told The Federalist that while the meeting did not resolve the conflict, it 'clarified things for me. It became patently obvious that the charges against Schulz are ridiculous. And by the end of the meeting I said, 'Is this all you guys got? ... when the church sees this, nobody's going to take this thing seriously."
"Scaer described the charges against Schulz as 'petty,' based on 'feelings,' and most importantly ignoring the core issue of Concordia's apparent indulgence of anti-Christian racial separatism."
Cario's Complaint

3b "Monday, February 28, 2022 ... Dr. Schulz described the discussion that occurred at the reconciliation meeting... he additionally shared the memorandum that I sent detailing the grounds for placing him on administrative leave."

Reported in The Federalist
4a "[According to a spokesman for LCMS President Matthew Harrison], 'This controversy erupted when the Board of regents rejected the very capable, theologically competent candidates given to it by the Prior Approval committee.'"

Cario's Complaint
4b "Section C of the Employment Agreement between Dr. Schulz and Concordia states that the agreement "is subject to all regulations of Concordia University now in force or which the Board of Regents may enact in the future." The regulations expressly referenced include the faculty Handbook and the LCMS Handbook..."

Secondly, it is not the case that this is a "personnel matter" to be handled privately. Not at all. To see why and how this is true, consider the text of the Manual on the foundational matters of the Governing Authority and Governing Principles, points A and B under III. General Principles and Regulations:

A. Governing Authority
The complainant and respondent, the president and board of regents of the involved college or university, and the review committee involved in the complaint resolution process shall be governed in all their actions by the Holy Scriptures, the Lutheran Confessions, the Constitution and Bylaws of the Lutheran Church—Missouri Synod, and this *Model Operating Procedures Manual*.

B. Governing Principles
Matthew 18 and the Eighth Commandment undergird this process for bringing and resolving complaints against members of faculty and administrations of the Synod's seminaries. While Matthew 18 provides the structure for carrying out church discipline in a local congregation, it also provides guidance and a pattern that is to be observed in this procedure *whenever applicable*. And in accord with the Eighth Commandment, everything possible should be done to protect the reputations of complainants and respondents (my italics).
Contrary to the pseudo-theological claims of the complaint, this is not a per-

sonnel matter. As the Scriptures make clear and as the synod president indicated in his Letter to the Board, what I addressed in my open letters and my essay is a matter of doctrine to be addressed publicly in the church.

As I put it in my essay: "As I have been arguing, Woke–ism is afflicting the consciences of students, faculty, and supporters of Concordia. Therefore, programmatic, systemic Woke–ism merits reconsideration. It also merits personal and institutional repentance." As President Harrison put in in his Letter, "[Because of Bylaw violations and faculty handbook alterations, and mission drift in regard to the anti-Scriptural philosophy of Wokeism, as evidenced in deep faculty frustration] many pious laypeople and congregations of the Synod have lost trust in the university's faithfulness to Lutheran doctrine…" This is the ultimate ecclesiastical supervisor of our church university identifying the problem as a theological problem concerning the entire church.

In careful biblical shorthand, the matter at hand is not "a Matthew 18 matter;" on the contrary, it is "a 1 Timothy 5" matter. It is not a matter for private reconciliation but a matter for urgent public attention by the pastors and people of the church at large. That's why President Harrison refers to *the involvement of the people and congregations [with their called pastors] of the entire synod.* As the apostle Paul writes in a section of this pastoral letter concerning *elders* or the leaders in Christ's church: "Do not receive an accusation against an elder except on the basis of two or three witnesses. Those who continue to sin publicly, rebuke publicly so that the rest too will be filled with fear" (1 Tim 5:19–20).

In the first place, then, A. Governing Authority states that the be–all–and–end all authority for the Manual (and therefore of our faculty handbook, and therefore the language of faculty contracts, and so on) is the Holy Scriptures and the Lutheran Confessions. My accuser's failure to acknowledge this biblical and confessional authority in practice does not license him to redefine terms such as *harassment, insubordination, or conduct unbecoming a Christian* as if these terms can be used in any way that suits his purposes as interim president and executive officer of the board.

I have not sworn fealty to the university president, nor to the board of directors; rather, as I have said, my oath of ordination is faithfulness to Holy Scripture per se and to the Lutheran Confessions because they are scriptural in every doctrinal matter they address. For example, in the first principle of Nisi Per Verbum in Apology AC 4. On Justification. Please see also Apology AC 14. Of Ecclesiastical Order.

In the second place, though, as B. Governing Principles, makes clear, the guidance and pattern of Matthew 18 is not an absolute, one–passage–fits–all portion of the Word for every conflict that might conceivably arise at our university. The text says that the administration of Matthew 18 provides "guidance and a pattern that is to be observed in this procedure [that is, concerning faculty and administration complaints and appeal of termination in our LCMS colleges and universities] *whenever applicable* (my italics).

Now, since our synod president has confirmed that this incursion and promotion of Wokeness at our university is a 1 Timothy 5 matter for publicly rebuking those who have been publicly sinning by promoting "a philosophy that is anti-Scriptural," I submit to the review committee that this is precisely the reason for the Manual's qualification "whenever applicable." Again, if my Lord and Master had not commended me to go the extra mile, I would stop right here.

In this connection, it will help to read and discuss what Kurt Marquart taught us about 1 Timothy 5 and doctrinal controversies in the church in Pr Jason Braaten's Gottesdienst posting of Marquart on The Question of Procedure in Theological Controversies. Incidentally, CUW recognized Dr. Marquart's exceptional contributions during theological controversies by awarding him as Doctor of Divinity in 2001. If this article does not make things clear, I would respectfully recommend that the review committee visit with Dr. Dean Wenthe, a close colleague of Marquart throughout a fair amount of controversy.

Given the constant drumbeat of "Matthew 18! Matthew 18!" by my accuser—and realizing that this is the only Bible passage he mentions in his complaint and has ever even mentioned during "the Schulz matter," one would assume that he has been relying on that chapter of Scripture to address me, as he told The Federalist, but that is not the case. *The interim president has not spoken to me once about anything in Matthew 18 or indeed about any other word of Holy Scripture whatsoever.* All he has done with Matthew 18, as far as I have seen and as far as his complaint indicates, is to brandish Matthew 18 as a weapon for the exclusive purpose of presuming / asserting / imposing one gag order after another. The complaint's accusations depend upon on this disingenuous tactic.

Moreover, I have not heard from him or read a single reference in his emails or letters to what Luther says in our Lutheran Confessions about the requirement for public calls to repentance which our Lord teaches in Matthew 18. For example, these are the concluding paragraphs of Luther's exposition of the Eighth Commandment in his *Large Catechism*:

> But if that [speaking with an offending sinner along with two or three more] do not avail, then bring it publicly before the community, whether before the civil or ecclesiastical tribunal... This is the right and regular course for checking and reforming a wicked person... All this [the earlier steps in Matthew 18] has been said regarding secret sins...

For where the sin is public, the reproof must also be public, that everyone may learn to guard against it.

In the last sentence of this quotation, you will recognize that Luther is referencing 1 Timothy 5:20. For the record, and as is evident in my emails which my accuser thoughtfully includes in his "Exhibits," I maintain that my words and actions have been in accord with Scripture and the Confessions all along. This ought to be crystal clear to anyone who reads the pastoral epistles and Luther's *Large Catechism*.

President Harrison's Letter agrees with this, right down the line. Accordingly, it is my contention that, according to the Scriptures and Luther on Matthew 18 and 1 Timothy 5, (1) the complaint against me is *doctrinally* misleading, in addition to its other flaws that I have already addressed. Furthermore, as I have already shown, the complaint (2) is in contradiction to the Manual because it disingenuously ignores the language of the Manual's text in regard to II. B. Governing Principles, which states, "While Matthew 18 provides the structure for carrying out church discipline in a local congregation, it also provides guidance and a pattern that is to be observed in this procedure *whe-*

never applicable."

It is time to conclude my response. I must provide a minimum of replies to several (though not all) of the falsehoods haunting the laundry list of allegedly termination-worthy offences (and insinuations of offences) that the complaint provides.

These rebuttals have to do with the complaint's part III. Grounds for Termination.

(a) alleges that I acted unethically by exploiting and harassing students, but this is not the case. Three questions for your consideration: Q 1. In which possible world does teaching students to think biblically and honestly for themselves—and to express their confessional Lutheran disagreements with a deeply flowed presidential search process such as the synod president depicts in his Letter count as unethical and exploitative? (This is rhetorical.) Q 2. Where will you find an administrator who would consider such teaching as described in Q 1. to be unethical and exploitative? A. In every university in America with Woke administrators, and diversity, inclusion, equity directors, officers, Woke board members, and Woke programs. By their anonymous bias reporting systems ye shall know them. Q. 3. What does it mean that the interim president, appointed by the board chaired by the disgraced Mr. Laabs (see the synod president's Letter), has suspended and now wants to terminate one of the Eleven synod-certified candidates for president of the university for the "unethical" and "harassing behavior" of teaching and encouraging pre-seminary students to think and act like confessional Lutheran pastors in the face of the violation of synod Bylaws and the promotion of an anti-Scriptural philosophy at their university?

(b–d) have two threads. One thread alleges that I have been acting insubordinately about directives from our district president, but this is not the case. This does not pass the smell test. Everyone in the district knows that Pres. Wille is not shy. Everybody in the greater Midwest knows this! He can and always does speak for himself. I respectfully recommend that the review committee contact our district president and ask him. I can, if needed, respond to each allegation under these points in turn. For example, is it plausible that the two of us, Dr. Peter Scaer from our Fort Wayne Seminary and I, would both be speaking as carefully and clearly as we did if a district president had expressly told us not to? Meanwhile, this allegation is in effect moot because of our synod president's Letter. Please consult my chart, *What is the case: A Comparison of the Complaint with what Schulz and Harrison Have Written*, row 7, on page 7–10 above.

The second thread of (b–d) largely alleges that I have been acting insubordinately because when the president says or assumes that I should be silent, I had better be silent, but this is not the case. In large part, I have refuted this allegation by explaining how and why his various demands for silence contradict CUS and therefore CUW policy because his demands contradict the Manual. (Here I must insert, as gently and briefly as possible another response to the complaint's assertions that I have been defying our interim president's expressed wishes. Regrettably, the interim president is simply not always clear in his communications. Please see, for example, Pres Cario's confusing explanation of the key terms of Wokeism, which concerns the very subject I have been addressing as a pernicious anti-Christ philosophy at CUW and in the public communications of the board's postings in the search for our next president.)

I have already explained based on 1 Timothy 5, and Matthew 18 *in Luther's explanation of the Eighth Commandment* how Dr. Cario's demands for silence are theologically wrong. As succinctly as possible, let me remind everyone that, while administrators and board members may be used to the notion that they can determine among themselves what constitutes insubordination, sometimes even after the fact, neither the Manual nor the Holy Scriptures and the Lutheran Confessions on which authority the Manual rests, allow for such revisionism.

(e) alleges that I am guilty of conduct unbecoming a Christian, but this is not the case. Please see my chart, *What is the case: A Comparison of the Complaint with what Schulz and Harrison Have Written*, rows 1–7, pages 7–10 above. One question here: It looks like the complainant is getting set to say that the synod president is guilty of conduct unbecoming a Christian. Is that my accuser's intent? To put it another way: Is it right to accuse a professor of conduct unbecoming a Christian, of insubordination, of harassment when it turns out that what he was saying and writing all along is precisely what the university's church body and the president of the LCMS have also said?

Final Summation

My response has exposed three fatal flaws in the assertions of Dr. Cario's complaint:

First, that he is in fact seeking to terminate me because of my writings against the Wokeism promoted by the board of regents, its search committee, and its administration, especially during the still-ongoing presidential search. I have shown this (a) by observing that eighteen pages of his twenty-five-page complaint consist almost entirely my writings, and (b) contrasting the text of his complaint point–for–point with the texts of what our synod president and I have both written on the matter.

Second, that this effort to terminate me is a not personnel matter that is being handled according to the Concordia University System Manual, as the complaint asserts. I have shown this by (a) contrasting the text of his complaint point–for–point with the texts of what our synod president and I have written on the matter, and (b) pointing out that he has been and is acting in violation of Section 3.3 of the Manual which says that *only the Board of Regents—not the President*—may relieve a respondent of teaching and/or administrative duties pending final resolution of a conflict.

Third, that in fact the complaint misrepresents his actions (six months ago as today) in suspending me, while at the same time misrepresenting Holy Scripture. I have shown this by (a) providing a side–by–side contrast of Dr. Cario's claims with the investigative journalism published in The Federalist, and (b) providing a close reading of the text of the Governing Authority and Governing Principles, points A and B under III. General Principles and Regulations, accompanied by a relevant passage from our Lutheran Confessions. Luther explains, based on Matthew 18 and with reference to 1 Timothy 5 that my public rebuke of the public sin of those pushing the secular ideology of Wokeism at CUW was *theologically necessary*. In this connection I also addressed some (but not all) of the many charges which the complaint alleged as ground for termination.

My response has also exposed a prevalent, methodical disingenuousness to the complaint. As I have shown, my accuser's complaint depends on the suppression of relevant and authoritative texts in order to make its case that I should be terminated. The relevant texts omitted include Luther's Explanation of the Eighth Commandment from his *Large Catechism* (part of our authoritative Lutheran Confessions), as well as LCMS President Matthew Harrison's official letter to the board and Dr. Cario.

As our synod president wrote to Dr. Cario and the board on 2 May 2022, "As the result of these very serious concerns [over Wokeism, mission drift, faculty frustrations] many pious laypeople and congregations have lost trust in the university's faithfulness to genuine Lutheranism and her mission…" and "[the board must] demonstrate repentance for Bylaw violations and adoption of secular worldviews and agendas."

Postscript to Regents and Your Executive Officer

A final observation to share with our review committee and other readers of my response: With the copious references to Matthew 18, and given all these disingenuous accusations in the complaint, I ask you regents and Dr. Cario, *Where is the fear of the Lord?*

Matthew 18 is not a proof text for imposing silence at a university or in the church—or at a university of the church! It is about children and education in Christ Himself. It is about the infinite worth of every individual because of the incarnation of God in the Person of Jesus of Nazareth. The chapter begins with our Lord telling us all to fear Him.

He called a child to Himself and set him among them, and said, "Truly I say to you, unless you change and become like children, you will not enter the kingdom of heaven. So whoever will humble himself like this child, he is the greatest in the kingdom of heaven. And whoever receives one such child in My name, receives Me; but whoever causes one of these little ones who believe in Me to sin, it is better for him that a heavy millstone be hung around his neck, and that he be drowned in the depths of the sea (3–6).

I submit to you regents who are reading this and overseeing this process that is no process at all: It is impossible to see this complaint as anything other than an effort to discredit a confessional Lutheran professor who is perhaps the second-most prominent voice in the church against this anti-Christian philosophy at CUW. Wokeism is an ideology that has been designed and implemented specifically to be a stumbling block to our sons and daughters, our grandchildren and our neighbors' children at places such as this university. There are advocates of Wokeism on the board right now, defenders of Wokeism in the present administration, individuals whose job descriptions are to carry out Woke programs and the financing of them.

Why your refusal to repent and to bring forth the fruits of repentance that Dr. Harrison called for in his Letter? That letter is as close as a Lutheran bishop or synod president will ever come to an *ex cathedra* proclamation of apostolic authority. Why your refusal to repent, as I have been urging you to do for nearly a year?

Enough with the distraction of this complaint business; it's past time for contrition and repentance. The confessional pastors and pious laity of our district and of our entire LCMS have already spoken. Honestly, what do you think is going to happen to Concordia University when they get word of Dr. Cario's move to terminate me and realize how unrepentant, how unresponsive, and how Woke the leadership at our university still is? What success can you possibly expect from any campaign to position CUWAA as a conservative Christian alternative to the Woke universities of Wisconsin and America after this?

The words of our Lord and Savior in Matthew 18 should terrify everyone connected with our university who has been promoting or putting up with or providing cover for this "philosophy laden with ideas antagonistic to the sacred Scriptures, including great lies about human sexuality and race" (Letter).

That said, let me in my turn echo the words of our synod president to you, that although God's grace is immeasurable, "I fear you will continue to reject my advice, to the continued detriment of Concordia and our life together."

Now then. Who among you knows what prescription and therapy thus came forth from those in charge in this university town which was both like but also unlike Wittenberg?

"They quoted the Scriptures to buttress their pseudo-learned pronouncements because of their pridefulness, their lack of professional character, and their own hurt feelings!" called out the students and all the townspeople, "Since the Scriptures speak of muzzling the ox who teaches or preaches publicly, and since this doctor taught publicly, they muzzled Dr Ox!" And thus it is, even to this day in that university town so like and so unlike Wittenberg.

Cordially, and as a pastor–professor in the Ministry of the Word,
Rev Dr Gregory P Schulz, DMin, PhD Professor of Philosophy

A Kierkegaardian Parable on 1 Corinthians 9:9

There was a doctor who taught in a university town which was like but also unlike the university town of Wittenberg. One academic year he diagnosed the beginnings of a fatal viral contagion manifesting itself among certain selectmen of the town and threatening the health of the entire community. He wrote to these elected leaders, alerting them to the contagious properties of their illness and offering to treat them with his skills as an experienced doctor. As they ignored his letter, he wrote again and again.

Now, it was long the custom of the citizens in this place to express public concerns, warnings, and courses of treatment for public health and spiritual welfare matters by posting their concerns, warnings, and courses of treatment publicly on the church doors in their town, as well as on the doors of their university chapel. And so, this is exactly what the doctor who taught at the university proceeded to do.

In response to his public posting, those in charge came upon him unawares while he was sleeping, and forced him into exile. Next, they barred their university and town against him. They forbad him to minister to his students.

Thereafter, they posted postings of their own invention, claiming that this doctor was himself the only one in need of treatment—that he was in need of whatever ministrations they might concoct in secret and then prescribe to such practicing professionals who dared to post concerns, warnings, and courses of treatment on their doors.

In this manner, all the while wheezing and fainting from the progression of their potentially fatal viral contagion, they propagated against the doctor their own pseudo-learned, lay pronouncements—pronouncements regarding the doctor's pridefulness, his professional character, the hurt feelings he had caused to fragile-minded townspeople and on and on. This they did, not allowing for everyone to read and discuss while congregating around the church doors, but in what they called "town hall meetings" and via churchly graffiti.

Appendix L

Brief to the Review Committee Hearing Determining the Outcome of the Reconciliation Process Seeking my Termination

Rev Gregory P Schulz, DMin, PhD
27 November 2022

Members of the Review Committee on the matter of "Concordia University and Prof. Schulz,"

In one of the first emails from your committee to me the topic was *integrity*. From decades of teaching military core values and leadership to people in uniform I know that this virtue is almost always misunderstood. Integrity is not a matter of being an officer with superior rank who successfully imposes his will and vision on his subordinates. Integrity is a matter concerning which authority a military officer lives, leads, and is ready to die by.

A matter of integrity

This understanding of integrity and daily authority applies as well to officers in an institution such as this university. The relevant question to pose when someone asserts that, or acts as if he is "a leader of integrity" is this: "Fine, but *what exactly are you integrous with*? What is your ultimate and daily authority, really?" Think for instance of what the Scriptures tell us of the integrity of the centurion stationed in Capernaum. "Lord ... just say the word... For I also am a man under authority" (Matthew 8:5–13). Think as well of the opening verse of Job, where we learn that Job was a man of integrity, meaning that he was integrous *with the LORD God, his Kinsman–redeemer*.

This committee is not itself the final authority on the matter before you, of course. As I have written in my response, "But to me it is a very small thing that I may be examined by you ... the one who examines me is God" (1 Corinthians 4). What, though, is the authority under which you must conduct your deliberations and reach your conclusions? The authority under which you ought to operate is a well-defined sort of integrity such as we learn from the Bible.

Here is a definition of the integrity expected of you in the matter of Cario's complaint seeking Schulz's termination:

All authority over Synod activities and agencies is a sacred trust granted by the Synod's congregations to specific officers and boards in the interest of actively maintaining and furthering the congregations' common confession and constitutional objectives in all aspects of the work of the Synod and its agencies. Our Bylaws make clear: All are to carry out responsibilities "in a manner reflecting the highest degree of integrity and honesty consistent with the Scriptures, the Lutheran Confessions, the Constitution, Bylaws, and resolutions of the Synod" (LCMS President Matthew Harrison, et al to the president and board of Concordia University Texas in response to their secession from the LCMS, 11 November 2022).

According to the president of the university's church body, the officers and boards of CUW (and thus committees operating at the university) are to conduct themselves "in a manner reflecting the highest degree of integrity and honesty with the Scriptures, the Lutheran Confessions, and the Bylaws."

The central question for you is this: *As you read and consider the interim president's written complaint and then my written response, which of us has been carrying out his responsibilities "in a manner reflecting the highest degree of integrity and honesty consistent with the Scriptures, the Lutheran Confessions, the Constitution, Bylaws, and resolutions of the Synod"?*

According to the words of our synod president in an earlier letter to a Concordia university, a letter addressed to the regents and sent as well to the administration of CUW this past May, my accuser, Dr William Cario, has been involved in at least two coordinated assaults on the biblical and synodical integrity of our university. To spell it out, (a) the board and his administration (at least tacitly) have been guilty of violating numerous Bylaws of the synod during its presidential search from 2021–2022, altering the texts of LCMS Bylaws and establishing a presidential search committee that both contradicted those bylaws and was engineered to install an academically unqualified and aggressively Woke senior member of the Ferry–Cario administration as the university's new president. In addition (b) my accuser has been instrumental in the introduction of the heresy of Wokeism into the programs and curricula of the university. See my response and its elaboration in Exhibit #1, the official letter of the synod president to the board, copied to Cario).

What is Wokeism? The synod president has identified Wokeism much as I have in my essay "Woke Dysphoria at Concordia," published only a few days before my suspension without due process by the interim president, my accuser in the matter before you.

Wokeism (also known as Critical Social Justice and Social Justice) is an anti-Christ, anti-Bible, anti-authority ideology. When accepted and promoted by officers and boards responsible for the Lutheran integrity of our Lutheran institution of higher learning, the religion of Wokeism is a heresy. For us professors and our students, Wokeism is a political and racist dogma that threatens our pursuit and teaching of truth everywhere at the university, but in theology, philosophy, and the sciences most obviously. These two reasons (a–b) explain why we professors in those disciplines (which are housed within the Arts and Science School of CUW), we theologians, philosophers, and scientists at the university, have been outspoken and urgent in our opposition to Wokeism. (See my Exhibit #6 for the investigative reporting of The Federalist on the racism and disregard for truth promoted in Wokeism.)

Cario's complaint: Without fear (1 Timothy 5:20)—fear either of God or of Man

My accuser has promulgated the heresy of Wokeism. As such, he is a secessionist. As a supporter of Wokeism, whether tacitly or actively, he is a CEO without biblical and confessional integrity. As further proof of this, you will see that in his submitted complaint there are positively no references to, and no reliance to speak of on the Scriptures and the Lutheran Confessions, as the authorities on which the Constitution, Bylaws, and resolutions of the Synod are based—or of the South Wisconsin District resolutions from its June 2022 Convention on the CUW campus. There is no engagement whatsoever with these authoritative texts. In other words, the complaint is utterly without integrity with the Bible and our Lutheran theology. Pres Cario's complaint is a model complaint for Woke governance.

The consequences of the interim president's suppression of these extremely relevant and authoritative texts such as the Holy Scriptures and our Confessional and theological writings, are a lack of honesty and integrity, not to mention an offensive and unjust argument for the termination of a divinely-called pastor and professor whose criticism of this secular ideology have all along been based on the authority of explicit Bible passages and the confessional and biblical stance of the university's church body. See my response as well as Exhibits #4–9.

The complainant's dishonesty and disregard of God's and His church's authority haunts the entire complaint, from its demonstrably false claims that the complainant has been following the procedure of the Model Operating Procedures Manual, to its implicit contradiction of and disregard for the Scriptures and the Lutheran Confessions in regard to Matthew 18 and the Eighth Commandment, to the arrogance of putting the complainant's idiosyncratic definitions and understandings of "insubordination" and "conduct unbecoming a Christian," etcetera, etcetera ahead of the definitions and understandings of these matters as taught in the Scriptures and the Lutheran Confessions, not to mention in the theology and practice of the Lutheran Church Missouri Synod. See my response and Exhibit #3, On the Question of Procedures in Theological Controversies.

Therefore, the complaint is inherently and obviously dismissive of the doctrine and practice of Christ's Church in the LCMS. It is also as Woke as can be in its disregard for the authoritative text of the Bible. Jesus tells us that all authority has been given to Him in heaven and on earth (Matthew 28:20), but there is not a hint of this biblical reality in the allegations put forward in the complaint. See my response as well as Exhibits #2–3.

In the complaint you will see that there are merely incidental, perfunctory mentions of the LCMS Handbook, the Faculty Handbook, and almost–incidental citations of the Model Operating Manual under which the claimant suddenly and belatedly claims to be following. These perfunctory mentions serve primarily as window-dressing for the complainants' contentions that whatever he personally regards as prohibited speech should prohibit me from teaching, preaching, writing, and confessing.

He especially wants to censor any writing and speaking from a professor that is critical of what the synod president has already officially determined to be Woke dysphoria at Concordia. Above all, due to the anti-Scriptural ideology of Wokeism which he has claimed he cannot explain but which he nevertheless has supported by supporting Jameson, supporting Laabs, and supporting a rogue presidential search committee. After tolerating and thus supporting for months and months the online posting of the presidential prospectus, the prospectus condemned by the synod president, my accuser now feels justified in terminating the most prominent anti-Woke voice on the faculty.

What seems to bother my accuser, the university president, is that the ultimate spiritual supervisor in the university's church body, the president of the LCMS, followed up on my essay against Wokeism at Concordia by visiting Mequon and Ann Arbor, as well as producing a letter, my Exhibit #1, which called for his administration and board to repent of their adulterous affair with Wokeism as promulgated by the individuals named in Pres Harrison's letter and others whom Pres Cario supports.

The interim president utterly deplores free speech when it involves doctrinal and educational objections to Wokeism. He does not want criticism or debate. He wants silence and at least tacit obedience to *his* authority so that he and the board and other schemers can do whatever they want to do to the rest of us, say what they want to say, and then deny what they want to deny without criticism. Especially regarding the heresy of Wokeism.

Crucially—and this is the reason I began my written response expressing my concern for his physical and spiritual well-being—Pres William Cario is maintaining a stance against God's inerrant and powerful Word. He took his stance against the apostolic imperative in February, and he is maintaining it with this effort to terminate me today.

In 1 Timothy 5:20 God the Holy Spirit had the apostle Paul write this: "Those elders who continue to sin publicly, rebuke publicly so that the rest too will be fearful." The promulgation of Wokeism (aka Social Justice, Cultural Marxism, etc) is the promulgation / promotion / teaching of heresy. Promoting Wokeism is heresy. I am continuing to rebuke publicly the elders or leaders at CUW who are sinning publicly. This is the free speech that the interim president feels he must prohibit at all costs.

Pres Cario wants to silence me as a professor and as a pastor. This is evident in the original document hastily cobbled together by Cario and Senior Vice President Prochnow. That Memorandum is the context from which my accuser has belatedly culled a few of their charges which he apparently believes he can get away with before he leaves office. See Exhibit #4.

The complainant, it seems, realizes at some level that he has to exile the apostle Paul, the evangelist Matthew, and Martin Luther from the discussion, for much the same reason that Pres Cario and Mr Prochnow had to exile me from campus, from teaching, and from all contact with my students and colleagues. This Memorandum *which is still in effect*, please note, goes so far as to prohibit the contact which normally occurs when I preach and commune my students and colleagues in area churches.

These senior administrators cannot bear my stubborn obedience to 1 Timothy 5:20, "If an elder sins publicly he is to be rebuked publicly," and Luther's application of the Eighth Commandment. Accordingly, Pres Cario weaponized Matthew 18, to make of this passage of Holy Scripture a convenient gag order to be wielded as needed by institutional officers at CUW.

The interim president evidently does not care that he is also inflicting harm on every professor at CUW and likely at every Concordia in the system with his war on academic freedom. He does not care that his efforts at this late stage to terminate me will harm the new incoming administration and, Lord willing, the recovery of the university from the Woke scandal which he aided and abetted.

What are you on the review committee going to do? That too is a matter of integrity. It's a matter of integrity as spelled out by President Harrison. Where will you take your stand?

Pres Cario's complaint comes to you more than a year after the time when my alleged disloyalty to the Woke-leaning board and administration were supposed to have taken place. His complaint, as mentioned, comes without proper documentation of these alleged actions.

For as often as the interim president speaks of himself as "a history professor," his written complaint as well as what my department chair has called his "draconian and Kafkaesque" campaign against me since mid-February are the words and actions of an all–too–common modern administrator. True to his Woke leanings, he writes as an executive officer who does not accomplish things with authoritative texts and honest, rigorous discussion and debate; but rather with a determination to suspend, to cancel faculty and place them under threats of termination if they should cross him. His made-up definitions of "telling the truth," "insubordination," "student harassment," and "conduct unbecoming a Christian" trump the normal definitions in his writing. He feels free to alter or misrepresent texts to accomplish his purposes.

In my case, he is seeking the termination of a pastor and professor because I have been fulfilling my contractual and moral obligations resolutely. I called on his administration and board to repent and not to teach and contrary to the Scriptures, the Lutheran Confessions, and the Bylaws and theology of our LCMS by turning CUW into Concordia University Woke.

Pres Cario's response has not only meant the violation of Scripture and our Lutheran Confessions and theology, but violating the lesser authorities of the LCMS Bylaws and the Faculty Handbook, As the lawyers on faculty at Princeton University's Academic Freedom Alliance wrote to President Cario nearly one year ago,

The Faculty Handbook explicitly sets out policies respecting academic freedom. The Bylaws of the Lutheran Church—Missouri Synod specifies at 3.10.5.7.3 that appointments of university faculty should be made only with such "limitations of faculty freedom" that are necessary to the religious and confessional nature and aims of the seminary." The Faculty Handbook in Section 4.5 specifically recognizes ... that the university has "specific expectations regarding the presentation of doctrinal teachings." ... *Of course Professor Schulz has a responsibility not to "advocate a position contrary to that of the Synod," but here is participating in a public debate on what the implications of the Synod's positions might be for the university* (my italics). See Exhibit #9.

When he writes in his disingenuous complaint under Grounds for Termination, "I am not seeking discipline because of the content of Dr. Schulz's messages and opinions..." my response is, "I do not believe you, Meletus, and I do not think anyone else will" (Plato, *Apology* 25e). This is what Socrates said to his accuser, Meletus, who was seeking to terminate him.

One thing more. The claim maintains (supported by a patent lie on the first page of his complaint, in a section ironically titled "Factual Background") that even a duly nominated and synod-vetted candidate for president of the university should be severely punished for expressing criticism of his Woke administration and the Woke board of regents committee of which board he, the claimant, is the executive officer. This is shameless.

My good faith teaching and writing as a bona fide presidential candidate and my faithfulness in fulfilling my faculty contract by not contradicting the doctrine and teaching of the Bible and the LCMS church—in brief, my faithful adherence to the Scriptures, notably 1 Timothy 5:20—these are the reasons for which President William Cario is seeking to terminate me.

Schulz's response: We ought to obey God rather than administrators (Acts 5:29)

My response addresses the complaint's strategy of arbitrarily and capriciously suppressing relevant and authoritative texts on three levels. First, my response diagnoses the claim's rhetorical sin of omission (that is, the claimant's suppression of relevant biblical, synodical, and legal texts) by identifying the complainant's strategy as *disingenuous* in both senses of the term.

On a second level, my response exposes the complaint's lies concerning, for example, the interim president's assertion that I was not a presidential candidate at the time he alleges that I was "harassing students" by teaching and encouraging them to be men of honesty and confessional integrity in the face of the board's very public determination to install a Woke president and Woke programs at their university. This, of course, is a page straight from the playbook of the former interim president and board of Concordia University Texas.

So that you don't misunderstand, in my response and in this brief, *I am addressing the complaint against me directly*. First, it is in the process of debunking the specific falsehoods of my accuser's claim that I have needed to provide you with the primary texts and documents which further reveal (a) his role in precipitating what the synod president refers to as "the Schultz(sic) matter" and (b) his role in fomenting the unrest and grief (that is the "dysphoria" or restlessness of consciences referred to in my essay) within the CUW community, our church body, and within academia on a national scale.

Second, despite an earlier effort to impose a *reconciliation* process on the "Schulz matter," and now in this *reconciliation* process of the Manual, I explain how and why <u>the reconciliation process is theologically inappropriate to the matter at hand because my writing and teaching is about a matter of biblical and Lutheran doctrine versus the doctrinal heresy of Wokeism at the university.</u> *Contrary to the assertions of the complainant, contrary to the board's referral of this matter to the review committee for reconciliation, and contrary to the prejudicial February 25, 2022 letter to the Michigan District by President Cario's regent designee to this review committee, this is not and has never been a "personnel matter" or a squabble between two persons at CUW; on the contrary, all along it has been matter of doctrinal importance that requires public reproof, rebuke, and repentance.* In fact, the right way to address this matter is with a church tribunal. See Matthew 18 and 1 Timothy 5:20, as well as Luther's biblical counsel for such a situation as this. Here too again see my response and Exhibits #2–3.

On the third, most fundamental level of my response, I overthrow the complainant's suppression of texts by lining up the relevant texts according to their "chain of authority" from Scripture (the ultimate and divinely infallible authority), down to the lesser authorities of the Manual, and then to the (incredibly fungible) Faculty Handbook.

When I wrote and submitted my response, it had been my hope that the interim president and board of Concordia University Wisconsin and Ann Arbor would repent and act in this matter with honesty and integrity. That is, with the biblical and doctrinal integrity sorely lacking in the secessionist president and board of Concordia University Texas, for one timely example.

Accordingly, at this third level I provide an exegesis or unpacking of the

Manual's text regarding authoritative texts, particularly III. General Principles and Regulations, A. Governing Authority and B. Governing Principles. I apply Scriptural and Lutheran Confessions texts suppressed from the complaint; but notwithstanding, extremely relevant to the claim's accusations and to the claimant's words and actions as university president.

My accuser has long been under censure by national university and legal foundations because of his war against academic freedom. As I have said, this complaint is the continuation of the university's attack on my academic freedom. Just as certainly, this complaint is establishing precedent; therefore, it is attacking the academic freedom of every professor in every Concordia. The consequences of your integrity in this matter (or lack thereof) will be far reaching indeed.

I also argue that the "process" instigated by the interim president in his written complaint contradicts the actual process in the text of the Operating Procedures Manual. If my argument is true and valid, the regents and review committee are violating the process established by the Concordia University System.

Conclusion

While twice noting on the basis of the authoritative texts (the Bible, the Lutheran Confessions, and then the lesser authority of the Manual) that there should be no need for me to respond further, I nevertheless do my best in my written response to go the extra mile (in line with my Lord's command in the Sermon on the Mount) by writing extra pages to point out to the board and the review committee *the double scandal (academic and ecclesiastical)* for the university *of the interim president and board's months-long actions against me.*

I document this in my response by linking and engaging with authoritative texts from within the church, such as texts from the synod president and from Seminary professor and churchman–author Kurt Marquart, as well as legal texts from the lawyers at FIRE and ALA which have an obvious bearing on the complaint itself and Cario's continuing efforts to stifle, to cancel, and to terminate me. Ten of my Exhibits reiterate and amplify the points of my argument in my response against the complaint. (Exhibit #11 concerns the integrity of the review committee itself given the very public partiality of Cario's designee from the board.)

To quote our synod president (as I do in the postscript of my response to the interim president and his regents), "I fear you will continue to reject my advice, to the continued detriment of Concordia and our life together." But I, along with many others, are still praying and working for the interim president and his wayward regents and others to repent, even at this late, late hour.

And so, I leave you to digest the pages of the careful work on the authoritative and exceedingly relevant texts that I have put into your hands in my response and in my reinforcing Exhibits. You have the opportunity to do your work with the assistance of two eminently faithful pastors, one a stalwart regent, one of the university's and the synod's most capable and experienced theologians. Assuming that things are done decently and in good order, four faithful and authoritative men in our LCMS, two exceptionally well-respected parish pastors and two highly-qualified professors of the church will be speaking as witnesses to help the review committee to deliberate with integrity.

Please read carefully and discuss the matter honestly.

To paraphrase a truly great president of biblical integrity: Now we are engaged in a great civil war, testing whether this Lutheran university, or any university so conceived and so dedicated, can long endure. We are met on a great battle-field of that war against Wokeism and Social Justice so-called.

Wokeism, as I have written and as anyone can learn for himself, is a witches' brew of Marxism and Progressivism, and salted with Harvard's pernicious CRT mythology. Wokeism is the delivery medium for antiracism racism, for the mutation of our sons and daughters in body, mind, and spirit. Christians who promulgate Wokeism are heretics. By their rejection of authority and authoritative texts such as the Holy Scriptures ye shall know them.

On which side of the battle line do you stand?

The administrative and board leaders named in President Harrison's May letter to the regents and to President Cario, namely, Gretchen Jamesen, EdD, and Board of Regents Chairman Richard Laabs are two individuals who took their places on the side of Wokeism or Social Justice and against Christ and His Church. They lied and they connived with others, named and unnamed, to accomplish their mission of overthrowing the identity of Concordia University as "a Lutheran institution of higher learning."

There are also collaborators with these Woke, Social Justice warriors in their campaign against Christ's authority and His Word at Concordia University Wisconsin. While mouthing ostensibly Lutheran and biblical commitments, these collaborators are people who nevertheless sought to further the Woke heresy by their terrorist attacks against those who deploy the Word of God and the confessional clarity of Lutheran doctrine against their (that is, the collaborators') Woke friends. The Woke collaborators remain active today.

These collaborators are even now aiding and abetting the cause of Wokeism and its attack on the bodies, minds, and spirits of our children and young people. These collaborators include those professors, administrators, and program directors who fund and implement the secular and antibiblical ideology of Wokeism in the curriculum and programs at the university such as its Maoist bias reporting system.

The Woke collaborators include President Cario and Vice President Alan Prochnow. See the details of their Memorandum in Exhibit #4, which is the first draft of the interim president's belated complaint seeking to terminate me. It appears that another collaborator is former District President David Maier, a regent and a member of this review committee, to go by his official letter informing the entire Michigan District that my suspension was "not for publishing a concern/complaint, but for his refusal to meet with Dr. Cario." See Exhibit #11.

Because my accuser invited District President Wille to be a witness for him in this matter, and because the president of the South Wisconsin District agreed to testify, we will have the opportunity to see where he stands during this hearing—assuming that I will be allowed to question him and assuming as well that he will respond forthrightly.

But there is no doubt where I have taken my stand. Realizing that presidents, senior administrators, and regents at the university appear not to have much regard or time for authoritative texts, I have narrowed the issue before you to two applicable Bible passages (Matthew 18 and 1 Timothy 5:20) and one passage from the Lutheran Confessions which addresses these passages in terms of the Woke matter at the church's university.

As every person of biblical and Lutheran confessional integrity will realize, even if you assume that Cario's allegations about my disobeying his or some other official's demand for silence on the matter of Wokeism at CUWAA—something I do not grant and which I disprove in my Response—I have been doing nothing other than obeying the authority of Christ and His apostle by speaking and writing publicly against the wickedness and anti-scriptural character of Wokeism. The written commands of Christ in the Bible take precedence over every other authority (Matthew 28:20).

The Scriptures tell every divinely called pastor–teacher such as I am, "If an elder [leader in the church] sins [continues to go against God's Word] publicly, he is to be [repeatedly] rebuked publicly" (1 Timothy 5:20).

This is where I stand. It is for maintaining this confessional stance that President William Cario wants you to help him fire me.

Appendix M

Luther's *Large Catechism*: The Eighth Commandment Regarding Matthew 18 and 1 Timothy 5

The Ten Commandments
BookOfConcord.org

Further, Christ teaches: But if he will not hear thee, then take with thee one or two more, that in the mouth of two or three witnesses every word may be established. So he whom it concerns is always to be treated with personally, and not to be spoken of without his knowledge. But if that do not avail, then bring it publicly before the community, whether before the civil or the ecclesiastical tribunal. For then you do not stand alone, but you have those witnesses with you by whom you can convict the guilty one, relying on whom the judge can pronounce sentence and punish. This is the right and regular course for checking and reforming a wicked person. But if we gossip about another in all corners, and stir the filth, no one will be reformed, and afterwards when we are to stand up and bear witness, we deny having said so. Therefore it would serve such tongues right if their itch for slander were severely punished, as a warning to others. If you were acting for your neighbor's reformation or from love of the truth, you would not sneak about secretly nor shun the day and the light.

All this has been said regarding secret sins. But where the sin is quite public so that the judge and everybody know it, you can without any sin avoid him and let him go, because he has brought himself into disgrace, and you may also publicly testify concerning him. For when a matter is public in the light of day, there can be no slandering or false judging or testifying; as, when we now reprove the Pope with his doctrine, which is publicly set forth in books and proclaimed in all the world. For where the sin is public, the reproof also must be public, that every one may learn to guard against it.

Thus we have now the sum and general understanding of this commandment, to wit, that no one do any injury with the tongue to his neighbor, whether friend or foe, nor speak evil of him, no matter whether it be true or false, unless it be done by commandment or for his reformation...

Appendix N

The Question of Procedure in Theological Controversies

Rev. Dr. Kurt Marquart
From the April–September, 1966, Australasian Theological Review

This paper does not pretend to be anything like a systematic treatment of some such *locus* of Moral Theology as "*De Controversiis.*" Nor is it intended as an assortment of conceivable *casualia*, or as an attempt to construct Canon Law from precedents. The object is, rather, to treat certain fundamental principles, and to do so with special reference to (1) the democratic, congregational type of church polity with which we are familiar, and (2) genuine, serious theological controversies, rather than mere silly squabbles or purely local agitations.

I. Truth and Love

It would appear that theological controversies cannot proceed very far before charges of "lovelessness" are raised by one or the other side. It behooves us therefore to examine the relevance and validity of such charges.

It is clear that even the best of Christians daily violate love. i.e. fall short of perfect charity. It is equally obvious that any sort of controversy will tend to excite not only righteous wrath, but also a whole clan of its less noble, carnal cousins! Since this failing would, presumably, be the common property of both sides of any dispute, it is difficult to see how it could be exploited by the partisans of one side! And it is safe to predict that not many will want to assume a sort of divine comedy, or miracle–in–reverse, whereby false doctrine becomes a guarantee of immunity from the propensities of the flesh, so that, given a dispute between the adherents of true and false doctrine respectively, only the former suffer from the malaise of lovelessness, while the latter are veritable Knights of Charity.

Obviously it cannot be this sort of thing which is meant by charges of "lovelessness." The real target of the attack seems to be that unbending adamance which is characteristic of the confessional attitude. For genuine Biblical commitment, broad, secular "reasonableness" has neither understanding nor tolerance. The ire of the world and of worldly churchmen is aroused not so much by the divine truth itself—that, after all, could be accommodated somehow in the pantheon of "views"—as by the inconvenient determination of its confessors to take that truth seriously, to live and die by it. Dr. C. F. W. Walther put it this way:

> *'It has always been not so much the pure doctrine per se, which has aroused hostility against its representatives, much less is that the case in our indifferent age, but taking it seriously, the exclusive adherence to it, the rejection and condemnation of the opposite doctrine, and above all the practical implementation of this doctrinal position, that is was "which at all times provoked hostility... So also the Cardinal of Salzburg said that Luther's doctrine 'he would tolerate, but to allow oneself to be reformed out of a corner (aus dem Winkel), that was not to be tolerated.' So*

it still is today. What doctrine isn't one prepared to tolerate nowadays, if only it will stand peacefully beside the other doctrine! And just those who want to be orthodox accomplish the most incredible fears in this tolerance. Only observe the harmonious relation, which shows itself in the academic colleges, the peaceable sitting together in pastoral conferences, the tone in the reviews!' (Lehre und Wehre, Jan. 1879, p. 1).

The world's love is a curious amalgam of sentimentality, callousness, and expediency. How different from Biblical *agape!* Ibsen put these flaming words into the mouth of Pastor Brand: "What the world calls love I neither know nor want. I know God's love, and that is not weak and mild. That is hard even unto the terror of death; it offers caresses which leave wounds" (Brand, condensed by Dorothy Hoyer Scharlemann, Act III). True, Biblical love is always dominated from above. It throws with the crimson of fire and of blood, and has no kinship whatever to the fraudulent pastels of sentimental philanthropy or egalitarian humanitarianism—and their religious counterpart: unionism. Only God may be loved absolutely. The First Table of the Law precedes and determines the Second, as the First Commandment precedes and determines all the others. When this anchorage in God is given up, and the Second Table, or love of Man, is absolutized, then God is no longer love; instead. Love is god! Such "love" is but an egalitarian, relativistic quicksand, which swallows up all distinctions between truth and error, right and wrong. But when objective standards and norms are gone, and the principle, *quod licet Jovi non licet bovi* (what is permissible for Jove is not permissible for an ox), is no longer intelligible, much less workable, such an oozing, undifferentiated "love" easily and quickly becomes an oppressive paternalism, i.e. tyranny. George Orwell, in describing the nightmarish police-state of 1984, adds a masterly touch when he has the horrible, heavily armed "law" enforcement agency called, officially, the "Ministry of Love"!

There is an important sense in which I must love Unitarians and Communists. But this does not mean that I have the right, much less the duty, to admit them into my pulpit. Love and ecclesiastical recognition are neither synonymous nor coextensive. No Christian churchman should dream of complaining when Truth is given precedence over Love, or, more accurately, love for God and His Word over love for man. This relationship is elementary in the Kingdom of God. "Pure love to the individual has its roots in the love to God, love to the disciple in love to the Master, love to the member in love to the Church, and the broader love must be the determiner of and controlling force to the narrower" (C. P. Krauth, quoted in S.E. Ochsenford, *Doctrinal History of the General Council of the Lutheran Church in North America).*

Luther asserts, in his typically blunt way, the supremacy of Truth over Love in countless passages. Here are a few examples:

"Faith and love are two different things. Faith tolerates nothing, love tolerates everything; faith curses, love blesses; faith seeks revenge and punishment, love seeks to spare and to forgive. Therefore, when faith and God's Word are involved, there can be no more loving or being patient, but only anger, zeal, and scolding. All prophets also acted in this way, that in matters of faith they showed no patience or mercy." (St. Louis ed., V, 38).

"Therefore in mere ceremonies love shall be judge and mistress, but not in matters of faith or of the promises of God... Rather, faith shall be

lord over love, and to it love shall yield, but faith shall not yield to love" (Theses against the Council of Constance. 1535).

"Nothing must be allowed to harm God and His Word. This must take precedence over everything else. All things must be sacrificed for it. Here we must give consideration neither to friend or foe. For this is something that does not belong to us, nor to the neighbor, but to God Himself... Therefore I say to my most bitter enemies: ... Since you do not want to submit to that Word, I will speak this prayer and blessing over you. May God hinder you and bring you to shame! I will gladly serve you, but not when you want to overthrow God's Word. Here you will not prevail upon me to give you one drink of water... The Bible says. Thou shalt love thine enemy and do good to him. But I must be an enemy of God's enemies, lest I attack God with them" (VII, 481).

"There are two kinds of sins, the first against the Word, or the Christian doctrine and creed; the other, against love. Sin against the doctrine should in no way be tolerated. But with the sin against love, we should have patience, for in such a sin one acts against the neighbor without any harm to the doctrine or the creed. But where something is done against the Word, the creed, and God's Honor, there one should under no circumstances remain silent, there must be far less patience, and one must oppose it vigorously" XIX, 1182).

In a day when saccharine "devotional" booklets have displaced the Psalter in the spiritual life of even many orthodox Christians, it is not to be expected that Luther's rugged language will find wide acceptance. Yet this ruggedness was one of Luther's most Christ-like traits! Consider Dr. M. Franzmann's eloquent reminder:

"Where the Christ is proclaimed, there will always be both, confessors and deniers, for... the Christ is the Christ who sunders and divides...The Messiah is the Prince of Peace... But He brings no cheap peace, half peace, no peace by compromise. He can create peace only by destroying evil; and since men love evil and cling to that which excludes them from the whole peace of God, His coming forces a decision between good and evil and proves to be, for all its peaceful intent, the sundering sword...

The division cuts through all human connections and dissolves every nexus that human life knows. And since it is an absolute division, the decision and the renunciation which it involves are agonizingly absolute...

This is no soft and mellow Jesus, no pink–and–blue Christ; there is no such Jesus Christ in our records of Him. And these apostles are not suavely robed young saints looking beatific against a bright Italian sky" (Follow Me, p. 96).

Since our Lord Himself, Perfect Love Incarnate, on occasion acted in ways (cleansing the Temple, for example) which did not, on the surface, make the presence of love apparent, it is clear that genuine, God-pleasing love cannot simply be judged by general outward appearances, such as someone's experience of embarrassment, unpleasantness, or even acute distress. True love may appear outwardly to be *its*opposite, while seeming love may turn out to be that false kind which Luther rightly calls "accursed." Love cannot be converted into a brittle code of external regulations!

It was no doubt for this reason that Dr. F. Piper penned these wise words:

"The principle all Christians must acknowledge... But not in every particular case may one command a Christian that he must practice love, and much less, in what measure that must happen. That one must leave to Christian judgment" (Vortraege, p. 120).

In the final analysis love is a mystery of the heart, over which God has not appointed human judges (St. Mat. 7:1). *De occultis non judicat ecclesia.* Only in those relatively rare cases when Scripturally defined external criteria have been breached demonstrably, should a charge of lovelessness be levelled, lest the charge itself be more loveless than the act condemned.

It is clear that in the context of a genuine theological controversy the charge of "lovelessness" is singularly inept, and should never be raised in isolation from the substantive question *of* the truth or falsehood of the doctrines debated. History teaches us to suspect that he who bases his case mainly on appeals to love, unity, etc., is trying to dodge an issue. Attention should be focused on the objective doctrinal issues, not on the entrails of the participants, which are irrelevant in this connection. After all, when someone claims that there is a bomb aboard an airplane, it is the verification of this allegation, and not the caller's state of mind that is of urgent, immediate, and primary interest.

To conclude this section, here are two quotes, one from Dr. C. F.W. Walther, and the other from a 1935 *Lutheran Witness* editorial:

"Never has there been so much talk about 'love' as in our day. 'Love' has become the slogan and watchword of those who claim to be Christians as well as those who do not care to be called Christians. Now what do such Christians mean when they speak about 'love'? They mean, above all, as they express it, that in matters of faith one must exhibit tolerance, that is, endurance, indulgence, and the spirit of compromise: that one must not be so exact in regard to purity of doctrine, nor criticize the departure from the Word of God as strenuously as was done in olden times; and that we ought, therefore, also recognize those as brethren who are not willing to obey the Word of God in some points, as long as they accept a few especially important articles of faith. But how? Should that really be a true description of Christian 'love'? Does not the Word of God say the very opposite: "Charity rejoiceth not in iniquity but rejoiceth in the truth"? (I Cor. 13:6). Such Christians (who out of 'love' tolerate false doctrine) are like the man who was very liberal and charitable toward the poor. What he gave them, however, he did not take from his own goods, but what he had secretly stolen from others. That he openly gave to the poor. For what are those Christians doing but robbing God of His Word, His Truth, His Glory, and thereby giving the impression that they have more love than others (who adhere strictly to God's Word)? Just how little 'love' such people really possess may be seen by their attitude toward those who take them to task for their indifference to the Truth. Against such (true disciples, John 8:13ff), they are mostly filled with rancor, venom, and bitter enmity" (Hausandachten, p. 92, quoted in Lutheran Loyalty, July, 1951).

"During the Spanish–American War unscrupulous greed led certain men to sell tainted meat; many of our soldiers became ill, suffered torture and a great number died. The culprits were exposed and punished. Was it lack of charity to expose them and to hand them over to justice?

... A gang of robbers had carefully planned an armed robbery of one

of the banks. They were a notorious band. A few murders did not seem to mean anything to them. By devious ways somebody learned the plot. He exposed it to the authorities. Because of that exposure some of the robbers are dead, while the others are in prison. Was it lack of charity to expose the plot? ...

Is it lack of charity to warn against false doctrine? There are some who will most emphatically reply in the affirmative. Is it an act of charity for a child of God to remain silent in order to spare the feelings of people with good intentions?

If that be charity, our Savior was most uncharitable... The same thing applies to all the apostles... God Himself makes it the duty of His children to contend for His honor. For those who fail Him in this He has words of the severest condemnation, calling them 'dumb dogs.' ... swayed by the ungodly spirit of unionism, some would not only remain silent themselves, but expect silence on the part of others lest somebody be offended... May God give us true charity!" (L.W. Nov. 5, 1935).

II. The Eighth Commandment and St. Matthew 18

There is a certain pietistic tendency to blunt and smother confessional impulses with "the Law of Love." No one will deny that the phrase has some meaningful and important uses. It may even happen that pastors or church officials and committees feel constrained to administer public rebukes in the name of the Law of Love. But one thing that should not be done with the phrase is to make it the basis of disciplinary proceedings. For that function the expression, by itself, in isolation from other more specific Scriptural injunctions, is entirely too vague and broad. For disciplinary purposes there is no abstract "Law of Love" floating above and beyond all specific commands and prohibitions. Such a construct is dangerously arbitrary and infringes upon the responsible, legitimate freedom of Christian conscience. Devoid of concrete, Scripturally verifiable content can serve only to tyrannize consciences through the imposition of someone's personal, arbitrary judgments and/or prejudices. As no secular court would accept and act upon a charge of "violation of the law of the land," without reference to a specific statute alleged to have been broken, so the Church should not countenance any disciplinary action on the basis of a conveniently ethereal "Law of Love."

The usual purpose of such references to the "Law of Love" is the protection of the reputation and honor of embattled theologians. But this purpose is served much better by referring to the Eighth Commandment, which represents, concretely and specifically, the Law of Love at that particular point. And the procedure of admonition given by the Lord in St. Mat. 18 may be regarded, in this connection, as a subsidiary provision of the Eighth Commandment. The question now arises whether and to what extent theologians involved in controversy may claim protection for themselves and their utterances under the Eighth Commandment. Without entering upon the details of casuistry, it is safe to offer three generalizations:

- 1. Error has no rights in the Church. With respect to doctrine the Christian Church is not a republic, in which all views enjoy equal rights, but an absolute monarchy, in which all subjects are irrevocably committed to the Word of their divine King, as promulgated in His Prophetic–Apostolic Constitution. Luther writes, in his comments on the 82nd Psalm:

"We read that the holy Fathers at the Nicene Council, as soon as they heard the Arians' doctrine read, hissed unanimously (zischten sie alle eintraeschtiglich) and would not hear it, nor let it be demonstrated or defended, but condemned them forthwith without any debating, as public blasphemers. Moses in his Law also commands to stone such blasphemers, indeed all false blasphemers. So also here one should not make much disputing but condemn such public blasphemy even without a hearing and defense (unverhoert und unverantworter); as also St. Paul commands in Tit. 3, that a heretic is to be avoided, when he has been admonished once or twice; and he forbids Timothy logomachy and disputing, which does nothing but pervert the hearers. For such universal article of all of Christendom have already been sufficiently examined, proved, and decided through the holy Scripture and the confession of the whole of universal Christendom, confirmed with many miraculous signs, sealed with much blood of the holy martyrs, witnessed and defended in the books of all teachers, and need no more mastering and probing (Kluegeln)" (Porra, Pastorale Lutheri, 577–8).

Needless to say, this does not mean that hitherto Orthodox theologians may be condemned without a conclusive demonstration that they have in fact fallen into heresy.

- 2. Public doctrinal error normally requires public correction, and by no means always necessitates previous personal dealings. Likewise, secret doctrinal error may and must be revealed, with or without personal dealings if the Church's doctrinal integrity is threatened. "I spake openly to the world: I ever taught in the synagogue, and in the temple whither the Jews always resort; and in secret have I said nothing. *Why askest thou Me? Ask them which heard Me*, what I have said unto them; behold, they know what I said" (St. John 18:20,21).

> "Them that sin rebuke before all, that others also may fear" (I Tim. 5:20).
> St. Paul issued specific rebukes On the basis of the testimony of others:
> I Cor. 1:11: "It hath been declared to me of you..."
> I Cor. 5:1: "It is reported commonly..."
> I Cor. 11:17; "I hear that..."
> I Cor. 15:12: "How say some among you..."
> I Thess. 3:11: "We hear that there are some..."
> Cf. also Gal. 1:6 and 4:10 ff.. which record rebukes written, evidently, on the strength of witnesses' reports.

The Large Catechism says:
"All this has been said regarding secret sins. But where the sin is quite public, so that the judge and everybody know it, you can without any sin avoid him and let him go, because he has brought himself into disgrace, and you may also publicly testify concerning him. For when a matter is public in the light of day, there can be no slandering or false judging or testifying; as when we now reprove the Pope with his doctrine, which is publicly set forth in books and proclaimed in all the world. For where the sin is public, the reproof also must be public, that everyone may learn to guard against it" (8th Commandment, par. 284).

That the various stages of Matt. 18 need not apply to public sins, is an accepted principle of Pastoral Theology: "*Whenever the committing of a sin has become generally known and public offense has been given, it is not necessary to observe the three degrees of admonition prescribed in Matt. 18" (Fritz, Past. Th. 232).* Very interesting is Luther's statement in his Reply at Worms:

"*The third kind consists of those books which I have written against private individuals, so-called, against those, that is, who have exerted themselves in defense of the Roman tyranny and to the overthrow of that piety which I have taught. I confess that I have been more harsh against them than befits my religious vows and my profession. For I do not make myself out to be any kind of saint, nor am I now contending about my conduct but about Christian doctrine. But it is not in my power to recant them, because that recantation would give that tyranny and blasphemy an occasion to lord it over those whom I defend and to rage against God's people more violently than ever" (Bettenson, Documents of the Christian Church, 2nd ed., pp. 281–282).*

Sometimes a situation arises in the Church which can only be described as conspiratorial. That happened, for example, at the University of Wittenberg after Luther's death, when the Crypto-Calvinists nearly succeeded in destroying the Lutheran Church from within. One of the conspirators, Peucer, wrote a letter to his friend Christian Schuetze, a crypto Calvinistic court-preacher in Dresden. By mistake, or rather by God's gracious direction, as Dr. Walther observes (*Concordienformel*, p. 54), the letter fell into the hands of another, orthodox, court preacher, Lysthen, who promptly transmitted the incriminatory document to the rather naive Elector August, thus at last opening his eyes to the conspiracy. Lengthy private dealings with the conspirators, and perhaps a gentlemanly gesture, such as returning the letter, would clearly have harmed the Church, and were therefore out of place.

The following instructive opinions were considered important enough to be included by Dedeken in his formidable compilation which bears the even more formidable official title: "*Thesaurus consiliorum et decisionum, d. i. vornehmer Universitaeten, hochloeblicher Collegien, Consistorien auch sonst hochgelehrter Theologen und Juristen Rath, Bedenken, Antwort, Belehrung, Erkenntnis, Bescheid und Urtheil in und von allerhand schweren Faellen, in Druck gegeben durch M. Georg Dedekennum. Hamburg, 1623.*"

In Vol. 1, pp. 864–865, an opinion by the ministerium of Riga is given regarding the question whether public sin must first be verified before being rebuked. This is vigorously denied, with the argumentation that John the Baptist did not ask Herod what he had done (he might have denied it), but condemned his public sin, as also Nathan did with David.

In Vol. II, p. 296, we have, beside a citation of Scripture's approval of spying for a good cause (as in the land of Canaan), the following opinion by Luther:

"*Whether sin and evil, or else secret things from which evil is to be feared, may be reported by a good Christian to the spiritual or temporal authority, according to the nature of the matter, or whether that is to be considered a betrayal?... it is no sin, but praiseworthy, when known and offensive sin and evil deed, or secret things from which evil can come, are brought before those before whom it belongs, such as authorities, spiritual and temporal, parents and teachers and the like... Thus Joseph brought before his father that there was an evil rumor against his brothers, Gen.*

37:2. To David it was reported that everyone's heart followed Absalom, and what other designs he had against his father, Il Sam. 15 and 17. Mordecai brought before King Ahasuerus that two chamberlains sought to lay hands upon the king, Esther 2:22. Saint Paul's sister's son brought the conspiracy which some Jews had made against him, before St. Paul, and through him to the captain; thereby Paul's life was saved. Acts 23:16ff.

"Such revelations of secret evil designs and deeds, whereby great damage can be prevented, are a piece of Christian love... Therefore one may not regard it as betrayal..."

And only last year the Texas District (Missouri Synod) Board of Appeals rendered an extremely significant decision (Texas District Praesidum vs. Pastor Francis Machina) which asserts:

"It is our judgment that the defendant has produced sufficient proof to sustain the position that personal confrontation is not always necessary, not even with respect to Matt. 18, when the matter is public. Authorities citied are Scripture, Walther's Pastorale, Fritz' Pastoral Theology, Luther's Large Catechism, and authorities in Synod. "Therefore it is our opinion that an offended brother may well publicly attack a public matter without personal confrontation."

This does not mean that contentious, censorious individuals are free to snatch up casual remarks of otherwise orthodox teachers and forthwith to broadcast them, together with invidious interpretations. Misunderstandings can easily occur, and even when some casual aberration of an otherwise orthodox theologian is real, genuine fraternal consultation offers the greatest hope of success.

The undersigned is convinced that some of the violent theological convulsions overseas are traceable, in part, to a certain unimaginative smugness in the past, coupled with an extreme and myopic brittleness and fussiness which fails to distinguish between divine truth and mere ecclesiastical tradition, the divine content and the particular historical form (though these terms are horribly abused nowadays). *Speaking the Truth in Love*, although designed to promote a disastrous theological fallacy regarding Church Fellowship, nevertheless contains at least one very valid paragraph:

"When the *Lutheran Witness*, in 1931, complimented a congregation on making its quota for Synod, a conference took note of the fact that this congregation had no parish school and that therefore "the entire tone and scope of said article is out of line with Synod's accepted principles. The conference asked the Witness to make proper explanations. From the editorial reply, 'I notice a growing tendency to elevate certain time-honored attitudes to the rank of principles, and then to make these principles serve almost as tests of good Missourianism or even of Lutheranism. I look with some alarm at such a free use of the term "Synod's accepted principles" as it occurs in your letter. I would caution against using such a line of argument whenever something has been done that displeases a brother. I would, of course, not take notice of this phrase, if I had not seen some very sincere and also intelligent brethren suffer reproach because of some deduction that was made which involved him in conflict, with the "standards of our Synod." The more of these yokes we hang upon the brethren, the more we shall produce a reaction of liberalism and radicalism... There must be utter freedom of expression and action, all governed by the principle of love, wherever the Word of God has not spoken the decisive word'."

Orthodoxy, far from being narrow, sterile, dead, etc., actually possesses a vast and thrilling catholicity of perspective, whose breathtaking grandeur dwarfs the tiny, confining superficialities of the ephemeral *isms*! We do the Church and her orthodox Faith a distinct disservice when we act as though the divine truth may be uttered only in one stereotyped way, and must be compressed into only one mold of devotion. The gifts of the Spirit are many and varied, but they all exist to edify the one Body. We must not be afraid of a healthy variety of expression—the New Testament itself is the best example of the strikingly different ways in which the one Gospel can be put—even while we jealously guard the continuing identity of our proclamation with the Apostolic, Biblical *depositum fidei* and with the unbroken teaching tradition of the orthodox Church.

Appendix O

Bad Company Corrupts Good Morals: The Only Way To Keep a Lutheran College Lutheran

Christian Preus
Christian Culture: A Magazine for Lutherans, Summer/Fall, 2022

There's a lot of talk about mission drift in our universities. President Harrison, God bless him, recently pointed it out in the case of Concordia University Wisconsin. The basic concept is that a college drifts away from its mission because of a self-survival instinct. It takes money to operate a college. What good is a mission if you can't fulfill it? But if you compromise it a bit, let it drift into something a little different, then more students will come, then the accreditors will be happy, then the institution can survive. This drift in mission was very obvious in the woke Diversity, Inclusion, and Equity push at Wisconsin, obvious enough to create the stir it did and invite a visitation from the president of Synod. But in all the talk of mission drift, what gets lost is a more important and far-reaching change that has taken place in all conservative Lutheran institutions of higher learning, not just in the LCMS, but in the ELS and WELS. And that is not simply a drift in mission, but a complete shift, a change. The shift was not so much in the change from two-year to four-year colleges,[1] but the unspoken assumption that went with that change, that all of these colleges needed to grow, get bigger. And in order for that to happen, they needed to attract non-Lutheran students. It started slowly, but it increased exponentially at the end of the twentieth century, until the Concordias all became majority non-Lutheran, and Bethany (ELS) and Wisconsin Lutheran (WELS) are at least approaching that mark. And this is the great shift: from being a Lutheran college preparing Lutherans for life in the church and the world to being a Lutheran college preparing anyone, even non-Christians, for careers in the world.

Every single Concordia was founded to be a Lutheran institution for Lutheran students with Lutheran professors. The main focus was to educate church workers, pastors and teachers. Since this paper was originally presented in Nebraska, I'll give a shout out to Seward, because it has retained a strong focus on this mission and continues to supply the majority of church workers to Synod. It also has the most Lutheran student body, at least among the undergraduates, at 50%. This is by far the best among the Concordias. Wisconsin is less than 40% Lutheran among its undergraduates. The others aren't even close. But all of the Concordias, Bethany, and WLC abandoned the all-Lutheran approach. Their mission ceased to be by Lutherans and for Lutherans. The professors aren't all Lutheran. In most cases, the majority of professors are non-Lutheran. And the students are majority non-Lutheran. It is this great shift that brings with it everything else—high cost of tuition, woke pressure, careerism, financial instability, and secular culture. The original mission is found in pockets—pre-sem programs and theology faculties and sometimes chapel worship—but the mission itself has not simply drifted; it has shifted entirely.

The great shift is a money problem as much as a theology problem. The two are completely intertwined. If you have seventy majors to attract thousands of undergraduate students, and if you have built many massive buildings to accommodate all these majors and students, it takes millions, even hundreds of millions, to meet budget each year. If you don't meet that budget or fall short of it by too much, you end up bankrupt and closed like Portland, Bronxville, or Selma. But in order to bring in that kind of money, you need not only to hike up your tuition, but to attract as many students as possible. And that means attracting more and more non-Lutheran students. The basic trend at the Concordias, Bethany, and WLC is that their Lutheran student population has remained static throughout the last decades, it hasn't changed, but their growth has been rapid and it is due entirely to non-Lutherans filling the ranks, until the Lutherans are a heavy minority and the entire culture of the campus changes. As of 2019, if you included graduate students, the percentage of Lutherans in the Concordia University System was only 11%.[2]

The tuition of the conservative Lutheran colleges and universities averages around $30,000 a year. Add to that room and board, books and fees, and the yearly price tag hovers around $50,000. As interim president of Concordia Wisconsin, Dr. Cario, recently pointed out, the expected decrease in student enrollment across all colleges and universities in the coming years is 15%. At Concordia Wisconsin that would be a reduction of over 300 undergraduates. Multiply 300 and $50,000 and you get a $15,000,000 loss in revenue a year. These are the kinds of differences, crushing differences, student enrollment makes when you charge these high prices for tuition. So the push is for growth. Grow bigger and you will be financially stable. But what does this growth mean for the mission of the college?

First, it means bringing in non-Lutheran students. I cannot stress how important this is for the mission of a Lutheran college. Most of the people you go to class with aren't Lutheran, don't go to chapel, don't pray before eating, don't have the same views about dating and sex outside of marriage, and this, even more than what you hear from your professors, shapes your reality, shapes your view of how the world works. When I attended Bethany Lutheran College twenty years ago, most of the students were Lutheran and the regular flow of campus life moved from class to chapel. You were the exception if you skipped chapel. It was normal to discuss the sermon afterward. Now at the same college the vast majority don't attend chapel, and despite the college being twice the size it was when I was there, the attendance at chapel is half what it was, even though the same number of Lutherans are there now as when I was there. The culture changed, not just for the non-Lutherans but for the Lutherans. The same trend exists, exponentially so, at the Concordias. Chapel life is not the life of the campus. It is the life of a tiny minority of the campus. The cohesion—shared Lutheran beliefs and shared moral assumptions—that prevailed years ago simply does not exist.

But this is not only the case with students. It's the case also with faculty and staff. The proliferation of majors needed to drive student population up requires the hiring of more and more professors. And there simply aren't enough Lutherans interested in these positions or qualified to take them. The number one complaint from the faithful presidents of our Concordias is the trouble they have finding Lutheran professors. The positions, though, are not very attractive to most Lutherans, even if the Lutherans are qualified. Let's look at business, for example. A college position might pay you $50,000 with benefits. But you can make twice as much and more with a job in the real world. And so the college positions are very often attractive only to professional academics, and very few of these are Lutherans. Concordia Chicago made the news this last year after the suspension of Paul Stapleton, an English professor at the university. Stapleton's theatrics after his suspension, which included open opposition against the biblical doctrine on marriage, showed him a pompous liberal and promoter of LGBTQ anti-culture. But he taught at CUC for years. Thank God for President Dawn at Chicago and Dr. Francisco who have consistently acknowledged the problem and taken big steps to correct it. Chicago cut 15 programs and dozens of faculty and staff in 2020 in order to make the university accord with a Lutheran mission. But the problem remains. Most of the faculty is non-Lutheran and more than eighty percent of the student body is non-Lutheran. In order to survive, they need to market themselves to non-Lutherans and they need to hire non-Lutheran faculty. In response to bad press attacking Concordia Chicago for lack of diversity in the wake of the Paul Stapleton fiasco, the university is quoted in the Chicago Tribune, "Concordia–Chicago has been very clear that it openly accepts students, faculty and staff of all faiths as members of the University community."[3] This is simply the reality all the Concordias have to work with, even when you have the best president and provost imaginable.

All the conservative Lutheran colleges and universities now have a campus community that is in fact religiously and philosophically diverse—different faiths, different worldviews—and this among both the faculty and the student population. It does not take a perceptive person to notice that this is a shift, not a drift, in mission from the original purpose of these institutions. The push for more majors was made without regard to the obvious fact that it would be impossible to fill the faculty positions with Lutherans and it was done without regard to the obvious fact that it would attract a non-Lutheran student population. The Lord Jesus asks, "For which of you, desiring to build a tower, does not first sit down and count the cost, whether he has enough to complete it? Otherwise, when he has laid a foundation and is not able to finish, all who see it begin to mock him, saying, 'This man began to build and was not able to finish.'" (Luke 14:28–31). We simply did not count the cost of these decisions. And the cost is the loss of the original mission: an all-Lutheran faculty with all-Lutheran students for the good of the Church.

Accreditation has played a role in this also. When Dr. Gregory Schulz publicly stated that accreditation concerns played a role in the woke agenda at Concordia Wisconsin, the administration openly retorted that this was a lie. It was not a lie. It was and is obvious and it's embarrassing not to admit it. The Higher Learning Commission (HLC), which accredits all of the Lutheran colleges in the Midwest, has a five-year plan called EVOLVE 2025, where it states that "an equity framework should permeate...all levels of institutions (e.g., students, staff, faculty and governing boards)" and then further states that "HLC will ensure that concepts of equity, diversity, access and inclusion are demonstrated in its mission and other foundational statements."[4] Their visitation teams lecture the administration and faculty on how overly white and non-diverse our Lutheran colleges are. The expectation is for more women in authority, more non-white faculty, staff, students, and regents, and more public acceptance or toleration of LGBTQ or BLM-type groups. If any of our Lutheran colleges or universities loses accreditation they will go bankrupt almost immediately. Enrollment will dip so drastically that it would be impossible to sustain their enormous budgets. Every regent knows this and every administrator knows this. The fact that HLC is openly woke and pushes wokeness on the institutions it accredits is a problem and an obvious factor in the leftward shift.

Sports have also played a role in shifting away from Lutheran culture. They have led to the active recruitment of non-Lutherans. They have sunk millions of dollars into stadiums and buildings that make the yearly operation of the universities far more expensive, which requires more students to pay the bills and so more dependence on non-Lutheran attendance. Once again, no one cared to count the cultural and missional cost of expanding organized sports on our campuses.

A word here about the "missional" argument for inviting so many non-Lutherans onto campus. The argument goes like this: We are a mission. We bring the unchurched and the non-Lutheran in and then they learn the Christian and Lutheran faith, and so we are spreading the Gospel. It does happen occasionally that people are converted to Christianity or become Lutherans because they attend these colleges. Thank God for that. But it happens rarely, because the non-Lutherans outnumber the Lutherans. And it is undeniable that the influence goes the other way too. When most people around you aren't Lutherans, there will be little encouragement to become one, especially when most majors do not require much instruction in the faith at all—one class, most of the time, and there is no chapel requirement at all.

But the theological and cultural problem is also the financial problem at these institutions. The business plan is unworkable. The times are coming, and are now here, when young men and women will not want to go into outrageous amounts of debt to get a college education. As I said, the estimate is a 15% decrease across the board. That's a conservative estimate. And it will hit institutions like the Concordias harder than other institutions. Hillsdale College, for instance, won't suffer. Hillsdale now has a 20% acceptance rate, compared to a 55% acceptance rate a few years ago. People really want to go there. But only one in five who apply get in. If the number of students applying decreases by 15% it doesn't matter at all. And in fact the number of students applying won't decrease. It will increase, because Hillsdale is known for being conservative and for being academically rigorous and for being pro-American. And it has already maxed out its student population. It's not growing any bigger. It has found a niche, acknowledged its limitations, been true to its mission, and so secured its future. It has no money problems at all. Lutheran money, a lot of conservative Lutheran money, has gone to Hillsdale instead of to our Concordias, because Hillsdale found a niche that the Concordias, Bethany, and WLC easily could have joined. That is the classical, conservative niche. But there is no classics department at any of these Lutheran colleges, and the word "conservative" is hard to find on their websites—at least not in any positive sense.[5]

Dr. Cario at Concordia Wisconsin openly acknowledged in a virtual town hall that other sources of revenue will have to be found in order to make up the enormous difference this impending 15% decrease in student population will bring.[6] The closures of Portland and Bronxville are the proverbial writing on the wall. Charging $30,000 a year tuition and relying on non-Lutheran students for tuition revenue, while trying to maintain massive campuses that were built for a much larger student population, is an unenviable position to be in. It is in recognition of the great shift and the financial issues that it involves that the

Board of Directors of Synod and the Board of the Concordia University System will be recommending through the 7-03 committee, that the LCMS vote in its 2023 convention to change its relationship with the Concordias. If the resolution passes, and it almost certainly will, the Concordias will receive theological accreditation from the LCMS and be associated with the LCMS, but the Concordia University System will be dissolved and the assets will be released to the individual universities.[7]

And so we come to the actual point of this essay, which is not how to make a Lutheran college non-Lutheran, but the opposite, how to keep a Lutheran college Lutheran. We are starting a new Lutheran college and we often get the question, "How can you be sure Luther Classical College will remain Lutheran?" How do we avoid the great shift that happened to every single Lutheran college in this country? We learn from history. Those who don't are doomed to repeat it.

1) First, a Lutheran college is for Lutheran students. It is not an outreach to unbelievers. Outreach happens elsewhere, and the students of Luther Classical will be eager to reach out to unbelievers, because they'll know their Lutheran doctrine and they will love it and they will want to share it with anyone who will listen. They'll experience the joy of singing Lutheran hymns with fellow Lutherans. They'll see the knowledge and happiness that liberalism and unbelief robs from people. And they'll learn from their professors and their fellow students what it means to be a city set on a hill and the light of the world, as Jesus says His Christians are.

So every student at Luther Classical College will sign a Lutheran faith statement, conservative, confessing the Bible as the inerrant Word of God and the Lutheran faith as they have learned it from the Small Catechism to be faithful and true. They will promise to attend church faithfully and chapel daily. They will promise by the grace of God, as they did at their confirmation, to live a godly life to the glory of God, and in faith, word, and deed, remain true to God, Father, Son, and Holy Spirit even unto death. Every single student at Luther Classical College will be a conservative, confessional Lutheran. No exceptions, ever.

This acknowledges the enormous importance of community at a college. The reason so many send their kids off to college and then receive them back changed—liberal and rebellious against what they had learned at home—is not mainly because of what they are taught at university, but because of who they were with. When those around you think like heathen, you will not remain unaffected. Bad company corrupts good morals. God said that. But good company creates good morals. I've seen it. The reason Lutheran hymns ring out in my house every day is not because anyone told me to sing hymns with my family. It's because I saw it again and again and I loved it and then I did it naturally. And that is what happens on a college campus filled with Lutherans who love Lutheran theology and hymnody and who sincerely want to live virtuous, Christian lives. Beautiful culture is lived and it gets handed down and shared and then invigorates every congregation these students end up making their home.

2) Second, a Lutheran college has Lutheran professors. If we are seriously going to say that every subject taught in college has something to do with Christ, then we had better make sure that every professor teaching is a Lutheran, specifically, an LCMS Lutheran. And more specifically, an LCMS Lutheran who agrees completely with our conservative, Lutheran mission, because

every single class at Luther Classical College will be taught from a Lutheran perspective. The lie is that there is such a thing as neutrality in teaching. There isn't. Everyone is biased. You can't teach literature without one bias or another, or you wouldn't be able to speak or comment at all. And the selection of literature to read is already a theological, biased decision. Why read Milton's *Paradise Lost* and not, say, James Joyce's *Ulysses*? Because one teaches virtue and censors vice and the other teaches vice and censures virtue. And you certainly can't teach science, the study of God's creation, without bias, or what our moderns call "theory." Your theory is either that God is Creator or not, that He is actively involved still in maintaining His creation or not. So you never compromise on this. Not a single professor can be anything but a confessional, conservative Lutheran, who lives his life like it and is an example to the students.

3) Third, a Lutheran college has Lutheran goals. The careerism that has taken over higher education is so obviously of the world. Jesus says, "Seek ye first the Kingdom of God" (Matt. 6:33), not second, after career. In fact, when He says that we should plan and count the cost before we build, He says, "Whoever does not take up his cross and follow Me cannot be my disciple" (Luke 14:27). Plan and count the cost, knowing what it takes to remain a Christian in this world. A college is not primarily for equipping students for a future career. It is for equipping them to live as Christians in the church and the home and the world. This has to be the goal of a Lutheran college or it will necessarily slip into worldliness, compromise the first things in order to gain the secondary. That's not to say the secondary considerations aren't there. Students, especially men, need to be able to provide for their families. God says that the person who doesn't provide for his own family is worse than an unbeliever (1 Tim. 5:8). But a classical education will give the type of intelligence, hard-work ethic, speaking ability, clarity of thought, and respect for authority that employers across the spectrum are looking for. But you never make the secondary primary. It is more important that our children remain Christian and Lutheran than that they gain the mammon of this world. (As a side note, no one is complaining about not getting a job after graduating from places like Hillsdale or Wyoming Catholic College or New Saint Andrews. Their rate of graduates getting jobs is better than our Lutheran colleges.)

4) Fourth, a Lutheran college doesn't get entangled in the world. A Lutheran college runs by Lutheran support, not by funding that comes from an increasingly hostile government. There are always strings attached to the money the government gives. And as our government—obviously the Democrats but also the Republicans, with very few exceptions—as our government becomes more and more friendly toward the LGBTQ agenda, we will see strings attached to the money it lends or grants to students. We've already seen this related to Diversity and Equity and Inclusion. It's already happening. Hillsdale can do what it does and say what it says, it can remain so vocally conservative, in large part because it doesn't accept government funds. The same is true of New Saint Andrews College and many others. It's far past time that we have a Lutheran college doing the same. I was informed recently that even if we at Luther Classical College tried to change our mind on receiving government aid or seeking more liberal accreditation, it's already too late. We've said too much. We're too conservative and unapologetically Lutheran. So we are blessedly locked in—no federal funding; and our accreditation will have to be friendly to Bible-believing Christians.

Besides this, the access to federal funding also drives up the cost of tuition. The kids can borrow the money from the government, so you can drive up the cost of attendance. That's what happens. It's time for us to realize that it's immoral to impose crippling debt on our children. I have a friend who ended up $200,000 in debt going to Concordias. He was irresponsible, obviously. But he was also a kid. No financial officer should have allowed that. And while that may be an extreme example, it's not uncommon to find a husband and wife coming out of a Lutheran college with well over $100,000 in debt. And then they make life decisions based on this debt—not based on the Bible, but based on debt. They put off having children, even though children are a gift from the Lord and would make their life so much happier, because a hundred thousand dollars can't give you a hug or say, "I love you, Daddy," or, "I love you, Mommy." They get sucked into careerism and make their goal in life paying off debt and then saving enough to retire. It becomes all about money. We have adopted a system that is systemically anti-family and pro-money. We are Christians. We are pro-family. We cannot allow our children to go into these loads of debt.

5) And this means a Lutheran college has to be an affordable college. Luther Classical College is purposely setting our tuition at $8,500 a year, because a student can make that amount in a summer of working. I made $6,000 a summer twenty years ago when I worked my way through college. You can make $8,500 a summer working at Walmart or waiting tables. And if you get scholarships, the cost will be easily manageable.

How can we afford to do this, charge only $8,500? The answer is twofold. First, we can't. We don't want to be able to afford it. We want Lutheran support that will make it possible. And we're getting it. Fifty congregations are supporting LCC right now. Our goal is a hundred by the end of the year, and we'll get it by God's grace. We don't want to survive as an institution without Lutheran—congregational and individual—support. Second, we actually can afford it, because Luther Classical College won't have a ridiculous number of faculty and staff. We'll only need twelve full-time professors. Twelve. Because everyone at Luther Classical College will take basically the same classes—80% or more of the classes. There will be only one major. We won't have a business major, a marketing major, an underwater basket-weaving major. Employers aren't even looking for these majors anymore. They're looking for competence. Teach everyone to be competent, to speak well, think well, to be hard working, to be respectful, and they will be able to learn just about anything. Ask anyone whether he learned more in college or more on the job, and the answer is always the same. You learn by doing, so long as you have a good foundation. And that's what a classical education gives: a beautiful foundation. This is how New Saint Andrews does it in Moscow, Idaho and Wyoming Catholic College in Lander, Wyoming, and they've had amazing success. You cut out the bureaucracy and the proliferation of majors[8] and the sports and the pampering programs, and college becomes affordable again.

6) The great shift took place in all three synods because the colleges wanted to get bigger than their mission allowed. It is puzzling to me why this was ever a goal, getting bigger. Why? But it was a goal and it spelt not only the shift in mission and the non-Lutheran population but also the rising tuition. So it's also essential that a Lutheran college remain small, in the same way as a Lutheran congregation should remain relatively small. If you get much over 300 regular attenders, start a new congregation. A pastor can't take care of 1500 souls. He

can't even know all their names. So it goes with a college. Once Luther Classical College has to start turning down qualified applicants, we'll start another college. We've got a few places in mind already.

7) Finally, a Lutheran college can never be impressed by the academic elite. The LCMS and Lutherans in America have an inferiority complex. We have the greatest doctrine, the pure teaching of Scripture, but we want to flirt with sectarians. We have the best music—we have Bach!—and we adopt schmaltzy fluff or embarrassingly repetitive soft rock from our inferiors. So it goes with academia. We have the greatest knowledge and tradition in the world, and we apologize for it and seek after the recognition of fools who are wise in their own eyes. Religious academics are famously terrified of being called fundamentalists, of being *that* type of Christian: so ignorant as to believe in the verbally inspired Word of God, so backward as to believe in a young earth, so bigoted as to believe in the divinely created differences between men and women. It's time we defend the fundamentals and scoff at an academy that believes sci-fi theories of humans evolving from slime and searches for nothing in history, the Bible, or literature but gender and gay theory. We know the better way, the best way. And we need to be unapologetic about pursuing it. We have nothing to hide when we pursue knowledge purposefully as confessional, Bible-believing Lutherans. And that, by the way, is all "classical" means: an honest, God-fearing, patriotic, conservative pursuit of knowledge in every area, from math to science, literature, history, theology, music, and language.

It is not only possible to keep a Lutheran college Lutheran. It has to be done. And it has to be done with purpose from the very start. That is exactly what we are doing at Luther Classical College. We start classes in Fall of 2025. Professors are excited to come on board and students can't wait to attend. We conservative, confessional Lutherans have to be done wringing our hands. It's time to build up the good and the beautiful and the bold and look forward to the bright future of the Lutheran Church in our native land.

1 As J.A.O. Preus pointed out fifty years ago, this spelled the end of the "system" and the senior college.
2 https://files.lcms.org/file/preview/27Hs9niRSnV7flL5Xj5RaQqPeBq3dziJ?
3 https://www.chicagotribune.com/suburbs/river-forest/ct-rfl-concordia-tl-0519-20220517-t7y3wgwwpfgvjl6thexb4zgrju-story.html
4 https://www.hlcommission.org/About-HLC/evolve-2025-equity.html
5 Compare the following from CUW's vice provost, Dr. Michael Uden, "Yet even amid a shared global experience, our sinful human nature still attempts to divide and conquer us. We focus on measurements and definitions regarding our differences—vaccinated vs. unvaccinated, conservative vs. progressive, caring vs. calloused." This is typical of LCMSers, as if the conservative vs. progressive is not also Christ vs. Satan! https://blog.cuw.edu/advent-preface/
6 February 24, 11am CST, virtual townhall.
7 https://files.lcms.org/file/preview/27Hs9niRSnV7flL5Xj5RaQqPeBq3dziJ?
8 CUW boasts over 70.

Appendix P

"The Successful Man"
Bonhoeffer, D. (1995): *Ethics*. New York: Simon & Schuster.

Emphasis added

Ecce homo!—Behold the man sentenced by God, the figure of grief and pain. That is how the Reconciler of the world appears. The guilt of mankind has fallen upon Him. It casts Him into shame and death before God's judgement seat. This is the great price which God pays for reconciliation with the world. Only by God's executing judgement upon Himself can there be peace between Him and the world and between man and man. But the secret of this judgement, of this passion and death, is the love of God for the world and for man. **What befell Christ befalls every man in Him**. It is only as one who is sentenced by God that man can live before God. Only the crucified man is at peace with God. It is in the figure of the Crucified that man recognizes and discovers himself. To be taken up by God, to be executed on the cross and reconciled, that is the reality of manhood.

In a world where success is the measure and justification of all things the figure of Him who was sentenced and crucified remain a stranger and is best the object of pity. **The world will allow itself to be subdued only by success**. It is not ideas or opinions which decide, but deeds. Success alone justifies wrongs done. Success heals the wounds of guilt. There is no sense in reproaching the successful man for his unvirtuous behaviour, for this would be to remain in the past while the successful man strides forward from one deed to the next, conquering the future and securing the irrevocability of what has been done. The successful man presents us with accomplished facts which can never again be reversed. What he destroys cannot be restored. What he constructs will acquire at least a prescriptive right in the next generation. No indictment can make good the guilt which the successful man has left behind him. The indictment falls silent with the passage of time, but the success remains and determines the course of history. The judges of history play a sad role in comparison with its protagonists. History rides rough-shod over their heads. With a frankness and off-handedness which no other earthly power could permit itself, history appeals in its own cause to the dictum that the end justifies the means.

So far we have been talking about facts and not about valuations. There are three possible attitudes which men and periods may adopt with regard to these facts.

When a successful figure becomes especially prominent and conspicuous, the majority give way to the idolization of success. They become blind to right and wrong, truth and untruth, fair play and foul play. They have eyes only for the deed, for the successful result. The moral and intellectual critical faculty is blunted. It is dazzled by the brilliance of the successful man and by the longing in some way to share in his success. It is not even seen that success is healing the wounds of guilt, for the guilt itself is no longer recognized. **Success is simply identified with good**. This attitude is genuine and pardonable only in a state of intoxication. When sobriety returns it can be achieved only at the price of a deep inner untruthfulness and conscious self-deception. This brings with it an inward rottenness from which there is scarcely a possibility of recovery.

(2) The proposition that success is identical with good is followed by another which aims to establish the conditions for the continuance of success. This is *the proposition that **only good is successful***. The competence of the critical faculty to judge success is reaffirmed. Now right remains right and wrong remains wrong. Now one no longer closes one's eye at the crucial moment and opens it only when the deed is done. And now there is a conscious or unconscious recognition of a law of the world, a law which makes right, truth and order more stable in the long run than violence, falsehood and self-will. And yet this optimistic thesis is in the end misleading. Either the historical facts have to be falsified in order to prove that evil has not been successful, which very soon brings one back to the converse proposition that success is identical with goodness, or else one's optimism breaks down in the face of the facts and one ends by finding fault with *all* historical successes.

(3) That is why the arraigners of history never cease to complain that all success comes of wickedness. If one is engaged in fruitless and pharisaical criticism of what is past, one can oneself never find one's way to the present, to action and to success, and precisely in this one sees yet another proof of the wickedness of the successful man. And, if only in a negative sense, even in this one quite involuntarily makes success the measure of all things. And if success is the measure of all things, it makes no essential difference whether it is so in a positive or negative sense.

Note: The figure of the Crucified invalidates all thought which takes success for its standard. Such thought is a denial of eternal justice. Neither the triumph of the successful nor the bitter hatred which the successful arouse in the hearts of the unsuccessful can ultimately overcome the world. Jesus is certainly no apologist for the successful men in history, but neither does He head the insurrection of shipwrecked existences against their success rivals. He is not concerned with success or failure but with the willing acceptance of God's judgement. Only in this judgement is there reconciliation with God and among men. Christ confronts all thinking in terms of success and failure with the man who is under God's sentence, no matter whether he be successful or unsuccessful. It is out of pure love that God is willing to let man stand before Him, and that is why He sentences man. It is a sentence of mercy that God pronounces on mankind in Christ. In the cross of Christ God confronts the successful man with the sanctification of pain, sorrow, humility, failure, poverty, loneliness and despair. That does not mean that all this has a value in itself, but it receives its sanctification from the love of God, the love which takes all this upon itself as its just reward. God's acceptance of the cross is His judgement upon the successful man. But the unsuccessful man must recognize that what enables him to stand before God is not his lack of success as such, not ***his position as a pariah, but solely the willing acceptance of the sentence passed on him by the divine love. It was precisely the cross of Christ, the failure of Christ in the world, which led to His success in history, but this is a mystery of the divine cosmic order and cannot be regarded as a general rule even though it is repeated from time to time in the sufferings of His Church. Only in the cross of Christ, that is, as those upon whom sentence has been executed, do men achieve their true form.***

Appendix Q

Professor Banned For Calling Out Racism At Christian University Negotiates His Return

Joy Pullmann
thefederalist.com
23 February 2023

Pastor Greg Schulz said he is in talks with Concordia University Wisconsin about its recent offer to let him back after suddenly ejecting him from campus a year ago.

It's been more than a year since Dr. Greg Schulz was suspended from Concordia University Wisconsin for publicly objecting to its board of regents inserting racial prejudices into its criteria for a new president. Interim president Dr. William Cario suspended the tenured philosophy professor on Saturday, Feb. 19, 2022, immediately banning Schulz from campus and his university email, according to legal documentation.

"The issue is not my personality, it was not some clash with people and their feelings. This is a doctrinal issue," Schulz said in a phone interview. Racial partiality is forbidden by the Bible and the theology of the Lutheran Church—Missouri Synod (LCMS), the denomination that appoints regents to Concordia's 18-member board.

"I think a lot of the wokeness depends on us being cowardly and inclined to be quiet for the sake of temporary peace," Schulz said.

The LCMS is one of the few large U.S. Protestant churches that still profess traditional Christianity. It claims approximately 1.8 million U.S. members as well as affiliations with biblically faithful Lutheran churches all over the world.

Campus free speech advocates called Schulz's sudden suspension with no opportunity even to hear the complaint against him "an unacceptable departure from [the university's] commitment to due process." It was also a violation of his contract and of university policy, noted Aaron Terr, a lawyer at the Foundation for Individual Rights in Education.

Instead of immediately reinstating Schulz upon discovering these violations, the board of regents kept him suspended. After LCMS President Matthew Harrison rebuked CUW last May for including "equity" and "diversity" in its criteria for a new president, last August the regents moved forward with a dispute resolution process that has never before been used in the LCMS, said a regent who spoke to The Federalist on condition of anonymity. That has dragged out Schulz's restoration and the university's execution of Harrison's demand that the university publicly repent for publicly endorsing sexism and racism.

Schulz is in talks with newly installed CUW President Erik Ankerberg about the university's recent offer to let him back into the classroom, Schulz told The Federalist Monday. He said he would dearly love to return to his students, but wants written commitments that the university would protect him and other professors from being treated as he was last year.

"A necessary ingredient would be a genuinely secure guarantee of academic freedom," Schulz said.

Decades of Unrepented Support for Heresy

Another key commitment, Schulz said, would be a public repudiation of racism tolerated in the name of buzzwords such as "diversity," "equity," "inclusion," and "anti-racism" that excuse giving preferences for a person's skin color or ancestry. The denomination's leader called for Concordia to do exactly that last May. It has yet to happen.

"If they don't abide by woke–ism, why don't they say so?" Schulz asked.

Concordia–Wisconsin maintains a Black Student Union and amid Schulz's suspension added a Hispanic Student Union. Concordia's accreditation agency requires that its "processes and activities demonstrate inclusive and equitable treatment of diverse populations."

The university also maintains a "bias reporting system." Those are widely known to enable attacks against students or colleagues. Campus trainings on the system led by CUW administrators under the previous president, Patrick Ferry, allege "unconscious bias" as a cause for filing such a report.

Last year from March 23–25, Harrison and 10 other pastors, scholars, and lawyers visited Concordia to investigate concerns about cultural Marxism affecting the university. They interviewed approximately 80 people—but not Schulz.

"Each district president is responsible for the ecclesiastical oversight of all called workers in his district, and [South Wisconsin District] Pres. John Wille is overseeing the process for dispute resolution between Dr. Schulz and the administration," said Harrison's assistant,

Rev. Jeffrey Hemmer, in an email to The Federalist Wednesday. "Therefore, President

Harrison has not engaged the matter of Schulz's suspension."

Harrison's May 2022 public letter called on Concordia to repent for tolerating racism and for several regents who had willfully violated church bylaws and theology to resign. "[T]hroughout our visit, concerned faculty, staff, and students expressed concern over the introduction of secular diversity, equity, and inclusion language and initiatives into the mission of the university. This philosophy is laden with ideas antagonistic to the sacred Scriptures, including great lies about human sexuality and race," Harrison wrote.

Racially divisive actions, committees, and public statements from CUW that The Federalist highlighted last year are still present on university websites:

The Office of Multicultural Engagement … 'strives to advance Concordia's efforts to embed diversity as a transformational force,' according to its web page. That page also states the office trains faculty, staff, and students in 'social identities, microaggressions, and implicit bias' and in being 'culturally competent.'

The university's Black Student Union recommends the fact-challenged and racially biased 1619 Project to students, as well as making purchases based on a vendor's skin color. It also recommended author Ibram X. Kendi's work.

Christian School Endorsing Anti-Christian Ideology

With 8,000 students and a beautiful campus in a suburb of Milwaukee, ConcordiaWisconsin is considered one of the denomination's better universities. Another LCMS university recently attempted to leave the denomination to pursue identity politics more freely, a move the church rejected. The denomination has closed three of its nine universities since 2018, all of which endorsed identity politics.

CUWs criteria for a new president described as "essential" that Ferry's successor have a "Demonstrated belief in and commitment to equity and inclusion." The initial search process prompted survey respondents to select "diversity" as a top priority of the new president.

Objecting to this—first privately, in emails to regents, and then publicly, in an article in Christian News—is what prompted Schulz's suspension. Schulz, an ordained minister, was on the denomination-approved list of 11 potential replacement presidents for CUW.

Through university spokeswomen, Ankerberg declined multiple requests for comment. He became Concordia's president on Jan. 9, 2023, and had an installation ceremony on Feb. 6."The regents wisely returned to the table to follow the church's process to elect a new president," Harrison said in an email statement Hemmer sent. "I, the church, and the LCMS South Wisconsin District are delighted by their election of Dr. Erik Ankerberg."

Shoot the Messenger

In addition to violating his contract, due process, and university policy, Schulz says, his suspension violates scripture. The Christian university is punishing him for obeying the Bible's commandment to publicly rebuke church leaders for public sins. Multiple regents and denomination officials The Federalist spoke to on the condition of anonymity said the case against Schulz is based on him criticizing the university in public.

That's another theological issue. The Bible commands that sin be rebuked privately first, unless the sin is public or the person who commits it is a church leader (Matthew 18, 1 Timothy 5). Schulz argues he met those biblical conditions and those who say he's part of the problem are simply covering their refusal to address the public sins the university continues to promote.

While his Wisconsin Institute for Law and Liberty lawyer told The Federalist Schulz has an easily winnable breach of contract case, so far Schulz has not sued. Schulz did have to threaten to sue to get his pay reinstated, he said. In June, Schulz was allowed back on campus for a regional church meeting held there only after the intervention of several pastors, he said.

'If What I Have Said Is True, Why Are You Striking Me?'

The South Wisconsin district's June 12–14, 2022 convention was alive with the Schulz issue, considering multiple resolutions to provide greater accountability to LCMS universities. The convention passed a resolution calling for their religious leaders to "identify and eliminate the promotion of social justice, or woke, ideology from the Concordia University System."

"The margin for their acceptance was something like 80–20," Senior Pastor Peter Bender of Peace Lutheran Church in Sussex, Wisconsin, told The Federalist of the 2022 anti-woke resolutions in South Wisconsin, his district. He also noted that former board of regents chairman Richard Laabs, one of the people Harrison called on to resign, wasn't on the ballot for the two CUW regents positions the convention filled.

The theological issues Schulz raises appear to be amplifying heading into the LCMS's next national convention on July 29–Aug. 3, 2023. This February, the LCMS's publishing house released a new edition of one of its key theological documents, Martin Luther's "Large Catechism." A few of the many dozens of theological essays in the book were written by non-LCMS authors who commune at so-called churches that condone obscene acts such as abortion and ordaining transgender people, prompting numerous pastoral and laity complaints.

The 2023 LCMS convention will be held in CUW's neck of the woods, in Milwaukee. At that triennial meeting, LCMS voters will elect two more regents to Concordia's board. That is expected to make the board more theologically sound, Bender said.

"I want things to work out," Schulz said. "My major concern has been to stop the wokeism at Concordia University. We know how this goes with professors at universities after they get back in the classroom. Soon they come up with some anonymous complaint and then you're out."

Appendix R

Reply to the President–Provost

12 March, 2023
Rev Gregory P Schulz, DMin, PhD

Dear Chairman Donovan and Voting Members of the Board of Regents:

Terry and friends in Christ, this is my response to the 13 March 2023 memorandum detailing our president and provost's "Reinstatement Agreement Following Board of Regents Decision" (attached for reference on the last three pages below).

1. Speaking the Truth, Best Construction, and Crucial Clarifications

In the spirit of speaking the truth in Christ[1] while putting the best construction on their speech and actions, I recognize that the last paragraph of President Ankerberg and Provost Dvorak's Memorandum/Reinstatement Agreement truly cannot be read as part of a respectful negotiation, but only as a one-sided demand that I must agree with their stated conditions right now, or else.

Here is an important clarification: *I have a valid and active legal contract— my tenure, in effect—with CUWAA, in addition to my divine call. Although CUWAA has been in breach of this contract since February 2022 (by suspending me in violation of the contract and the applicable handbook and bylaws), this Memorandum treats me as the party in breach* by demanding that I must sign and date "no later than Monday, March 20, 2023," and further, that "if I do not return it by 5:00 on Monday ... Concordia will interpret this as a refusal to abide by the final decision of the BOR."

Further clarification: To date, there has been no formal decision of the Board determining that I violated any provision in the contract. More significantly, to date there has been no acknowledgement by the Board that CUWAA officials suspended me without authority and in violation of the due process and aca-

---

[1] The words are from Holy Scripture, Ephesians 4:11–16, which is normative for our conduct at CUWAA and in our church body, the LCMS. According to Saint Paul, speaking the truth is the work which the Lord has given to every divinely called pastor–teacher. According to biblical and Lutheran doctrine it means speaking and confessing that which is doctrinally correct— especially to those who need reproof, correction, and training in righteousness because they are erring publicly. In a word, "speaking the truth in love" means faithfully addressing those in need of *repentance*, as Luther says in the first of his Ninety–Five Theses and as further defined in our Lutheran Confessions. A confessional Lutheran pastor–teacher such as I am is bound by his vow as a called and ordained servant of the Word to do his work according to these apostolic words.

demic freedom guarantees in my contract.

For the record, *I agree with and appreciate the Board's very recent decision to reinstate me* in keeping with the report from the Review Committee. As you know, this followed that committee's complete rejection of Pres Cario's year-long efforts to terminate me. The Board's recent decision was a decision to do what is good and right; this memorandum, however, purports to be only the work product of the president and provost. This memorandum is thus another matter entirely and should not be conflated with the Board's decision. Contrary to what the memorandum claims in its concluding paragraph, a rejection of the memorandum is not at all a rejection of the Board's recent decision to reinstate me.

To be crystal clear: I reject the memorandum per se. It is not at all in the spirit of reconciliation. To go by their words and threatened actions, the university's president and provost are not concerned with doing what is good and right, as the board has recently been; on the contrary, as one of my lawyers pointed out, their memo "memorializes punishment" for all academic speech that the administration may want to silence, whether in my case or at any future time. If I were to sign this memorandum I would be aiding and abetting a dreadful anti-academic freedom precedent, a thing even worse than Cario's immoral attack on my academic freedom and the illegitimate, shady anti-clericalism of the Laabs–Polzin Board regarding all of us LCMS clergy on the CUWAA faculty duly nominated and vetted for consideration for the office of CUWAA President. Therefore, I cannot in good conscience sign.

To my great disappointment and regret, the university administration's memo is simultaneously (a) a rejection of my publicly expressed, good faith willingness to negotiate with CUWAA and (b) a continuation of the university's year-plus war on academic freedom.

This continuing attack on academic freedom is serious and, unless corrected, merits continuing criticism from the lawyers at national organizations such as the Wisconsin Institute for Law and Liberty (WILL), The Academic Freedom Alliance (ALA), and The Foundation for Individual Rights in Education (FIRE) for which Concordia has already been under censure for more than a year owing to Cario's words and actions against me.

In lockstep with the disingenuous "reinstatements" of faculty that we see implemented by Woke American universities, the President / Provost Memorandum is a roadmap for further unethical treatment of me at their discretion. It is also a written declaration of their disposition toward every professor whom they (as senior administrators) at any point may feel the need to discipline or dispose of for any reason whatsoever, or indeed for no reason at all. (For an example of an exemplary policy of academic freedom in contrast to the Ankerberg–Dvorak Memorandum see my attached page titled "Model Academic Freedom and Free Expression Policy" at the end of this response.)

In addition, the memo contains factual inaccuracies, and seeks to impose a retirement date on a professor of the church who has no plans or reason to retire. The memo smacks of age discrimination, which is prohibited by state and federal law.

The Memorandum also asserts a blanket confidentiality allegedly based on the CUS Model Operating Procedures Manual, 1.1. Notwithstanding this assertion, as I explained to you in my written Response to Cario's Complaint against me, this is not valid or true. The memorandum's citation of the Manual 1.1 is presented in culpable ignorance of the Manual, III. A–B. Asserting confidentiality in this matter contradicts 1 Timothy 5:20 and Luther's *Large Catechism* on the Eighth Commandment.

According to biblical and LCMS doctrine, *confidentiality does not apply to the situation at CUW, for biblical and Lutheran doctrinal reasons*. The CUS Manual itself acknowledges this contingency. The LCMS President has publicly identified the situation as *a public concern for the entire church*: "... many pious laypeople and congregations of the Synod have lost trust in the university's faithfulness to genuine Lutheranism and her mission to raise up both church workers and faithful citizens in other vocations, all while reaching the lost with the Gospel of Christ."

Nor, by the way, according to the attorneys at FIRE, does my article constitute anything in violation of the university's own policies. All in all, the Memorandum as written—and I am speaking charitably here—is remarkably unreasonable, as any objective reader will acknowledge.

2.

Chairman Donovan and voting Regents, in the spirit of good faith and transparency on my part, here follows my proposal. Rather than disagreeing point–for–point with this disagreeable memorandum, let me simply present you with my charitable and well-reasoned position. I respectfully urge the Board to adopt these two steps (1–2) for the good of the university and the peace of Christ among us.

"Schulz has an easily winnable breach of contract case" (Atty Dan Lennington in The Federalist)

To go by Cario's words and actions, and to go by the tone and substance of the Ankerberg–Dvorak Memorandum, I urge you to consider the possibility that the interim president and now our new president have been ignoring and perhaps mischaracterizing to all of you on the Board of Regents what LCMS President Harrison referred to as "the Schultz (sic) matter," *which (as Harrison wrote)* <u>*the university's administration precipitated*</u>. The cause, the epicenter of this tsunami affecting the university and the LCMS at large, is not my essay; in point of fact, it is the CUWAA administration and its breach of my contract.

I am not here with my hat in hand, desperate and hoping against hope that CUWAA may be merciful to me. I was right to profess the truth of the Woke Social Justice shenanigans going on in the presidential search *which were seriously eroding the university's identity as "a Lutheran institution of higher learning" and thereby putting our university and our students at risk*. Harrison has agreed. The South Wisconsin District in Convention has agreed. Myriad parish pastors and parishioners, students, and alumni—along with publications for the person in the pew such as *Christian News*, and an upper tier publication such as The Federalist—have agreed with me.

I have been more than patient and forgiving during a year of manifestly unjust treatment by the university, and its interim president and senior administration. It is unjust and unreasonable to expect me now to accept the draconian and vindictive conditions laid out in the Memorandum by the two most senior members of the current administrative regime.

Here is what I am proposing instead:

(1) First, so that the university can make a start at redressing the very public and documented injustices committed against me regarding my academic freedom, my due process rights, my professional reputation, and other personal harm committed against me by CUWAA, I am willing to return to full status for one fully paid sabbatical year (AY 2023–2024) under the subsidiarity principle.

It follows from this principle that Dr Angus Menuge, my department chair and immediate supervisor, will be the one to approve and then to supervise my scholarly production. In this way, the university will be able to report that it has reinstated me to the LCMS in its upcoming National Convention, to its various "stakeholders," and to the national legal groups, namely, AFA, FIRE, and WILL, which currently have CUWAA under censure for its attack on academic freedom.

(2) Second, because it is manifestly evident from the Memorandum that both the President/CEO and the Chief Academic Officer of the university do not want me to continue as Professor of Philosophy unless I am under their thumb—and obviously that I therefore cannot trust the authors of this Memorandum to act professionally or ethically toward me as a professor—I respectfully request that the Board buy out my five-year contract as a full professor, calculated as beginning immediately after my paid sabbatical year, that is, on 1 July 2024. This will be a reasonable (if far less than ideal) conclusion to "the Schulz matter" at CUWAA.

For Lutheran doctrinal reasons it is inappropriate for this LCMS university or its voting Regents to impede me from fulfilling my divine call from Christ through His Church (see once more the footnoted Ephesians passage), so (1–2) will necessarily include a peaceful release from my call to CUWAA without qualification on 1 July 2024 so that I can continue to teach or pastor elsewhere in Christ's Church.

Since the president and provost have concluded their memorandum forthrightly, I shall do the same:

If the Board is unwilling to authorize and guarantee my proposal (1–2), or if the president and provost somehow succeed in voiding the Board's decision to reinstate me as they threaten because I will not sign the Ankerberg–Dvorak Memorandum, or if the Board backslides from its recent good and right decision to reinstate me, I have instructed one of my lawyers to move forward with legal action against the university and its administration in order to redress CUWAA's breach of my contract.

I've no intention of being vindictive—that is, at present my lawyers and I are not contemplating legal action for financial reparations and defamation, and I certainly forgive the transgressions against me, as our Lord teaches us to pray—but the university has done and is still doing significant harm to me and to my family. To go by the Memorandum, President Ankerberg and Provost Dvorak intend for this to continue ad infinitum—or at least until my forced retirement.

I've done everything asked of me, from staying off campus and doing without my books and personal property in my university office, to participating in the university's many "processes" to terminate me or to get me to resign, etc., etc. The Review Committee has vindicated me.

Enough is enough. I have more than a prima facie case. One of my lawyers has been quoted in The Federalist as saying, "Schulz has an easily winnable breach of contract case." He is not the only Christian and Lutheran lawyer who has told me the same thing.

"Where the sin is public, the rebuke must also be public…" (Luther's *Large Catechism*)

The matter of CUWAA's breach of my contract is one thing; the university leadership's war against me for professing the truth and calling pastorally for repentance over the false doctrine of DIE and Wokeism promoted via the presidential search, and so on, is another (see Ephesians 4:11–16 cited and footnoted above). Sooner or later, Harrison's detailed 55-page letter is going to become available to the pastors and congregants of the entire LCMS and to every Concordia parent and potential parent, every student and potential student, every donor, every online podcaster and editor, every conservative commentator, and every reporter.

Before that detailed analysis comes out, it would be good, right, and salutary for the Regents and the university president to acknowledge publicly and in print that what I said in my essay for which Cario suspended, banished, slandered, and threatened me for almost the entirety of calendar year 2022 was true (see Luther's explanation of the Eighth Commandment in his Large Catechism, which includes reference to 1 Timothy 5:20).

After all, my "Woke Dysphoria at Concordia" is the essay with which Harrison agreed, point for point, in his Letter to the CUWAA Board of Regents of 9 May 2022. I documented this for all of you in graphic detail in my written Response to Cario's Complaint to the Board sent to the entire Board back in September.

What I professed, what Harrison wrote to the Board, what the South Wisconsin District affirmed almost unanimously in its June 2022 resolutions—all confirm that I was right regarding CUWAA's drift from Lutheran identity and mission toward secular and anti-biblical Woke Social Justice.

Assuming that the university's breach of contract is addressed as I have proposed, I would be willing to make myself available as part of my paid sabbatical to help the Board think and pray things through and to see how and why Wokeism / Social Justice / Cultural Marxism is utterly opposed to the Word of God and therefore inimical to Lutheran higher education. I am uniquely well-qualified to help you to draft your repudiation of the secular and Marxist ideology of Wokeism in order to get the university back on track with its *missio Dei*, its God-given mission.

First things first, though. Considering the unreasonable form and content of the Ankerberg–Dvorak Memorandum/Agreement and its timestamped demand, I am compelled to ask—assuming as I do, contrary to the Ankerberg–Dvorak Memorandum, that the Board intends to negotiate—that from here on you direct your comments, questions, and communications to one of my lawyers. Lord willing, this can be resolved in negotiation. Still, because of the tone and content of the Memorandum we are reluctantly preparing for legal action.

Attorney Mark Leitner, a member of the FIRE network, is my designated representative who will speak on my behalf with you (and then the university's legal counsel, if necessary) regarding CUWAA's breach of contract, the civil dimension of "the Schulz matter," and my good-faith proposal. This is his contact information:

Mark Leitner, Attorney at Law

Model Academic Freedom and Free Expression Policy

Freedoms to engage in research and scholarship, to teach and to learn, to express oneself and to be heard, and to assemble and to protest peacefully and lawfully, are essential to the function of the University as an educational institution. Because the University is committed to free and open inquiry in all matters, it guarantees all members of the University community the broadest possible latitude to speak, write, listen, challenge, and learn. Except insofar as limitations on that freedom are necessary to the functioning of the University, the University fully respects and supports the freedom of all members of the University community "to discuss any problem that presents itself."

The University's fundamental commitment is to the principle that debate or deliberation may not be suppressed because the ideas put forth are thought by some or even by most members of the University community to be offensive, unwise, immoral, or wrong-headed. It is for the individual members of the University community, not for the University as an institution, to make those judgments for themselves, and to act on those judgments not by seeking to suppress speech, but by openly and vigorously contesting the ideas that they oppose.

This University subscribes to the 1940 Statement of Principles of Academic Freedom and Academic Tenure issued by the American Association of University Professors and the Association of American Colleges, as amended in 1970. This policy applies to all individuals insofar as they are involved in teaching or scholarship at the University.

The scholar is entitled to full freedom in scholarship, research, and creative expression and to disseminate the results, subject to the adequate performance of the scholar's other academic duties.

The instructor is entitled to freedom of expression in the classroom on matters relevant to the subject and the purpose of the course and of choice of methods in classroom teaching.

Members of the faculty are entitled to the freedom to speak or write on any matter of public concern and on any matter related to professional duties and the functioning of governance of the University without fear of institutional censorship or discipline. The University assumes no responsibility for the personal statements of individual members of the faculty.

Source: Academic Freedom Alliance, provided by Wisconsin Institute for Law and Liberty

Appendix S

CUR VERBUM VERBA, The Word Reveals Himself in Words Or, The Lutheran Disputation Option

Gregory P. Schulz

Presented in Casper Wyoming at the invitation of the First Luther Classical College Convention, June 2023

"[Twelve] score and seven years ago our fathers brought forth on this continent a new nation, conceived in Liberty, and dedicated to the proposition that all men are created equal. Now we are engaged in a great civil war, testing whether that nation, or any nation so conceived and so dedicated, can long endure." Once we bring the scores of years up to date, President Lincoln's Gettysburg Address stands as an argument against the Woke Marxism that has generated a Cold Civil War in our nation in our century. In our great civil war, the self-evident proposition that all men are endowed by their Creator with unalienable rights is imperiled by the Woke replacement of equality under the law with diversity, inclusion, and equity. It is a great civil war against the sacrosanct texts of our country (the Declaration and Constitution) and the God of that self-evident proposition. Woke Marxism violently attacks anyone who dares to dispute with them because of these sacrosanct texts.

The insurgency of Woke Marxism is not limited to our native land, may God be gracious and bless her, even now. Our entire Western culture, which gave birth to our one nation under God, indivisible and with liberty for all under that proposition, has also been under attack for some time. In the words of T.S. Eliot,

Knowledge of words, and ignorance of the Word.
All our knowledge brings us nearer to death,
But nearness to death no nearer to God.
Where is the Life we have lost in living?
Where is the wisdom we have lost in knowledge?
Where is the knowledge we have lost in information?
[*Where is the information we have lost in lies?*]
The cycles of Heaven in twenty[-one] centuries
Brings us farther from God and nearer to the Dust.

Once we bring the century up to date—Eliot's poem said, "twenty centuries / Bring us farther from God;" but I read "twenty-one centuries"—and add one line to identify "the information we

have lost in lies," these early lines of *Choruses from "The Rock"* present an argument against Woke Marxism on the more global, European Union scale in our century. Again, it is an argument against the Woke replacement of the God of the canonical texts of Western culture, an attack that takes us ever farther from Christ the Life by replacing the Bible with the lies of Marxism. Woke Marxism violently attacks anyone who dares oppose their ideological lies with the authority of the sacrosanct texts of Scripture and the Western canon.

"Live not by lies," as Solzhenitsyn said.

In these latter days we also discover that Woke Marxism, this insurgency against God as well as against the sacred texts of our nation and culture, has been promulgated on the campuses of our Lutheran universities. Lord, have mercy upon us! While the powers that be assure us that all is well, our administrators and regents refuse to relinquish their power to censor and punish anyone who dares oppose them because on the basis of the divine authority of the sacrosanct texts of Scripture and the Lutheran confessions. Their reactions to anyone who opposes them have been both punitive and deceitful.

The President of Concordia University Texas wrote recently, "Our Lutheran identity is central to all we do, including our Diversity, Equity, and Inclusion (DEI) work. We recognize that DEI is an important issue and believe that our efforts in this area align with Lutheran theology" (April 21, 2023 Open Letter). Administrators and regents at our Concordia, Mequon, Wisconsin, have recently been founding and funding a variety of Woke programs. They have also been working publicly for Woke Marxist leadership in senior administrative positions of my university: "Concordia University Wisconsin and Ann Arbor seeks a president characterized by a demonstrated belief in and commitment to equity and inclusion" and who promotes "diversity in all its myriad forms" (official online announcement, publicly posted from 2021–2022).

On top of this, the academic freedom to argue against Woke Marxism and to dispute on the basis of Christ's words and our confessions, is denied to us confessing Lutheran professors: After a six-month trial of one professor determined that there were no grounds for his termination or suspension and recommended his reinstatement, the current President and Provost at Concordia University Wisconsin wrote, "With written permission of the CUWAA President and Provost and *at their sole discretion*, you will be invited to resume teaching in the Department of Philosophy ..." (March 13, 2023 Memo, italics added).

We underwent a similar battle at one of our seminaries in the last century. Of that explosion Kurt Marquart wrote, "What ought to be clear is that any retreat from biblical facts and history is a retreat from the Incarnation itself. Any driving of wedges ... between fact and faith, between history and theology, hits at the inmost nature of biblical Christianity. The written Word is about the Incarnate Word and is of a piece with Him" (*Anatomy of an Explosion*, 125).

Considering Marquart's analysis of the Seminex explosion in our Lutheran seminary two generations ago, how shall we respond to the incursion of Godless Woke Marxism in our Lutheran universities today, accompanied by the censoring of debate and disputation against this retreat from the Incarnation? Well, let us live not by lies. Let us instead oppose the lies with the truth Himself.

I propose to lean on Marquart's proposition that the written word is about the Incarnate Word and is of a piece with Him. Adopting and adapting the title of a recent book by Jeremy Holmes, *Cur Deus Verba*, I shall unpack Marquart's proposition by asking with a slightly different accent, *Cur Verbum Verba*, "Why has the Word revealed Himself in words?" In this way I intend to expose and then refute the presupposition on which Woke Marxism depends—to refute Wokeism with Christ the incarnate Word and thereby establish that the means of grace are the only means by which we can do Lutheran education. A come-along feature of my refutation of Wokeism is to reestablish disputation or argumentation as the hallmark of Lutheran teaching and learning. This will be of help not only to Lutherans, but to every Christian praying and laboring to save Christian schools from the anti-Christian assault of the latest version of Marxism.

First, a few crucial terms. *Woke Marxism* (also known as Cultural Marxism, Identity Marxism, Diversity/Inclusion/Equity, Critical Social Justice, etc.) has two components, one obvious, the other suppressed. On the one hand, it involves the Marxist social engineering of society by means of disruption and violence resulting from the invention and incitement of diverse identity groups (see Karl Marx, *The German Ideology* and *The Communist Manifesto*). This is the obvious component.

On the other hand, there is a component that is *presupposed*, meaning that it is so widely taken for granted that it hardly ever comes up for debate or discussion (even where debate and discussion are possible). If anyone asks about this presupposed foundation, his question will most often be poo pooed. (*Poo pooing* is an actual philosophical term that amounts to an outright dismissal of someone's argument by the ad hominem tactic of insinuating that he is being ridiculous.) The presupposition of Woke Marxism is postmodernism's cynical disbelief regarding the inherent meaningfulness of the divine gift of language. This presupposition has to do with the means–by–which Wokeism or Woke Marxism is promulgated. Woke Marxism is anti-text because it is anarchic, or anti-authority. Just look at Woke Marxism's cavalier overthrow of personal pronouns, sacred propositions, and all words, as they see fit.

Education in our universities, secular and religious, has been neglecting philosophy of language and shunning sacrosanct texts, particularly the Scriptures, for a long while. The pre-censoring of classical texts in theory and in practice is a major reason why contemporary universities are vulnerable to Marxism. In C.S. Lewis's essay collection, *The Abolition of Man*, of which his book, *That Hideous Strength*, is a novelization, he puts the problem this way: "The task of the modern educator is not to cut down jungles, but to irrigate deserts." Wokeism thrives in a desert environment. Therefore, it detests irrigation and sources of living water.

Western culture is a term that must be understood normatively, that is, in terms of moral authority. This is important because our Woke adversaries almost always follow the understanding of culture taught by the social sciences (such as professional anthropology or political science or linguistics). But the social science understanding of culture is merely descriptive. It is without authority and without moral content. You cannot make any moral judgments based on scientific data or hypotheses, no matter how detailed or widely believed your hypothesis may be. This is the nature of science. As Marquart wrote about our earlier crisis in Lutheran education, "Science has neither use nor room for privileged authorities or sacrosanct texts. It recognizes only observations, experiments..." (120).

As T.S. Eliot wrote just before lamenting the Life of Christ that we have lost in living,
> Endless invention, endless experiment,
> Brings knowledge of motion, but not of stillness;
> Knowledge of speech, but not of silence;

> Knowledge of words, and ignorance of the Word.
> All our knowledge brings us nearer to our ignorance,
> All our ignorance brings us nearer to death,
> But nearness to death no nearer to God.

Trafficking on widespread ignorance of the Word, of the texts and ultimate authority of the Word of Christ, Woke Marxism is a social science experiment conducted with utter disregard for any individual person and utterly void of moral authority. It is a global transgression of the Nuremberg Code regulating human experimentation after the ghastly social and physical experiments of the Nazis. Readers of C.S. Lewis's *That Hideous Strength* will recognize that N.I.C.E., the National Institute for Continuing Experimentation on animals and human beings, is a foreshadowing of ideologies and social phenomena such as Woke Marxism, with its queer undermining of all morality and its physical and mental experimentation on the bodies and souls of our children at all levels of formal and media education.

Western culture is best defined as a *culture* in the normative or authoritative sense of the passing on of moral judgments and values from one generation to the next. This is a philosophical definition in contrast to the mere descriptions that come from the social sciences. What distinguishes it as *Western* culture is that it passes on moral judgments (a) in Greek forms of thinking and (b) with the material content of the Hebrew and Greek texts of the Scriptures (Roger Scruton).

The Greek forms of thinking that formed Western culture are Socratic and Platonic dialog, argumentation, logic—the stuff of argumentation, debate, and disputation for the sake of capital-T Truth which take place, of course, *in the medium of language.*

Woke Marxism is an insurgency against Western culture in its arrogant and immoral attack on what the Greek philosophers and the apostle John identify as *the logos*. This is the heart of Woke Marxism's social experimentation on human subjects, utterly without their informed consent. This is what Eliot identifies poetically as the "Endless invention, endless experiment, / [which] Brings ... / Knowledge of words, and ignorance of the Word." That is, in Latin, ignorance of Christ the incarnate Verbum (John 1:1 & 14).

One more thing before we get to the winsome and powerful response of the incarnate *Verbum* and His very *verba* of Holy Scripture, which is the means-by-which Lutheran education is Lutheran and educational. I deal with this biblically and logically, as an intellectual and professional heir of Martin Luther. There are at least three fallacies at work in the compromising of Lutheran— and indeed of all Christian education by the anarchic (that is, the anti-divine Logos authority, see John 1:1) ideology of Woke Marxism, and without the informed consent of parents of school age children and of young adult students of higher education.

Woke Marxism is human experimentation in defiance of any and every moral and ethical norms, but especially those of Western culture. For example, as the first proposition of the Nuremberg Code, codified in 1945 to oppose the horrors of Nazi experimentation on Jewish persons in their millions, as on other peoples of the Bible, declares,

> The voluntary consent of the human subject is absolutely essential. This means that the person involved should have legal capacity to give consent;

should be so situated as to be able to exercise free power of choice, without the intervention of any element of force, fraud, deceit, duress, over-reaching, or other ulterior form of constraint or coercion; and should have sufficient knowledge and comprehension of the elements of the subject matter involved, as to enable him to make an understanding and enlightened decision. This latter element requires that, before the acceptance of an affirmative decision by the experimental subject, there should be made known to him the nature, duration, and purpose of the experiment; the method and means by which it is to be conducted; all inconveniences and hazards reasonably to be expected; and the effects upon his health or person, which may possibly come from his participation in the experiment. The duty and responsibility for ascertaining the quality of the consent rests upon each individual who initiates, directs or engages in the experiment. It is a personal duty and responsibility which may not be delegated to another with impunity.

There is no informed consent for the Woke Marxist experimentation in education. The experimentation being conducted upon our children and young adults is therefore immoral and unethical. Furthermore, it is anti-educational. Woke Marxism is arrogantly and pridefully anti-rational and anti-logical in the–means–by–which it operates. It is an affront to our shared humanity, a weapon of mass destruction, the abolition of man (C.S. Lewis). It is, remember, based upon the presupposition that language is inherently meaningless. At every turn, Wokeism intends, with malice aforethought, to abolish language, the means–by–which we human beings have fellowship with one another (Aristotle, *Politics*, Book 1).

There is more. Language, in the case of the unsurpassable authority and verbally inerrant Word of Christ, that is, the biblical text, is the means–by–which God—that is, the *Creator* of the Declaration who has created all us human beings equal and endowed us with unalienable rights such as Life, Liberty, and the Pursuit of Happiness—has established and still maintains His fellowship with us human beings. In Lutheran thought and education, we identify the Bible (and the Sacraments which it authorizes) as *the means of grace*. There are no other means–by–which God relates to humanity since the incarnation of the Verbum, the Word, His Son (see the Greek New Testament, including the opening paragraph of the Epistle to the Hebrews).

At the most superficial level, Woke Marxism depends upon the fallacy of equivocation. For example, Woke "justice" is not the justice of the God of the Bible who, according to the prophet, "Has told you, O man, what is good; and what does the LORD require of you but to do justice, to love kindness, and to walk humbly with your God" (Micah 6:8). It's not the justice of Plato's *Republic*. It's not the justice of Western thought as recently as John Rawls. It is not justice at all. It is racialized vengeance. It is institutionalized racism.

Equivocation is Woke Marxism's stock–in–trade, its weapon of choice for its Marxist opposition to the Scriptures, opposition to the Western canon, opposition to the texts of the Hebrew and Greek Scriptures. As we read in Isaiah, "Woe to those who call evil good and good evil, who substitute darkness for light and light for darkness" (5:20). In the insurgent mantras of Woke Marxism, "Equity" means certain groups are more equal than others. "Diversity" means the carving up of our common humanity into manmade categories of skin color and sexual proclivities. "Inclusion" is the legitimization of the exclusion of

Christ, of His words, from education and media. It seeks to normalize government persecution of Christians, in deliberate contradiction of the First Amendment.

At a more profound level, compromise with Woke Marxism is commitment to a treacherous slippery slope fallacy. The compromise with Woke Marxism is a philosophy of education that rejects the words and Person of the Way Himself (John 14:6) in favor of an increasingly cozy fellowship of appeasement with the wicked, the sinners, the scoffers of the world. In other words, compromise with Woke Marxism is a paradigm of the slippery slope depicted in Psalm 1: "How blessed is the man who does not walk in the counsel of the wicked, nor stand in the seat of sinners, nor sit in the seat of scoffers, but his delight is in the law of the LORD, and in His law he meditates day and night."

At its most fundamental level, the compromise of Lutheran education with Woke Marxism is an appeal to false authority, a shameful *ad Verecundium* of biblical proportions. (The Latin name of this fallacy means "shameful.") Jesus of Nazareth, God in our human flesh, says in Matthew 28, "All authority has been given to Me in heaven and on earth." Woke Marxism scoffs at Him and His words at every turn. Woke Marxism is social experimentation conducted on the flesh and the souls of uneducated and vulnerable people to see if anything will happen when you teach them to "throw off the fetters," the words and the divine authority, of the Messiah Himself. For the guaranteed outcome of this dehumanizing experiment, see Psalm 2.

Strictly speaking, I am not simply making an argument here in favor of believing the biblical faith—although I believe, teach, and confess the Bible and the Christian creeds without qualification as a pastor and a professor. So far, I have been offering for your consideration an analysis of Wokeism as an assault on the founding proposition in the opening words of the sacrosanct text of our American Declaration of Independence. Because of Woke Marxism, as President Lincoln said, "We are engaged in a great civil war, testing whether that nation, or any nation so conceived and so dedicated, can long endure." I have also explained that Woke Marxism is opposed to the canonical texts of Western culture. In both cases, it is more than plausible to conclude that Woke Marxist education in media and especially in our American schools and universities is an attack on the God of the founding proposition and of the canonical Scriptures.

In the following paragraphs, I offer for your consideration how we in my Lutheran church body are failing to hold the line against Woke Marxism in our universities, along with a prescription for what we need to do if we are to remain faithful to the God of Scripture, the God who has spoken to us by His Son, the God who created us all and gave us the divine gift of language for fellowship first with Him and then with one another. So, I turn next to my church body and its Lutheran Christian inheritance.

Can we hope for a bright future for Lutheran education in the middle of this Woke Marxist insurgency against nation and culture, logic and language? In this month's *Reporter* (June 2023) our synod president states, "[Our remaining Lutheran] universities have the strongest theological and administrative presidents we've had in decades." That is not saying much, given the lightweight theologians who recently led these institutions, and given the current class of lay presidents we have in most of our (rapidly diminishing number of) Concordia universities.

He goes on to say, "Concordia Wisconsin and Ann Arbor's future is bright. My only goal is that we ... confess and live the authority of inerrant Scriptures and our confessions. *This precludes Wokeism*" [my italics]. His statement against Wokeism is on target. Praise the Lord. But on the one hand, neither Concordia University Wisconsin (CUW or CUWAA) nor any other Concordia, to my knowledge, has repudiated Woke Marxism.

On the other hand, the comment of bright optimism misses the point. The reality is that we must address the *conditions* at our Lutheran universities that allowed Woke Marxism to take root in the first place, otherwise this exceptionally evil ideology will continue to fester.

After all, the pressure to Go Woke or Go Broke is immense socially. It is immense financially. There is a predictable consequence for a religious university's dependency on federal funding—funding from a federal administration that is maniacally imposing Woke Marxism on every institution in our constitutional republic.

As far as I can tell, the synod president's visitations to investigate Wokeism at Mequon and Ann Arbor were helpful as far as they went, but there has been none of the repentance for which he called in May 2022. It also seems that no one is willing or capable of acknowledging the elephant on campus, namely, government funding. This is funding leveraged by a federal government that is striking at the heart of Christianity, the authority of the written Word of the Word made flesh. Just look at the White House's declaration of transgendered surgeries and experimental hormones for all made the week before Holy Week in 2022, and its plans for reconfiguring Title IX this year.

With or without the elephant of federal funding (and, again, no Concordia University president has announced a plan to dislodge our religious universities from federal or state funding) it is the case that our Lutheran universities which promulgate Woke Marxism, DIE, and so-called social justice are, as I argued in the first pages of this essay and have argued at length elsewhere) "hitting at the inmost nature of biblical Christianity. The written Word is about the Incarnate Word and is of a piece with Him."

Woke Marxism deplores the Incarnate Word and His personal, authoritative words to us human beings. For a Lutheran institution of higher learning to become so vulnerable to such an antithetical, anti-Christ ideology as Wokeism or Critical Social Justice is outrageous and mind-boggling. How could this have happened? *This* is the question.

Due respect, when our church body president says, "Concordia Wisconsin and Ann Arbor's future is bright" this is a naive and unwarranted assertion. He has failed to provide (or to acknowledge) a diagnosis. Here is one: A Lutheran or other religious university that goes Woke has a compromised theological immune system. *The* question is, "How did we wear down our immune system? *The missing ingredient* in our universities—and in our church body as a whole—*is Lutheran disputation.*

Lutheran disputation. The administration and board at my university, CUWAA, for example, *will not have it. They abhor it. They are actively censoring, prohibiting, and attacking it for all to see, in the church and far beyond. Their ongoing attack on academic freedom is a public scandal.*

Let me show you what I mean by pursuing the question, *Cur Verbum verba*, in terms of Martin Luther's 1536 Disputation Concerning Man. My dispute with

Woke Marxism and Lutheran universities that accept it is based on three theses from the heart of this disputation, a disputation in which Luther in fact sets out forty propositions for logical and edifying debate—a means of doing church and education for which "reconciliation processes" (the soup of the day for dealing with problems in my church body) are a poor, unmanly and un-Lutheran substitute.

A word on the Greek form of thinking exemplified in Luther's disputation: A disputation like this one is a powerful, pedagogical way of having a thoughtful discussion and dialog concerning a critical topic in mediaeval universities such as the University of Wittenberg. The online Stanford Encyclopedia of Philosophy (SEP) confirms that this type of teaching by disputation is essentially an academic form of philosophical dialog (the sort of teaching that Plato did in dialogues such as his *Republic*).

It's also significant that this disputation form "comes into the classroom as an outgrowth of the *lectio*, the careful reading and commentary on authoritative texts" such as Holy Scripture in the first place, but also culturally formative academic texts such as the writings of Aristotle. As the SEP explains in detail, disputation "is centered around a systematic rather than a textual question, and the supporting and opposing arguments are supplied by students".

By the way, what Luther calls *theses* in Lewis W. Spitz's translation are what we in philosophy today refer to as *propositions*, statements of fact to be judged as either True or False. Each proposition is an open invitation to say either, "This is true" or "This is false." Then the dialog begins! Disputation is the Three Acts of the Mind put to work by applying to the problem at hand authoritative texts: sacrosanct classic texts (such as Aristotle), but especially the normative text of the Scriptures, the *Verba* of the *Incarnate Verbum*.

Disputation, *Thesis 1*. *Philosophy or human wisdom defines man as an animal having reason, sensation, and body.* Luther is stipulating Aristotle's definition of man in *Politics*, Book 1. There the philosopher categorizes man as *zoon logon echon*, an animal type of being characterized by *logos*. Aristotle takes stock of all the different types of beings in the cosmos and sets about learning what a thing is, "always and for the most part", by determining its kind. A thing's kind of being is determined by asking, "What is this kind of thing *essentially*?" Today we call this *ontology*, the study of beings. The second word in the compound term for this discipline, onto–*logy*, preserves the fact that study and discovery take place in the medium of *logos,* that is, in language—that is, in informed conversation, in discourse, and in disputation.

Significantly, Aristotle also identifies *logos* or language as the medium of fellowship (*koinonia*) among human beings. What Aristotle could not dream of, but what is revealed in the Person and words of Jesus the incarnate *Logos*, is that language is also the medium of fellowship with God Himself.

The human being is, at the core of his being, a language being fitted by the Creator for the *verba* of the Redeemer by the work of the Sanctifier. An attack on language is, therefore, a crime against humanity, an abolition of man. The suppression of language—say, by canceling, censoring, restricting debate, disputation, and the thoughtful application of authoritative texts which inform these activities—is a violation of the rights with which our Creator has endowed all us members of the human, logos species.

If it is true that The Word reveals Himself in words (*Verbum verba*, according to our Latin title for this essay), then the suppression of language and words is insurgency against the second person of the Holy Trinity Himself. As Marquart said of the insurgency against the Word by the queer hermeneutics at St. Louis late last century, censoring and punishing professors and others "hits at the inmost nature of biblical Christianity. The written Word is about the Incarnate Word and is of a piece with Him". It is, to invoke Tolkien, the breaking of the fellowship.

Disputation, *Thesis 11*. *Therefore, if philosophy or reason itself is compared with theology, it will appear that we know almost nothing about man.* Here Luther is talking about what Paul refers to as "the hollow and deceptive kind of philosophy," or education and learning. It's hollow and deceptive because it depends entirely on human tradition and the basic principles of this world. For example, see atheistic Marxism.

Instead, the apostle mandates the kind of philosophy and education that depends on Christ (Colossians 2:8–10). Christianity is the true *philos–sophos*, or philosophy, because it is the befriending and loving of Christ, who is Himself the *sophos* of God in a singular Person (1 Corinthians 1:22–25). Thus, Luther's theology of the human being is also a Christological anthropology.

Luther is understandably leaning forward, toward a major upcoming thesis for disputing, debating, and understanding our human kind of being Christologically in terms of justification, Thesis 32. But there is an important point regarding his mention of reason and rationality at this point. When the Greek term *logos* is carried over into Latin, there is a fork in the road. As we all know, "When you come to a fork in the road, take it" (Yogi Berra). The fork in this case is that the one Greek word, *logos*, forks into two diverging Latin words, namely, *verba* and *ratio*.

Perhaps the medievals were able to keep both terms in mind, side by side, but the choice of *ratio* as the Latin translation for *logos* inevitably leads us moderns down the wrong road. It leads those of us after Descartes to think that *logos* is fundamentally about our mental processes; but on the contrary, our mental capacities *originate in and depend upon language*. *Ratio* invariably leads to Platonism and to thumbing one's nose at language and written texts, material liabilities and incidentals such as they are to Plato and Plotinus. We should take the road less traveled.

Verba is the better translation. It's also the road taken in our Lutheran Confessions. For example, the text of the Apology, the article on the chief article of doctrine, justification, reads "God cannot be treated, He cannot be apprehended, *Nisi per Verbum*, except via the Word."

Disputation, *Thesis 32*. *Paul in Romans 3[:28], "We hold that a man is justified by faith apart from works," briefly sums up the definition of man, saying, "Man is justified by faith."* Since this thesis is definitional, as Oswald Bayer says, we would do well to translate it as "The human being is human in that he is justified by faith."

In other words, while we have grown up learning to think of the human being as *homo sapiens*, on the basis of the thicker anthropology which we have only from the incarnate *Verbum* by way of His revelation of Himself in His own *verba*, it would be much more accurate to think of the human being as *homo justificans*, since we are the kind of being that seeks to be justified: Either we acknowledge that we are justified by God's grace alone in Christ or we waste our time of grace as language beings trying to justify ourselves apart from Christ and His words—a deeply frustrating and upsetting project for any member of the language species!

By the way, as Lutherans should see more clearly than most Christians because of our inherited commitment to the means of grace and faith in Christ's words alone (the *solas* of the Lutheran Reformation), the Woke Marxist notions of diversity, inclusion, and equity DIE) are ineffective replacements for the central doctrine of universal justification ("All .. are justified..." Romans 3, especially verses 23–24) brought to us solely by God and solely through His means of grace.

Woke ideology insists that people will find meaning and purpose, not in praising God for universal justification, but in constant revolution, class against class, everyone in unending violent rebellion against the sacrosanct texts and the God of creation and order. But Marxism is a lie.

In summary, the question is, *Cur Verbum Verba?* The answer is "God cannot be treated, cannot be apprehended *Nisi per Verbum,* "except through the Word" (Apology, Article 4, On Justification). This first principle of Lutheran education follows from Christ's own words, "No one comes to the Father *Nisi per Me"* (John 14:6 in Latin). We are members of the language species. Language is for the purpose of justification. It is for fellowship with the incarnate Word Himself. As the apostle Paul writes, "Faith comes by hearing, and hearing by the Word of Christ, the *verba* of the *Verbum*". Following this fellowship from God, language is the means–by–which we have human fellowship and flourishing.

A tightly linked question is, "How exactly can we read, mark, learn, and inwardly digest the *verba* of the incarnate *Verbum* in regard to the problems, issues, and conflicts that we experience?" Answer: "By means of Lutheran Disputation, the form of Greek thinking we have inherited from Luther and the Lutheran confessions."

This is what we mean by *Lutheran* and *Classical* and *Education.*

This is the Way (see John 14:6)!

Appendix T

The Dallas Statement on Social Justice and the Gospel
Summer 2018

I. Scripture

WE AFFIRM that the Bible is God's Word, breathed out by him. It is inerrant, infallible, and the final authority for determining what is true (what we must believe) and what is right (how we must live). All truth claims and ethical standards must be tested by God's final Word, which is Scripture alone.

WE DENY that Christian belief, character, or conduct can be dictated by any other authority, and we deny that the postmodern ideologies derived from intersectionality, radical feminism, and critical race theory are consistent with biblical teaching. We further deny that competency to teach on any biblical issue comes from any qualification for spiritual people other than clear understanding and simple communication of what is revealed in Scripture.

SCRIPTURE: GENESIS 2:18–25; PSALM 19:7–10; 1 CORINTHIANS 2:14–15; EPHESIANS 5:22–33; 2 TIMOTHY 3:16–4:5; HEBREWS 4:12; 13:4; 1 PETER 1:25; 2 PETER 1:19–21

II. Imago Dei

WE AFFIRM that God created every person equally in his own image. As divine image-bearers, all people have inestimable value and dignity before God and deserve honor, respect and protection. Everyone has been created by God and for God.

WE DENY that God-given roles, socioeconomic status, ethnicity, religion, sex or physical condition or any other property of a person either negates or contributes to that individual's worth as an image-bearer of God.

SCRIPTURE: GENESIS 1:26–30; 2:18–22; 9:6; 2 CORINTHIANS 5:17; COLOSSIANS 1:21–22

III. Justice

WE AFFIRM that since he is holy, righteous, and just, God requires those who bear his image to live justly in the world. This includes showing appropriate respect to every person and giving to each one what he or she is due. We affirm that societies must establish laws to correct injustices that have been imposed through cultural prejudice.

WE DENY that true justice can be culturally defined or that standards of justice that are merely socially constructed can be imposed with the same authority as those that are derived from Scripture. We further deny that Christians can live justly in the world under any principles other than the biblical standard of righteousness. Relativism, socially-constructed standards of truth or morality, and notions of virtue and vice that are constantly in flux cannot result in authentic justice.

SCRIPTURE: GENESIS 18:19; ISAIAH 61:8; MICAH 6:8; MATTHEW 5:17–19; ROMANS 3:31

IV. God's Law

WE AFFIRM that God's law, as summarized in the ten commandments, more succinctly summarized in the two great commandments, and manifested in Jesus Christ, is the only standard of unchanging righteousness. Violation of that law is what constitutes sin.

WE DENY that any obligation that does not arise from God's commandments can be legitimately imposed on Christians as a prescription for righteous living. We further deny the legitimacy of any charge of sin or call to repentance that does not arise from a violation of God's commandments.

SCRIPTURE: DEUTERONOMY 10:4; ROMANS 6:14, 10:5; GALATIANS 2:16, 3:10, 12; COLOSSIANS 2:1417; HEBREWS 10:1

V. Sin

WE AFFIRM that all people are connected to Adam both naturally and federally. Therefore, because of original sin everyone is born under the curse of God's law and all break his commandments through sin. There is no difference in the condition of sinners due to age, ethnicity, or sex. All are depraved in all their faculties and all stand condemned before God's law. All human relationships, systems, and institutions have been affected by sin.

WE DENY that, other than the previously stated connection to Adam, any person is morally culpable for another person's sin. Although families, groups, and nations can sin collectively, and cultures can be predisposed to particular sins, subsequent generations share the collective guilt of their ancestors only if they approve and embrace (or attempt to justify) those sins. Before God each person must repent and confess his or her own sins in order to receive forgiveness. We further deny that one's ethnicity establishes any necessary connection to any particular sin.

SCRIPTURE: GENESIS 2:16, 17, 3:12,13–15; PROVERBS 29:18; ISAIAH 25:7, 60:2–3; JEREMIAH 31:27–34; EZEKIEL 18:1–9, 14–18; MATTHEW 23:29–36; ROMANS 1:16–17, 3:23, 5:12, 10:14–17; 1 CORINTHIANS 15:3–11; 2 CORINTHIANS 11:3; GALATIANS 1:6–9; TITUS 1:12, 13; REVELATION 13:8

VI. Gospel

WE AFFIRM that the gospel is the divinely-revealed message concerning the person and work of Jesus Christ—especially his virgin birth, righteous life, substitutionary sacrifice, atoning death, and bodily resurrection—revealing who he is and what he has done with the promise that he will save anyone and everyone who turns from sin by trusting him as Lord.

WE DENY that anything else, whether works to be performed or opinions to be held, can be added to the gospel without perverting it into another gospel. This also means that implications and applications of the gospel, such as the obligation to live justly in the world, though legitimate and important in their own right, are not definitional components of the gospel.

SCRIPTURE: GENESIS 3:15; PROVERBS 29:18; ISAIAH 25:7, 60:2, 3; ROMANS 1:16–17, 10:14,15,17; 1 CORINTHIANS 15:1–11; GALATIANS 1:6–9; REVELATION 13:8

VII. Salvation

WE AFFIRM that salvation is granted by God's grace alone received through faith alone in Jesus Christ alone. Every believer is united to Christ, justified before God, and adopted into his family. Thus, in God's eyes there is no difference in spiritual value or worth among those who are in Christ. Further, all who are united to Christ are also united to one another regardless of age, ethnicity, or sex. All believers are being conformed to the image of Christ. By God's regenerating and sanctifying grace all believers will be brought to a final glorified, sinless state of perfection in the day of Jesus Christ.

WE DENY that salvation can be received in any other way. We also deny that salvation renders any Christian free from all remaining sin or immune from even grievous sin in this life. We further deny that ethnicity excludes anyone from understanding the gospel, nor does anyone's ethnic or cultural heritage mitigate or remove the duty to repent and believe.

SCRIPTURE: GENESIS 3:15; ACTS 20:32; ROMANS 3–4; EPHESIANS 2:8–9; GALATIANS 3:28–29; 1 JOHN 2:1–2

VIII. The Church

WE AFFIRM that the primary role of the church is to worship God through the preaching of his word, teaching sound doctrine, observing baptism and the Lord's Supper, refuting those who contradict, equipping the saints, and evangelizing the lost. We affirm that when the primacy of the gospel is maintained that this often has a positive effect on the culture in which various societal ills are mollified. We affirm that, under the lordship of Christ, we are to obey the governing authorities established by God and pray for civil leaders.

WE DENY that political or social activism should be viewed as integral components of the gospel or primary to the mission of the church. Though believers can and should utilize all lawful means that God has providentially established to have some effect on the laws of a society, we deny that these activities are either evidence of saving faith or constitute a central part of the church's mission given to her by Jesus Christ, her head. We deny that laws or regulations possess any inherent power to change sinful hearts.

SCRIPTURE: MATTHEW 28:16–20; ROMANS 13:1–7; 1 TIMOTHY 2:1–3; 2 TIMOTHY 4:2; TITUS 1:9; 1 PETER 2:13–17

IX. Heresy

WE AFFIRM that heresy is a denial of or departure from a doctrine that is essential to the Christian faith. We further affirm that heresy often involves the replacement of key, essential truths with variant concepts, or the elevation of non-essentials to the status of essentials. To embrace heresy is to depart from the faith once delivered to the saints and thus to be on a path toward spiritual destruction. We affirm that the accusation of heresy should be reserved for those departures from Christian truth that destroy the weight-bearing doctrines of the redemptive core of Scripture. We affirm that accusations of heresy should be accompanied with clear evidence of such destructive beliefs.

WE DENY that the charge of heresy can be legitimately brought against every failure to achieve perfect conformity to all that is implied in sincere faith in the gospel.

SCRIPTURE: JOHN 14:6; ACTS 4:12; GALATIANS 1:6–9; 1 JOHN 4:1–3,

10, 14, 15; 5:1, 6–12

X. Sexuality and Marriage

WE AFFIRM that God created mankind male and female and that this divinely determined distinction is good, proper, and to be celebrated. Maleness and femaleness are biologically determined at conception and are not subject to change. The curse of sin results in sinful, disordered affections that manifest in some people as same-sex attraction. Salvation grants sanctifying power to renounce such dishonorable affections as sinful and to mortify them by the Spirit. We further affirm that God's design for marriage is that one woman and one man live in a one-flesh, covenantal, sexual relationship until separated by death.

Those who lack the desire or opportunity for marriage are called to serve God in singleness and chastity. This is as noble a calling as marriage.

WE DENY that human sexuality is a socially constructed concept. We also deny that one's sex can be fluid. We reject "gay Christian" as a legitimate biblical category. We further deny that any kind of partnership or union can properly be called marriage other than one man and one woman in lifelong covenant together. We further deny that people should be identified as "sexual minorities"—which serves as a cultural classification rather than one that honors the image-bearing character of human sexuality as created by God.

SCRIPTURE: GENESIS 1:26–27, 2:24, 4:1, 19:24–28; MATTHEW 19:3–6; ROMANS 8:13; 1 CORINTHIANS 6:9–11; 1 TIMOTHY 1:10; JUDE 7

XI. Complementarianism

WE AFFIRM that God created mankind both male and female with inherent biological and personal distinctions between them and that these created differences are good, proper, and beautiful. Though there is no difference between men and women before God's law or as recipients of his saving grace, we affirm that God has designed men and women with distinct traits and to fulfill distinct roles. These differences are most clearly defined in marriage and the church, but are not irrelevant in other spheres of life. In marriage the husband is to lead, love, and safeguard his wife and the wife is to respect and be submissive to her husband in all things lawful. In the church, qualified men alone are to lead as pastors/elders/bishops and preach to and teach the whole congregation. We further affirm that the image of God is expressed most fully and beautifully in human society when men and women walk in obedience to their God-ordained roles and serve according to their God-given gifts.

WE DENY that the God-ordained differences in men's and women's roles disparage the inherent spiritual worth or value of one over the other, nor do those differences in any way inhibit either men or women from flourishing for the glory of God.

SCRIPTURE: GENESIS 1:26–28, 2:15–25, 3:1–24; EPHESIANS 5:22–33; 1 CORINTHIANS 11:7–9; 1 TIMOTHY 2:12–14; TITUS 2

XII. Race / Ethnicity

WE AFFIRM God made all people from one man. Though people often can be distinguished by different ethnicities and nationalities, they are ontological equals before God in both creation and redemption. "Race" is not a biblical category, but rather a social construct that often has been used to classify groups of people in terms of inferiority and superiority. All that is good, honest, just, and beautiful in various ethnic backgrounds and experiences can be celebrated as the fruit of God's grace. All sinful actions and their results (including evils perpetrated between and upon ethnic groups by others) are to be confessed as sinful, repented of, and repudiated.

WE DENY that Christians should segregate themselves into racial groups or regard racial identity above, or even equal to, their identity in Christ. We deny that any divisions between people groups (from an unstated attitude of superiority to an overt spirit of resentment) have any legitimate place in the fellowship of the redeemed. We reject any teaching that encourages racial groups to view themselves as privileged oppressors or entitled victims of oppression. While we are to weep with those who weep, we deny that a person's feelings of offense or oppression necessarily prove that someone else is guilty of sinful behaviors, oppression, or prejudice.

SCRIPTURE: GENESIS 1:26–28; ACTS 17:24–26; 1 CORINTHIANS 13:4–7; 2 CORINTHIANS 12:16–18

XIII. Culture

WE AFFIRM that some cultures operate on assumptions that are inherently better than those of other cultures because of the biblical truths that inform those worldviews that have produced these distinct assumptions. Those elements of a given culture that reflect divine revelation should be celebrated and promoted. But the various cultures out of which we have been called all have features that are worldly and sinful—and therefore those sinful features should be repudiated for the honor of Christ. We affirm that whatever evil influences to which we have been subjected via our culture can be—and must be— overcome through conversion and the training of both mind and heart through biblical truth.

WE DENY that individuals and sub-groups in any culture are unable, by God's grace, to rise above whatever moral defects or spiritual deficiencies have been engendered or encouraged by their respective cultures.

SCRIPTURE: ROMANS 1:18–32; EPHESIANS 4:17–24; COLOSSIANS 3:5–11

XIV. Racism

WE AFFIRM that racism is a sin rooted in pride and malice which must be condemned and renounced by all who would honor the image of God in all people. Such racial sin can subtly or overtly manifest itself as racial animosity or racial vainglory. Such sinful prejudice or partiality falls short of God's revealed will and violates the royal law of love. We affirm that virtually all cultures, including our own, at times contain laws and systems that foster racist attitudes and policies.

WE DENY that treating people with sinful partiality or prejudice is consistent with biblical Christianity. We deny that only those in positions of power are capable of racism, or that individuals of any particular ethnic groups are incapable of racism. We deny that systemic racism is in any way compatible with the core principles of historic evangelical convictions. We deny that the Bible can be legitimately used to foster or justify partiality, prejudice, or contempt toward other ethnicities. We deny that the contemporary evangelical movement has any deliberate agenda to elevate one ethnic group and subjugate another. And we emphatically deny that lectures on social issues (or activism aimed at reshaping the wider culture) are as vital to the life and health of the church as the preaching of the gospel and the exposition of Scripture. Historically, such things tend to become distractions that inevitably lead to departures from the gospel.

SCRIPTURE: GENESIS 1:26–27; DEUTERONOMY 10:17; ACTS 10:34; ROMANS 2:11; EPHESIANS 6:9; GALATIANS 3:28; JAMES 2:4

Appendix U

Luther's 1521 Speech at the Diet of Worms

The following translation comes from The History of the Reformation in the Sixteenth Century by Jean–Henri Merle d'Aubigne (1774–1872), translated by David Dundas Scott. Slight changes have been made in spelling and punctuation and passages clarified by Lyndal Roper's Martin Luther: Renegade and Prophet *and Roland H. Bainton's* Here I Stand: A Life of Martin Luther. *Biblical citations are from the original text. worldhistory.org*

Most Serene Emperor, Illustrious Princes, Gracious Lords:

I this day appear before you in all humility, according to your command, and I implore your Majesty and your august highnesses, by the mercies of God, to listen with favor to the defense of a cause which I am well assured is just and right. I ask pardon, if by reason of my ignorance, I am wanting in the manners that befit a court; for I have not been brought up in king's palaces, but in the seclusion of a cloister and I claim no other merit than that of having spoken and written with the simplicity of mind which regards nothing but the glory of God and the pure instruction of the people of Christ.

Two questions were yesterday put to me by his imperial majesty; the first, whether I was the author of the books whose titles were read; the second, whether I wished to revoke or defend the doctrine I have taught. I answered the first directly, and I adhere to that answer: that these books are mine and published by me, except so far as they may have been altered or interpolated by the craft or officiousness of opponents. As for the second question, I am now about to reply to it and I must first entreat your Majesty and your Highnesses to deign to consider that I have composed writings on very different subjects. In some, I have discussed faith and good works, in a spirit at once so pure, clear, and Christian, that even my adversaries themselves, far from finding anything to censure, confess that these writings are profitable, and deserve to be perused by devout persons. The pope's bull, violent as it is, acknowledges this. What, then, should I be doing if I were now to retract these writings? Wretched man! I alone, of all men living, should be abandoning truths approved by the unanimous vote of friends and enemies, and should be opposing doctrines that the whole world glorifies in confessing!

I have composed, secondly, certain works against the papacy, wherein I have attacked such as by false doctrines, irregular lives, and scandalous examples, afflict the Christian world, and ruin the bodies and souls of men. And is not this confirmed by the grief of all who fear God? Is it not manifest that the laws and human doctrines of the popes entangle, vex, and distress the consciences of the faithful, while the crying and endless extortions of Rome engulf the property and wealth of Christendom, and more particularly of this illustrious nation? Yet it is a perpetual statute that the laws and doctrines of the pope be held erroneous and reprobate when they are contrary to the Gospel and the opinions of the Church fathers.

If I were to revoke what I have written on that subject, what should I do but strengthen this tyranny and open a wider door to so many and flagrant impieties? Bearing down all resistance with fresh fury, we should behold these proud men swell, foam, and rage more than ever! And not merely would the yoke which now weighs down Christians be made more grinding by my retraction, it would thereby become, so to speak, lawful, for, by my retraction, it would receive confirmation from your most serene majesty, and all the States of the Empire. Great God! I should thus be like to an infamous cloak, used to hide and cover over every kind of malice and tyranny.

In the third and last place, I have written some books against private individuals, who had undertaken to defend the tyranny of Rome by destroying the faith. I freely confess that I may have attacked such persons with more violence than was consistent with my profession as an ecclesiastic; I do not think of myself as a saint, but neither can I retract these books. Because I should, by so doing, sanction the impieties of my opponents, and they would thence take occasion to crush God's people with still more cruelty.

Yet, as I am a mere man, and not God, I will defend myself after the example of Jesus Christ, who said: "If I have spoken evil, bear witness against me; but if well, why doest thou strike me?" (John 18:23). How much more should I, who am but dust and ashes, and so prone to error, desire that everyone should bring forward what he can against my doctrine. Therefore, most serene emperor, and you illustrious princes, and all, whether high or low, who hear me, I implore you by the mercies of God to prove to me by the writings of the prophets and apostles that I am in error. As soon as I shall be convinced, I will instantly retract all my errors, and will myself be the first to seize my writings and commit them to the flames.

God is wonderful and terrible in His counsels. Let us have a care, lest in our endeavors to arrest discords, we be bound to fight against the holy Word of God and bring down upon our heads a frightful deluge of inextricable dangers, present disaster, and everlasting desolations. Let us have a care that the reign of the young and noble prince, the Emperor Charles, on whom, next to God, we build so many hopes, should not only commence, but continue and terminate its course, under the most favorable auspices.

I might cite examples drawn from the oracles of God. I might speak of Pharaohs, of kings in Babylon, or of Israel, who were never more contributing to their own ruin than when, by measures in appearances most prudent, they thought to establish their authority! God removeth the mountains and they know not (Job 9:5). In speaking thus, I do not suppose that such noble princes have need of my poor judgment; but I wish to acquit myself of a duty whose fulfillment my native Germany has a right to expect from her children. And so, commending myself to your august majesty, and your most serene highnesses, I beseech you in all humility, not to permit the hatred of my enemies to rain upon me an indignation I have not deserved. I have done.

[At this point in the hearing, Luther was asked by Charles V to repeat what he had said in German in Latin. He was told to answer simply, and without the art of oratory, whether he would retract his statements or stand by them. He then concluded with the most famous passage of his speech.]

Since your most serene majesty and your highnesses require of me a simple, clear, and direct answer, I will give one, and it is this: I cannot submit my faith either to the pope or to the council, because it is clear that they have fallen into error and even into inconsistency with themselves. If, then, I am not convinced by proof from Holy Scripture, or by cogent reasons, if I am not satisfied by the very text I have cited, and if my judgment is not in this way brought into subjection to God's word, I neither can nor will retract anything; for it cannot be either safe or honest for a Christian to speak against his conscience. Here I stand. I cannot do otherwise. God help me. Amen.

Printed in the USA
CPSIA information can be obtained
at www.ICGtesting.com
LVHW021325180224
772034LV00011B/302